Seeking God for Daily Living and Destiny

Seeking God for Daily Living and Destiny

by
Gordon Magee
of Christ Light Ministries

Aventine Press

Published by Aventine Press
55 East Emerson St.
Chula Vista CA 91911
www.aventinepress.com

ISBN: 978-1-59330-814-8

Printed in the United States of America

Dedication

I dedicate this book to Jesus Christ, my Lord and Savior, Who has reconciled me to God the Father, called me to follow, set me free from slavery to sin, and has been and will be with me always throughout this journey.

Also to my readers, may this book stir and challenge you to put seeking God into practice, in the manner He intended. We who would know the salvation of Christ must break free from the deceptive patterns of our present time and truly follow Him, learning and appropriating God's daily will and living out our God appointed destiny.

Acknowledgements

My mother Goldie Magee and my daughter-in-law Amy Magee have my gratitude for their time and effort in providing editorial comments and review as well as the original cover art provided by Amy.

Many thanks as well to my first Pastor and father in the faith Harold Hendricks who took the time to provide me with feedback on content, flow, and spiritual quality.

Look for my first book:
"Breaking the Cycle of Slavery to Sin"

Table of Contents

Introduction

Don't skip the Introduction!

Dear reader,

You are reading these very words of introduction because the title 'Seeking God for Daily Living and Destiny' either: was recommended, caught your eye, or you were actually looking for a title on this subject. Plus of course my header 'Don't Skip the Introduction!', and yes, I promise to make this worth your while regarding whether or not you invest your time in reading this book.

Nevertheless, how you arrived at this point tells me something about you. Regardless of whether you are young or old, whether you are relatively new to following Jesus, have been His follower a long time, or are just checking out this 'God' thing, you were drawn to the title in one way or another. On the inside you know that there is supposed to be much more to life than what you see being commonly experienced by your fellow man and even by many who claim to know Jesus.

Who am I? Why am I here? What is this life really all about? How do I get to know God? Does God really have a plan for mankind? If so, does He have a plan and purpose for me? How do I interact with and 'hear' from God? These are the real baseline questions of life that cry out for real answers which can be brought down to earth in practical daily living to shape and fulfill our destiny.

We were created by God and He is the point of reference for all areas of this life. Because of this, it is in God alone that we will find real answers to these baseline questions of life. Once these are resolved we then move on to higher things which have to do with purpose. How do I set my feet on the path which fulfills my destiny? How do I share, and minister this life which God has given me to others?

The answers to all of these questions are found preserved for us in God's word the Bible. My intent is to assist us in bringing these truths into our lives becoming those who seek and understand God and truly follow Jesus Christ, a people who go beyond the initial foundation and embrace the whole experience. Jesus promised: *I have come that they may have life, and that they may have it more abundantly (John 10:10b).*

None of us wants to live a fruitless life. Goofing around with my children when they were little, they would ask for a bedtime story and I would say: 'a man was born he lived and died, the end'. Then of course, following their protests, I would bring a real story. But sadly, even tragically, the former is the story of most of mankind.

Few engage with God and drill down with Him into their real purpose for being here. In our western world, mainly North America and Europe, we share a set of values which includes intelligence. That is to say we often pride ourselves on having thought through the greater issues of life and many of us tend to have a need to feel that we know what we are talking about. While there is certainly a measure of value in this, it can also become a barrier. For if we do not then press on and actually live out discovered truth on a daily basis we miss the boat. Jesus appropriately asked the following question in regard to His second coming: *"when the Son of Man comes, will He really find faith on the earth?" (Luke 18:8)*.

God has placed you into this earth on purpose and in context. There is an individual context relevant to your life since God Himself chose to place you here. There is a historical context for your life based on what God has been doing over the centuries on behalf of mankind. There is a current context for your life based on what is happening in the Kingdom of God today. We are intended both to understand and be influenced in our decisions and actions by the context of these things.

In the Bible book of Judges, Chapter 7 verses 2-8, we read the story of Gideon's army. Gideon started with 32,000 men but God had Gideon send home all that were afraid, which left him with 10,000. Then God had Gideon test the rest of them through the manner in which they drank. Those seemingly un-mindful of being at war, who knelt down and put their face to the water, he sent home. Those who seemingly remained alert, bringing the water up to their faces to lap were retained.

In the end God used Gideon to rout an innumerable host of enemy troops with just 300 men. Which are you? I will bet that whatever drew you to the title of this book indicates that you are awake and alert, becoming so, or have the deep desire to be so.

To live awake and alert in Jesus Christ is to live somewhat apart from the crowd. Most of the people you and I know are going to choose to remain asleep, either in the darkness of sin or even under the light of Christ. They may talk a good fight, perhaps that has included you and me in the not so distant past, but they are not going to actually take action to change and become people who seek and follow God for daily living, laying hold of His destiny and purpose for them. *And do this, knowing the time, that now it is high time to awake out of sleep; for now our salvation is nearer than when we first believed. The night is far spent, the day is at hand. Therefore let us cast off the works of darkness, and let us put on the armor of light. (Romans 13:11-12).*

I remember the words of Billy Graham addressing a stadium of people, on the question of when Jesus will return. He said something to the effect of: I don't know but in 30 to 70 years He will have returned for each of you. I am 55 at the time of this writing. I was born again at age 18 and started earnestly following Jesus at age 21. I may have something like 20 years left, perhaps at the outside 40 years left to live out my purpose for Christ. How long do you have? You see we are only here a short while. What time is it? It is high time to awake. If you have no plans to do so then please pass this book on to someone else.

In the introduction to my last book; 'Breaking the Cycle of Slavery to Sin', I stated that I would not spend time trying to prove that God exists or that the Bible is His word to mankind. However, God Himself is able to satisfy you that He exists and that He has provided His word for you to live by.

The Bible contains many of what the Apostle Peter called: the great and precious promises of God. I am adopting perhaps the most important one of these as the theme verse for this book. God is talking and here is what He has to say: *And you will seek Me and find Me, when you search for Me with all your heart. I will be found by you, says the LORD (Jeremiah 29:13-14).*

From my own experience I can promise you that if you will step out in bravery and press into this promise of God by seeking Him, God will reveal Himself to you. You will find Him; you will end up knowing God, and as you continue you will experience His word in your life.

All of His fullness, along with the trials which may come along with it, is there for you to find. I can prove to you that God exists and that His words in the Bible can be trusted, but you have to do the work of seeking with all of your heart if you are to find out whether or not God is true to His promise. This is the point at which those who really do not ever plan to wake up call it quits.

Dear readers do your part; seek God, asking Him to reveal Himself to you. Read the Bible taking your questions to God each day in prayer. I suggest you start with the New Testament if you are not familiar with the Bible.

All Biblical quotations in this book are in *italics* and are taken from the New King James Version of the Bible (NKJV). It is a standard, word for word translation, which means that there is an English word for each of the original language words instead of a translator's opinion on what the Bible passages mean. You can still find the passages, which I have used, in any other translation by following the reference given. The end of this introduction will quote Hebrews 11:6, which you can find in any Bible by looking up the book of Hebrews in the table of contents, then the 11th chapter and 6th verse.

But without faith it is impossible to please Him, for he who comes to God must believe that He is, and that He is a rewarder of those who diligently seek Him (Hebrews 11:6).

Chapter One

Created on Purpose

At one time or another, most of us have heard of or read about incredible tales of survival or triumph against seemingly impossible odds. Pausing for a moment to consider these extreme cases, what is it that we tend to think? Were those involved just lucky? Did these things happen based on pure chance or physics? Did those involved pull it off completely from their own strength and ability? Or do we consider that some form of greater purpose and maybe even destiny had something to do with it?

The same questions can be pondered for the other extreme. We have all heard or maybe even experienced tales of terrible woe and destruction. Usually in these cases all other questions get dropped and we begin to automatically ask: where was God? Whether we have lived our lives as if He even existed or mattered, most humans will ask: why did God let this happen? In other words we just don't understand what greater purpose or destiny that event could possibly have served.

Don't we wish we had all the answers to the questions of life? The first level of questions which ring through the hearts of every human being are: Who am I? Why am I here? What is this life really all about?

Many discard these as quickly as they come up. Others try the various paths which have seemed right to mankind over the millennia, some persist, and others eventually give up. Yet whether we block or pursue them, the questions remain. Humans seem driven, even pre-programmed, to find some form of significance in life that satisfies.

The second level of questions are less often asked; usually depending on our upbringing, cultural acceptance, and maybe even our fear of what others may think about us. Yet, if we are brave, willing, and able to suspend some of our doubts we can then ask: How do I get to know God? Does God really have a plan for mankind? If so does He have a plan and purpose for me? How do I interact with and 'hear' from God?

Let's begin with an age old promise, expressed in a number of places throughout the Bible, recorded for us in the following words by Jeremiah who was one of the major prophets of the Old Testament portion of the Bible. God is speaking to His people who are lost and in trouble as a result of their own sinful choices.

For I know the thoughts that I think toward you, says the LORD, thoughts of peace and not of evil, to give you a future and a hope. Then you will call upon Me and go and pray to Me, and I will listen to you. And you will seek Me and find Me, when you search for Me with all your heart. I will be found by you, says the LORD, and I will bring you back from your captivity; I will gather you from all the nations and from all the places where I have driven you, says the LORD, and I will bring you to the place from which I cause you to be carried away captive. (Jeremiah 29:11-14)

Throughout the Bible in passage after passage God's desire is clearly expressed: that we whom He created would know Him as our God, our Heavenly Father, our Savior, our Helper, our Friend and He promises that the depths of such a relationship will happen as we seek and search for Him with all of our heart.

It is my express intention in the pages of this book to help each of my readers step in with both feet and become people who can say: 'I sought the Lord with all my heart and I found Him. He met me and continues to meet me. He was really there just as He promised. The Lord leads me daily showing me His plans for my life and the direction of my destiny.' Come now dear reader, it really is high time for us to move beyond mere religion and religious practice and into the life God truly intends for you.

Who is Gordon Magee? Yeah buddy, who are you anyway! I am nobody special in any particular way. Whatever the Lord saw in me, He probably sees in you as well. I started out as a product of a broken home and made all the wrong decisions about life. It is easy to look back now and see that God has been working in my life from the very start. God was not the author of all of my bad experiences and decisions but He did chose to use them to bring me to a point where I would start to ask the questions of life.

The year was 1975. I was an 18 year old soldier in boot camp, Fort Ord, California. Separated from the life I had known, all of my frames of reference were gone. I was sitting on the edge of my bunk and trying to remember something, anything, familiar and coming to grips with being a lost soul. Within the next few months, as I moved on to my new duty stations in Texas and then Germany, the questions began in earnest: Who am I? Why am I here? What is this life really all about? I can tell you now that this is the finger of God beginning to stir the soup of a person's life and get them ready for an encounter with Himself.

Destiny:
Teachings on pre-destination began during the protestant reformation of the 1500s. John Calvin (Calvinism) declared that we have no choice in our own destiny and that we are either 'saved' or 'damned'.

Strong reaction from the majority of Christian church leaders produced an opposite extreme we might label as 'free will', being the idea that it is totally up to me to chose my own destiny; to accept or reject God's offer of salvation through Jesus Christ.

How did these church leaders arrive at these views which continue to influence Christian thought even in our day?

Both views are taught side by side in the Bible in the same manner as other topics which defy our human desire for immediate and perfect definition. For example the scriptures clearly teach that those who share their substance by giving it away will receive more in return. Such thinking is counter intuitive to what we feel is our own human intelligence. *Luke 6:38 Give, and it will be given to you: good measure, pressed down, shaken together, and running over will be put into your bosom. For with the same measure that you use, it will be measured back to you."*

A discovery is made when a person moves forward embracing God's promise to become one who seeks Him with all their heart. At some point we discover that God has purposefully installed scriptural tensions into His word the Bible, which require us to live by faith, involving ourselves in a life that regularly seeks Him, rather than by the ability to fully understand the operation of all things before we proceed with life.

We are left then holding two things which seem very opposite: that God pre-destined our lives and that life also involves free-will, or choice on our part, if it is to operate as intended. I have come to be sure that both of these are true and necessary parts of the life of faith to which God has called us. I am not among those who would agree with John Calvin, that life is as simple as having been pre-destined to be 'saved' or 'damned', however I recognize in the scriptures that God's form of predestination holds a large sway over all of our lives and is very important to understand.

Beginning to answer the questions of life: Who am I? Why am I here? What is this life all about? We find that there are three things which God purposefully and deliberately chose, or pre-destined, for each and every one of us and that these things begin to provide a context for our lives:

Nurture or the lack of it. You did not choose the family into which your soul was born, God chose your family for you.

Environment. It was God who chose your people group: your race, skin color, and heritage, as well as the political and social circumstances into which you would be born.

History. It was God who specifically chose the era of time into which you would be placed. God will also have quite a bit to do with choosing the day and time of your exit from history.

Why Lord? There is a very direct answer to this question, but before we look at it let's take a moment to understand our own question. Because when humans cry out to God asking to know the reason for such a fundamental question, we do so out of two needs.

First, let us understand that within our hearts we truly do hunger for significance, for a reason and purpose to our existence. As deep as that often feels and as unanswerable as that often seems, we must learn to embrace this as a good thing and as a gift from God. A gift which is meant to keep us in a mode of searching, progressing, and ultimately achieving. Can you see that the very longing for significance has been installed by God to move us toward its fulfillment?

Secondly, we cry out to God with this question because of internal pain. Pain and hurt often so intense it can seem overwhelming. It is hard for us as humans to reconcile the concept of God being good and loving with the amount of pain and suffering we see in this world and which we often experience within ourselves. We experience pain and we suffer from all three of the areas over which we had no personal control: from the level of nurture we received or did not receive in our family of origin, from the political and social environment into which we were born, and from the points and events of history into which we entered this world.

Herein lies trust which is a big issue for all humans. Can we trust God that there is reason, meaning, and purpose wrapped up in His choices for our lives?

Why Lord? Why did you choose for me to be placed into this family, environment, and history? The direct answer from God's word the Bible is found in the Book of Acts Chapter 17 as part of the Apostle Paul's address to the people of Athens after seeing an altar dedicated to 'the unknown god'.

Therefore, the One whom you worship without knowing, Him I proclaim to you: God, who made the world and everything in it, since He is Lord of heaven and earth, does not dwell in temples made with hands. Nor is He worshiped with men's hands, as though He needed anything, since He gives to all life, breath, and all things. And He has made from one blood every nation of men to dwell on all the face of the earth, and has determined their preappointed times and the boundaries of their dwellings, so that they should seek the Lord, in the hope that they might grope for Him and find Him, though He is not far from each one of us; for in Him we live and move and have our being, as also some of your own poets have said, 'For we are also His offspring' (Acts 17:23-28).

God has made all of us from one blood. God has pre-appointed our times and boundaries. God has done this so that we: *should seek the Lord, in the hope that* (we) *might find Him.* This is God's hope, this is the reason that your soul and mine were placed into what may even have turned out to be a painful family, environment, and point of history. Understanding this hope on the part of God Almighty is intended by God to be foundational for understanding our individual human experience. Fulfilling God's hope by actually becoming people who seek Him, who seek the Lord, is intended by God as the mechanism that will fulfill His will in and through our lives and bring us, in whom He delights *'For we are also His offspring'*, into a completed sense of fulfillment.

In agreement with the Great Commission given to His followers by Jesus Christ *(Matthew 28:18-20)*: our discussion thus far begs a question which few consider and fewer embrace. In most cases we just get too focused on our own problems and pain to look up. The question is this: can I trust that God has placed me into this very painful stream to be His agent? To be one who brings the Light of Christ into darkness and the life of God into the midst of those perishing?

The Apostle Paul himself was a human just as we are; in fact he was a man who endured more difficulty in life than most. Paul understood and embraced a life of seeking God. Listen to the following statement he made at the end of his life and see if your own heart does not resonate with a desire to be just that sure that you did not waste your time and God's time down here. *I have fought the good fight, I have finished the race, I have kept the faith. Finally, there is laid up for me the crown of righteousness, which the Lord, the righteous Judge, will give to me on that Day, and not to me only but also to all who have loved His appearing (2 Timothy 4:7-8).*

Does God truly plan for each individual as opposed to creating mankind in general and hoping that whoever comes to life might seek Him? This is a fair question which can be answered through a number of scriptures revealing that God indeed does plan for and pre-destine the existence of individuals.

Starting at the top we understand that God planned for the Son's entrance into human history as our Savior Jesus Christ.

Luke 1:30-33 (God's word to Jesus mother)
Then the angel said to her, "Do not be afraid, Mary, for you have found favor with God. And behold, you will conceive in your womb and bring forth a Son, and shall call His name JESUS. He will be great, and will be called the Son of the Highest; and the Lord God will give Him the throne of His father David. And He will reign over the house of Jacob forever, and of His kingdom there will be no end."

Matthew 1:20-21 (God's word to Mary's husband)
But while he thought about these things, behold, an angel of the Lord appeared to him in a dream, saying, "Joseph, son of David, do not be afraid to take to you Mary your wife, for that which is conceived in her is of the Holy Spirit. And she will bring forth a Son, and you shall call His name JESUS, for He will save His people from their sins."

We also find the announcement of God's pre-planning, through an angel, regarding John the Baptist and the direct words of God regarding His pre-planning for the Prophet Jeremiah.

Luke 1:13-17 (God's word to John the Baptist's father)
But the angel said to him, "Do not be afraid, Zacharias, for your prayer is heard; and your wife Elizabeth will bear you a son, and you shall call his name John. And you will have joy and gladness, and many will rejoice at his birth. For he will be great in the sight of the Lord, and shall drink neither wine nor strong drink. He will also be filled with the Holy Spirit, even from his mother's womb. And he will turn many of the children of Israel to the Lord their God. He will also go before Him in the spirit and power of Elijah, 'to turn the hearts of the fathers to the children,' and the disobedient to the wisdom of the just, to make ready a people prepared for the Lord."

Jeremiah 1:4-5 (God's word to Jeremiah)
Then the word of the LORD came to me, saying: "Before I formed you in the womb I knew you; before you were born I sanctified you; I ordained you a prophet to the nations."

Lastly, coming to ourselves and the rest of mankind, the psalmist King David gives us general insight into just how intimately involved God becomes with the formation of each human life.

Psalm 139:13-16
For You formed my inward parts; You covered me in my mother's womb. I will praise You, for I am fearfully and wonderfully made; marvelous are Your works, and that my soul knows very well.
My frame was not hidden from You, when I was made in secret, and skillfully wrought in the lowest parts of the earth.

Your eyes saw my substance, being yet unformed. And in Your book they all were written, the days fashioned for me, when as yet there were none of them.

All of us have made something, even if it was just a breakfast omelet. When we started that process we had every intention of the end result being good because we ourselves are similar to our own creator. We will explore the meaning of being created in the image of God a few chapters further on.

God Himself made plans for your creation and He planned for it to be good. He placed you into this world on purpose, even into what may be difficult circumstances. No doubt He has put you into just such a time and situation to provide the best possible opportunity for you to both seek Him and discover your place in bringing about His purposes in this life. Expanding a bit on our theme verse let's take another look at Jeremiah Chapter 29.

For I know the thoughts that I think toward you, says the LORD, thoughts of peace and not of evil, to give you a future and a hope. Then you will call upon Me and go and pray to Me, and I will listen to you. And you will seek Me and find Me, when you search for Me with all your heart. I will be found by you, says the LORD (Jeremiah 29:11-14a).

There is no time like the present to begin to put God's call to seek Him into practice. It takes but a moment to decide to become one who seeks God's face and that decision can certainly become the starting point from which one never looks back. However, even the fastest race car takes some amount of time to get from zero to sixty. We were created to seek God but, as with physical exercise, lack of engagement and regularity lead to 'soft' seeking muscles. Be prepared to put in the effort to build yourself up into a seeker of God and you will be less likely to become discouraged at the start.

No one moves from the noisy city into the country and is immediately able to perceive all of the small sounds of quiet nature. The same is true when we choose to move from the noise of our daily lives into that space where we can hear from God. Have patience and in due time you will learn to perceive the: *still small voice (1 Kings 19:12).*

Of a certainty God stands willing to enrich and guide your life with His presence, wisdom, and insight. The facets of this gem are unlimited but most fall into one of three categories.

First and foremost, in seeking we need to learn to wait on the Lord just because of Who He is and with a readiness to serve on our part. It is important to remember that it is He who is the potter and we who are the clay *(Romans 9:20-21).* If there is a commonality to the human experience we call prayer, then it is certainly that we both talk too much toward God and listen too little to God. The ability to come into His presence just for Him and not because we want something will take you farther than you can imagine.

Next, unlimited insight about life is available when we come to the quiet and specifically meditate before God on what we may have read in His word the Bible. *I have more understanding than all my teachers, for Your testimonies are my meditation (Psalm 119:99).* Not to be confused with Eastern religious forms of meditation, this is not akin to Yoga or seeking oneness with god. In Christian meditation, we seek to understand what God is saying or indicating to us in His Word and by His Spirit. Bring the passage of scripture before Him and have patience while you let your questions hang out there before God. You may find He has other things to say or other thoughts He would have you process as part of that day's journey.

Appropriately enough for people who are approaching the Lord most high, God of all creation, ruler of Heaven and earth, the last main category has to do with what we want. There is nothing wrong with bringing our cares, concerns, and needs before God. Notice, if you have ever raised or witnessed the raising of children, you know how much better the experience is for the parent when the children have matured somewhat and bring their requests without selfishness and whining. Or do we imagine that the parenthood we humans may experience is really that different from the parenthood that our Father God experiences with His almost seven billion children at last count? In approaching God with our desires and needs a proper attitude consists in having consideration and respect for God our heavenly Father. The Apostle Peter wrote: Therefore *humble yourselves under the mighty hand of God, that He may exalt you in due time, casting all your care upon Him, for He cares for you (1 Peter 5:6-7).*

We may live in a world that loves instant gratification, however in God's economy there will always be a need for that fuel called patience and this is especially true when we are seeking God. *But let patience have its perfect work, that you may be perfect and complete, lacking nothing (James 1:4).*

Putting It into Practice:

Wherever you may be at this very moment it is certainly private enough for you to be reading a book. Close your eyes or leave them open as you prefer, there is really nothing special about that. Clear your mind of everything else, God is present, you are before Him right now, He has called you to peace. Right now simply wait on God, not asking for anything, not wanting anything, ready to receive whatever He might choose to reveal or not reveal. Do this right now for 60 seconds.

If seeking God is new to you then most likely those 60 seconds, a single minute, seemed longer than you expected. I have so much more to share but let me challenge you to begin to embrace the fullness of life in God. *Psalm 34:8 Oh, taste and see that the LORD is good; blessed is the man who trusts in Him!* Mankind that is, this is for you ladies too!

The challenge:
Set aside a specific time two days this week to wait on the Lord, not asking anything, not wanting anything, just bring your spirit before His Spirit and come to the quiet for as long as you can. This will be of value to your soul.

Set aside a specific time three days this week, read a section of scripture from the Bible each day, then quiet yourself before the Lord and meditate on the meaning and anything He shows you from that passage. If you are unfamiliar with the Bible start with the first New Testament Book named Matthew.

Chapter Two

Taking the Biggest Step

(Receiving the Gospel of Jesus Christ.)

At this point we have peeked behind the scenes just a little bit. We have seen that there is, or in dawning faith that there might be, a person called God. Hopefully we are beginning to embrace the idea that we have indeed been created by Him on purpose.

Stepping back a little further and examining the world in which we live and our own lives, it becomes apparent from what we see that few, including ourselves, have taken God at His word to seek Him. In fact, for the most part human behaviors show that we as a race remain confused, often uncertain, not particularly directed, and only mildly engaged with our own destiny and purpose in life.

Take prosperity away from humans and historically they cry out to God for a while but then settle into lives mainly focused on survival. At the other extreme, give humans even general prosperity and historically they tend to forget God and look for ways to be even more 'happy' than they already are. Historically it is rare to find more than a fraction of a percent of individuals who walk consistently with God and live out what they believe is their God given mission. In short, and in agreement with the record of God's word the Bible, humans are lost. We have many built in systems of thought, opinion, religion, and self-image which work to deny this fact. Most of these add up to a faint hope that we will one day be better or one day save ourselves, but it leaves us in the same place today.

The Bible is very clear about the lost condition of each person. Whether you accept the story of Adam and Eve as fact or simply an explanatory allegory, the premise that mankind has chosen to depart from the purity of a life with God and live in our own self-will which the Bible calls sin cannot be denied. Self-will with its tendency to lead a selfish and self-preserving life is deeply ingrained in every person born. By original creation we were not intended to be so and in the next chapter we will take a much deeper look at: how we were made, what changed when sin entered the picture, and how that is modified when a person returns to God.

The progression of what is commonly called the fall of man is laid out for us in God's word. Originally there was no separation between God and His creation.

In the first chapter of the Bible we read: *Then God saw everything that He had made, and indeed it was very good (Genesis 1:31).* Man was at one with God our Creator: *And the LORD God formed man of the dust of the ground, and breathed into his nostrils the breath of life; and man became a living being (Genesis 2:7).* There was no need for an extensive code of laws but there was one rule, whether of necessity or to test man's loyalty: *And the LORD God commanded the man, saying, "Of every tree of the garden you may freely eat; but of the tree of the knowledge of good and evil you shall not eat, for in the day that you eat of it you shall surely die" (Genesis 2:16-17).*

After our forefathers had broken that rule, making a conscious choice to disobey God, our relationship with God changed. *And they heard the sound of the LORD God walking in the garden in the cool of the day, and Adam and his wife hid themselves from the presence of the LORD God among the trees of the garden (Genesis 3:8).* Fear had entered in and with it a new thing called hiding. From there the next step away from God was easy as both Adam and Eve blamed others for their sin.

Adam had the audacity to actually blame God along with Eve. *Then the man said, "The woman whom You gave to be with me, she gave me of the tree, and I ate" (Genesis 3:12).* Eve took no responsibility either, 'the devil made me do it' was her reply. *The woman said, "The serpent deceived me, and I ate" (Genesis 3:13).* Do you see a familiar pattern here? What about the people you know and what about yourself? It is pointless to deny, because it is almost automatic within ourselves, that as soon as we are either directly confronted about or find ourselves facing the possibility of confrontation that we have done wrong, we instinctively hide and place blame. Hiding and blame shifting have become ingrained in what the Bible calls our sinful nature and it is evident both in ourselves and throughout human history.

We know from the story that God shuts Adam and Eve out of the Garden of Eden and away from the eternal life with God which had been originally intended. *So He drove out the man; and He placed cherubim at the east of the garden of Eden, and a flaming sword which turned every way, to guard the way to the tree of life (Genesis 3:24).*

Mankind, influenced by evil, by our own decisions and choices and with nowhere to hide and no one to blame, had become a race of lost souls. We were separated from God and had lost our connection to Him through His Spirit. Our lost-ness and need to re-connect with God is something that is certainly felt deep within. One of Adam and Eve's first sons Abel is recorded as a person who worshipped and sought the Lord, see *Genesis 4:4*. Shortly after the fall mankind began the practice of prayer: *Then men began to call on the name of the LORD (Genesis 4:26)*.

Indicated and expressed in many places in the Bible, the Prophet Isaiah put it to us directly: *But your iniquities have separated you from your God; and your sins have hidden His face from you, so that He will not hear (Isaiah 59:2)*.

Parents are intended to be every child's foundation and proper frame of reference for understanding life. We see the reverse effects of this in our modern society in the social fallout which comes from divorce and broken homes; it affects the children the most. As children of the Living God, we also suffer the effects of being lost because our family of Creation is not whole, and there is separation between ourselves and God our Heavenly Father.

Had God lost interest or His love for us the story would have simply ended there and we would not be wrestling with the topic of seeking God. However, such is not the case. Throughout the portion of the Bible we call the Old Testament we have the record of God's interaction with mankind, mainly and purposefully through the nation of Israel through whom God has chosen to bring salvation to all.

Recorded along with all of the sins, disasters, sufferings and triumphs, the thread of God's plan for the salvation and redemption of those who will turn back to Him is woven throughout story and prophecy. The birth, life, and sufferings of Jesus Christ on our behalf to purchase pardon for our sins are fully foretold, consider *Isaiah 7:14, 9:6-7, and Chapter 53*. Peeking into just one of the prophecies we see a continuation of God's great promise regarding what we shall find when we seek Him.

"Behold, the days are coming, says the LORD, when I will make a new covenant with the house of Israel and with the house of Judah not according to the covenant that I made with their fathers in the day that I took them by the hand to lead them out of the land of Egypt, My covenant which they broke, though I was a husband to them, says the LORD. But this is the covenant that I will make with the house of Israel after those days, says the LORD: I will put My law in their minds, and write it on their hearts; and I will be their God, and they shall be My people. No more shall every man teach his neighbor, and every man his brother, saying, 'Know the LORD,' for they all shall know Me, from the least of them to the greatest of them, says the LORD. For I will forgive their iniquity, and their sin I will remember no more" (Jeremiah 31:31-34).

It is in the portion of the Bible which we call the New Testament that God fully reveals the details of His plan to address our lost and sinful condition.

We covered the initial scriptures which describe the purpose and mission of Jesus in Chapter one. To Mary, the Lord revealed: *"And behold, you will conceive in your womb and bring forth a Son, and shall call His name JESUS. He will be great, and will be called the Son of the Highest; and the Lord God will give Him the throne of His father David. And He will reign over the house of Jacob forever, and of His kingdom there will be no end."* (Luke 1:31-33). And to Joseph the Angel said: *"Joseph, son of David, do not be afraid to take to you Mary your wife, for that which is conceived in her is of the Holy Spirit. And she will bring forth a Son, and you shall call His name JESUS, for He will save His people from their sins"* (Matthew 1:20-21). Clearly the one so long foretold was being sent as an everlasting King and the one who would save His people from their sins.

Yes, it is Jesus. All of the religions of mankind, wherever they are found, attempt in some way to connect with or appease the presumed anger of God or gods. Humans have tried so many ways to bridge the gap that we feel. A certain percentage of our religions have made attempts to achieve purity. Others have fallen into the depths of perversity in fulfilling human lust or even sacrificing others in our place. Even Christianity can become no more than a mere religion with rules and regulations when those who practice it do not truly seek after and follow the Lord. As a person, Jesus Christ makes no attempt to merely fulfill the sinner's felt need to appease God. Jesus stated His own mission in these terms: *"for the Son of Man has come to seek and to save that which was lost"* (Luke 19:10) and: *"I have come that they may have life, and that they may have it more abundantly"* (John 10:10).

As difficult as it may be for humans to face, there is no moral high ground for any of us. There is no group of humans who are better than others, no club to join where all are sin free and have no need of salvation. There is no set of laws, rules, or religion which will rescue us from the separation our sinful natures create between ourselves and our God. There is nothing we ourselves can do but take His hand, because only God has the power to save.

For the grace of God that brings salvation has appeared to all men, teaching us that, denying ungodliness and worldly lusts, we should live soberly, righteously, and godly in the present age, looking for the blessed hope and glorious appearing of our great God and Savior Jesus Christ, who gave Himself for us, that He might redeem us from every lawless deed and purify for Himself His own special people, zealous for good works (Titus 2:11-14).

Jesus Christ is the grace, the un-merited favor, of God toward man. He is God's provided way of salvation for mankind. What mankind could not do for their selves,

God has done for us. Jesus the Son paid the debt of sin we owed. He has cancelled the warrant for our arrest and conviction by satisfying our crimes through the substitution of His own death in our place and He has risen from the dead, defeating the grave, to provide us with the opportunity to return through Him to the eternal life for which we were initially created, a life of re-union and union with God. We understand this mentally first from Old Testament prophecy and then from New Testament reality, but we experience this salvation when we believe God at His word and take hold of His outstretched hand. The Apostle Peter wrote of the reconciliation to God and newness of life which Jesus brings us in this way: *who Himself bore our sins in His own body on the tree, that we, having died to sins, might live for righteousness — by whose stripes you were healed. For you were like sheep going astray, but have now returned to the Shepherd and Overseer of your souls (1 Peter 2:24-25).*

The waters rise and fall, the ocean with a dark and angry look rolls on as far as the eye can see. Lighting flashes from time to time to reveal its surface and in the midst of the waves we see lost souls each concerned with their own attempt to stay afloat. It is the ocean of sin, the great sea of the present and historical wickedness of mankind. The rising and falling and gasping and struggling of each soul takes many different forms but in one manner or another all of the souls who remain in these waters eventually perish.

But look, there is hope, we see a large boat and in the boat a figure. His wounded feet are firm upon the deck. He reaches out His damaged hand to those in the water. His voice explains the simple Gospel of repentance (turn from your sin) and salvation (take My hand) to those in the water. He is pulling into His boat anyone and everyone who will meet His grasp and take His hand.

They all take His hand immediately don't they? To be sure the boat has room for everyone. No, we are sad to say, they don't. Many of them never do and many of those He has pulled into the boat remember that at first they did not take His hand either. There are as many reasons for refusing His hand as there are people struggling in the waters. Some have become so busy with their struggles that they just cannot see the man in the boat. Others believe they have found a way already and that it will eventually lead them out of the waters. Still others have made a peace and even a sort of friendship with their struggles, after all better the devil you know than the devil you don't know, they say. Some just do not care and many question the motives, the message, or even the existence of the Person in the boat. If you really exist and are really a good God then you have to save us anyway because a good God would never send anyone to Hell, so we will just continue our struggles thank you.

The question is not: how could a good God send anyone to Hell? God has been and is fully engaged in the rescue of mankind. He has committed Himself to the point of enduring death for our sins on the cross. We perish by our own willfulness and our own sinful nature. The real question is: how is it that we can continue to refuse His hand?

Why would God go to these great lengths? If you and I were on the throne of Heaven, would we even try to redeem mankind at all? Would we throw out a life-line after they had turned from the way we had created for them and wreaked such historical destruction on themselves and our creation? Likely, given our own sinful condition we would not, and most probably this is not how we would treat our self-declared enemies. Instead we would wipe them out or let them perish.

So what is the difference between ourselves, if we were master of the universe, and God who actually is? Not a few leaders, generals, and dictators have found themselves in power over larger contingents of mankind over the years; it is very rare to read about that being a good thing in the history of mankind. The difference between us and God is simple and fundamental: God is Love and we are not. *For God so loved the world that He gave His only begotten Son, that whoever believes in Him should not perish but have everlasting life.* <u>*For God did not send His Son into the world to condemn the world, but that the world through Him might be saved*</u> *(John 3:16-17).*

My Testimony:
In hopes of adding some value to this chapter on a more intimate level here is how this played out in my own life.

In general I was lost as a young person. Having suffered various disappointments in life, I adopted self-destructive tendencies and began substantially masking my feelings with substance abuse around age eleven. At seventeen I wanted out and the week I turned eighteen I ran as far away from home as I could, literally halfway around the world by joining the Army and shipping out to Germany for three years. Naturally, as with all solutions which seem right to a man, this changed nothing. I was still a lost soul and drugs were still plentiful, only now I was in a new location with different responsibilities.

My lost-ness had begun to press in on me with the start of basic training. Stripped of my human identity and separated from the gang back home, long hair gone, clothes exchanged for the drab green 'pickle-suit' of the US Army, I began to really reach for anything to hang onto. My mother's voice, what was the sound of my mother's voice? As I moved on to advanced training I can remember sitting up under the big Texas sky while waiting for formation, the questions of life were crowding in on me. Who am I? What is this life all about? Is there any meaning or purpose to this world I find myself in?

In Germany our NATO missile base operated 24 hours a day, seven days a week. By this time I had found my footing as a soldier and of course, with no real changes having occurred, I was back to all my old self-destructive ways. But the questions would not leave me alone. One night as I lay in a bunk of the missile base ready bay, I looked over and saw a stack of Bibles next to the TV. My mind flashed back on a number of people who had tried to tell me about God over the years. For their troubles they had gotten the mouth, or spit on, or punched and kicked, and even a banana peel accurately landed on the open Bible of a street preacher. My friends and I had gathered Bibles that were handed out at high school and we took and made a bon-fire of them. I don't know about the others but I don't remember even having a reason for why we did that. Perhaps it was just Satan at his best?

Now I was lying there thinking: I have cursed everyone who has tried to tell me what is in that book… I think I will read it!

I cannot remember where I started to read but I do remember being truly amazed at what the Bible had to say. I remember thinking: wow, it really talks about a person called God, it really says stuff like this about hope and salvation and all that. I remember my decision: I'm going to take this down to my barracks with me and read from it.

Well, I did not know where to start. I had no church background except that churches were those places you met for Boy Scouts and which were open all day for boys to play around inside and find things to steal. But one of my army friends seemed to have some knowledge. He would smoke a big pipe of hashish and then read in the Book of Revelations. I still remember him turning the pages and saying: 'wow...Wow...Wow!', so I figured that Revelations would be a great place for me to start.

One night I was alone in my barracks room reading God's word and wondering about the things it said. All of a sudden, Jesus stood to the right of my desk. I did not see Him physically but, however He did it, His presence was so tangible as to be without doubt (see *1 Samuel 3:10*). Without spoken words He began to show me: this is what you are reading about, this is Who I am, this is who you are, you need me as your Savior. His presence left, I got up, locked my door, got down on my knees and asked: 'Lord save me.' I remember wondering: 'What is going to happen next?'

Well, what did happen next? I was still very uneducated with next to zero background in the things of God. As yet I had no clue that I had been living a self-destructive life or that any of my filthy behaviors would need to be changed. However, my whole teenage life I had gone about with a phony tough guy act; I had been hurt enough and no one was allowed to get past my guard. But as I awoke the next day I sensed a change, the phony mask on a stick that I had held up to protect myself from others was gone and I did not even know where it went. It would be the first of the Lord's miracles in my life. I was eighteen, born again, and I had a new best friend, Jesus. That was about all I understood at that point.

So much has happened over the last 37 years since I took Jesus' hand. Knowing Him has made all the difference in my life. In His own way, the Lord moved in and patiently began to lead me, bringing the changes which would shape me into the person He had intended me to be. As coarse as my beginning was, I was in God's boat and a member of Jesus' crew.

I can definitely assure you that sailing with Jesus beats perishing in our own sin. However, to continue to use my metaphor, you must know that this mighty ship of God's salvation is not a passenger cruise line but rather a working vessel. Salvation serves the purpose of God in Christ: *to seek and to save that which was lost" (Luke 19:10) and that they may have life, and that they may have it more abundantly" (John 10:10).*

Those who try to turn the grace of God into a cruise for themselves always end up disappointed because they find their self at cross purposes with the Master of the ship. Those who receive the blessing of being called into this grace and salvation and turn to assist the Master of the ship in His purposes end up living a fulfilling life with no need of regrets.

Is the invitation to take His hand open to everyone? The Apostle Peter tells us that: *The Lord is not slack concerning His promise, as some count slackness, but is long-suffering toward us, not willing that any should perish but that all should come to repentance (2 Peter 3:9).* Jesus said: *"And I, if I am lifted up from the earth, will draw all peoples to Myself." This He said, signifying by what death He would die (John 12:32-33).* The answer is yes. All of us are being called by God to leave our self-centered and sinful lives, which serve to trap us in darkness, and in which we do not know the Lord, and to take His hand and enter into new life to begin becoming those who do seek and know Him.

Then Peter said to them, "Repent, and let every one of you be baptized in the name of Jesus Christ for the remission of sins; and you shall receive the gift of the Holy Spirit. For the promise is to you and to your children, and to all who are afar off, as many as the Lord our God will call" (Acts 2:38-39).

"Most assuredly, I say to you, he who hears My word and believes in Him who sent Me has everlasting life, and shall not come into judgment, but has passed from death into life" (Jesus Christ- John 5:24-25).

All of the words of God and each of the promises of God are there for all who will join Him. *For you are all sons of God through faith in Christ Jesus. For as many of you as were baptized into Christ have put on Christ. There is neither Jew nor Greek, there is neither slave nor free, there is neither male nor female; for you are all one in Christ Jesus. And if you are Christ's, then you are Abraham's seed, and heirs according to the promise (Galatians 3:26-29).*

Putting It into Practice: (Taking the Biggest Step)

My goal throughout this book is to shine a spotlight on many of the areas of God's word, the Bible, that call us to a life of seeking, knowing, and following God. I know that there are so many voices calling us in so many different directions these days but I also know that if we ignore the basic and fundamental truths, which God has provided, we will not have a happy ending.

For example, if indeed Jesus Christ is trying to lead us somewhere and we choose not to follow Him, then we will not get to where He is trying to take us. On the other hand, regardless of our level of knowledge and regardless of who we are, where we have come from, or what we have done, if we will take His outstretched hand and simply receive into our hearts Jesus' gift of dying to satisfy the judgment and penalty for our sins and His gift of overcoming the power of the grave through His resurrection, then we can begin to walk with Him as seekers of God starting now and through eternity.

I am thankful if this writing finds that you are already in the faith and have taken the biggest step. Read on as we step even further into what it means to belong to God and to seek Him for daily living and destiny.

Perhaps you recognize that taking this biggest step is something that you have never really done. Perhaps this message of God's Gospel, or 'good news', of salvation through Jesus Christ is completely new to you or is being presented in a new light. I hope the words of this chapter and the beginning of my own testimony have made you wonder and made you hope that there is so much more to life than has appeared before. Does the message excite you? Do you find it scary? Perhaps doubts remain. In any case, I want to encourage you to seek the Lord about this until you are convinced one way or the other. I mentioned in the introduction that God Himself is able to satisfy you that He exists and that He has provided His word for you to live by. I also mentioned that this proof would come as you embraced God's promise made to you and to all mankind: *And you will seek Me and find Me, when you search for Me with all your heart. I will be found by you, says the LORD (Jeremiah 29:13-14a).*

The time for bravery has come: seek God, spend time with God, ask God to reveal Himself to you and to confirm to your spirit the truth or fiction of the words about salvation which I have written to you in this chapter. Search the scriptures to find out if they support what I have been telling you. *Then the brethren immediately sent Paul and Silas away by night to Berea. When they arrived, they went into the synagogue of the Jews. These were more fair-minded than those in Thessalonica, in that they received the word with all readiness, and searched the Scriptures daily to find out whether these things were so (Acts 17:10-11).*

God is not afraid of your questions, go ahead and ask them and, once you are convinced, ask Jesus to save you and join His crew with the understanding that there is no turning back. There really is nothing for us in the waters of sin.

Seek the LORD while He may be found, Call upon Him while He is near. Let the wicked forsake his way, and the unrighteous man his thoughts; let him return to the LORD, and He will have mercy on him; and to our God, for He will abundantly pardon (Isaiah 55:6-7).

But without faith it is impossible to please Him, for he who comes to God must believe that He is, and that He is a rewarder of those who diligently seek Him (Hebrews 11:6).

Chapter Three

Seeking God for Who He is

Hopefully you have already begun to take up the challenge of seeking the Lord. Spending time in His presence, asking Him to reveal more of Himself to you, bringing Him your needs and perhaps the needs of others and, above all, patiently listening to attune yourself more and more to His Spirit. The next leg of our journey takes us deeper into who God is.

It would be perfectly normal for me to head to the store, grab a gallon of milk, take it to the front, pay the checker, and walk out without coming to know who the checker is. It is not normal to show up in prayer before the Lord with a shopping list in hand but with no regard for a real relationship with Him. One of the first steps in any relationship is to learn about the other person. God already knows more about you and me than we know about ourselves, but what more can we know about God?

Well who is God anyway? Having a depth of understanding about this will definitely come in handy as we move forward in becoming people who seek God for daily living and destiny.

In Chapter One, we reviewed our own existence and understood that we are not here by chance or accident. God specifically planned for us to be. He chose our family of nurture, our environment, and the point at which we entered history. *Acts 17:26-27* taught us that God set this up so that we might seek Him.

Diving into the subject of who God is and what God is like, we turn to His word the Bible and a bit of human history to gain a firm foundation. It is of the highest importance for you and I to know what we believe about God so that we may be assured about the One Who holds our lives in His hands.

Let's start with the very first sentences of the Bible: *In the beginning God created the heavens and the earth. The earth was without form, and void; and darkness was on the face of the deep. And the Spirit of God was hovering over the face of the waters. Then God said, "Let there be light"; and there was light (Genesis 1:1-3).*

Wow! What a scene! The stage is set and the Master of the play calls for the curtain to part. Let's see who we have on this initial stage at the start of the heavens and earth. In this passage we see: God, the Spirit of God, and someone else, the Word of God is there. In fact as we continue to read the first chapter of the first book of the Bible, we see that all of God's creation was brought into being by His spoken Word.

The Gospel of John provides the most descriptive insight about the Word of God as a person. In speaking of Jesus he writes: *In the beginning was the Word, and the Word was with God, and the Word was God. He was in the beginning with God. All things were made through Him, and without Him nothing was made that was made. And the Word became flesh and dwelt among us, and we beheld His glory, the glory as of the only begotten of the Father, full of grace and truth (John 1:1-3, 14).*

Speaking further of Jesus Christ, the Apostle Paul would write: *He is the image of the invisible God, the firstborn over all creation. For by Him all things were created that are in heaven and that are on earth, visible and invisible, whether thrones or dominions or principalities or powers. All things were created through Him and for Him. And He is before all things, and in Him all things consist (Colossians 1:15-17).*

The Hebrew word used in the first verses of Genesis and throughout the Old Testament portion of the Bible for God is: 'elohihm, pronounced el-o-heem'. This word contains a bit of a surprise package in that it is actually a plural word, yet it is consistently used of the one supreme God.

From this as well as many passages of scripture in both the Old and New Testament we understand that there is one God eternally existent as Father, Son, and Holy Spirit. Traditionally this revelation of God is called the Trinity.

Jesus said of Himself; *'I and My Father are one' (John 10:30).* Jesus affirms this oneness of God in answer to Philip's question, *Philip said to Him, "Lord, show us the Father, and it is sufficient for us." Jesus said to him, "Have I been with you so long, and yet you have not known Me, Philip? He who has seen Me has seen the Father; so how can you say, 'Show us the Father'? Do you not believe that I am in the Father, and the Father in Me? The words that I speak to you I do not speak on My own authority; but the Father who dwells in Me does the works. Believe Me that I am in the Father and the Father in Me, or else believe Me for the sake of the works themselves' (John 14:8-11).*

It is clear through any reading of the scripture that the Israelites were taught this concept of God's oneness as in *Deuteronomy 6:4-5, "Hear, O Israel: The LORD our God, the LORD is one! You shall love the LORD your God with all your heart, with all your soul, and with all your strength.* This is also why as Christians we are commissioned by

Jesus to *"Go therefore and make disciples of all the nations, baptizing them in the name of the Father and of the Son and of the Holy Spirit, teaching them to observe all things that I have commanded you; and lo, I am with you always, even to the end of the age." (Matthew 28:19-20).* That is the name, singular tense, of: the Father, Son, and Holy Spirit, the one supreme God.

Moses was not just curious about Who God was, he was also a bit afraid and was wanting to make sure that he had his story straight. After all, God was telling Moses to return to Egypt from which he had recently fled for his life and walk straight up to Pharaoh the king and tell him that the Lord says 'let my people go'. (The Israelites had been slaves of the Egyptians for about 400 years at this time.) So while standing in front of the burning bush Moses, like any good seeker, asks the obvious question. *Then Moses said to God, "Indeed, when I come to the children of Israel and say to them, 'The God of your fathers has sent me to you,' and they say to me, 'What is His name?' what shall I say to them?" (Exodus 3:13).*

God understands Moses need to know and as we shall discover His response is short but it has very wide implications. *And God said to Moses, "I AM WHO I AM." And He said, "Thus you shall say to the children of Israel, 'I AM has sent me to you'" Moreover God said to Moses, "Thus you shall say to the children of Israel: 'The LORD God of your fathers, the God of Abraham, the God of Isaac, and the God of Jacob, has sent me to you. This is My name forever, and this is My memorial to all generations' (Exodus 3:14-15).*

Just a few chapters later in the book of Exodus, God reveals one last layer which ties this all together after which we will review and bridge together the importance of understanding God's name. *And God spoke to Moses and said to him: "I am the LORD. I appeared to Abraham, to Isaac,*

and to Jacob, as God Almighty, but by My name LORD I was not known to them (Exodus 6:2-3).
I AM WHO I AM, tell them *I AM* has sent you. The Hebrew word for I AM is hayah, pronounced haw-yaw, this a prime root meaning: to exist. In the Bible this word is always used emphatically with force or decisiveness of expression. Picture explaining to someone that you exist in a strong voice, head held high, shoulders erect, and pushing your fist out in front of you, it is a statement of decisive expression.

God's name, and He states it doubled, *I AM WHO I AM*, means: the existing one who exists! God goes on to speak of Himself as: *'The LORD God of your fathers'* and then states that their fathers knew Him as *God Almighty* which in Hebrew is 'el shadday, pronounced ale-shaddah'-ee. He also says that by His name *'LORD'* He was not known to them.

This name *'LORD'* is the Hebrew word Yehovah, pronounced yeh-ho-vaw', which comes from the root word hayah or I AM. Yehovah, or Jehovah as we commonly use it in English, means: the self-existent or eternal. It is found throughout the Old Testament portion of the Bible as the word LORD and the standard word for word English translations of the Bible make it recognizable through this all capitalized letter form. The Hebrew people considered the name of God to be so sacred that their scribes would not spell it out but rather used the abbreviated form of YHWH, in their own lettering of course.

So what does this mean to us and how does it help us to understand God? Even nature reveals to us that anything built to last requires a solid foundation. If I am going to take God at His promise and become a person who seeks Him with all of my heart, it is going to give me great comfort to know that God is solid and not 'squishy'.

Having Him reveal His name like this to us, and knowing that He is the self-existent existing One Who exists, makes me feel a lot better about my choice and lets me know that I am starting to build on solid ground and not sinking sand.

The Bible does not give us any details about where God might have come from or how He chose His personality. As we have read it just starts out with *'In the beginning God'*. I suppose we can ask Him on that day when each of us will stand before Him if at that point it even remains a relevant question. I suspect that the answer is as far above us as we are above the fish in our fish tank. Take care that you do not make that one unanswerable question into a barrier which prevents you from seeking God further. I have met a number of people who used unanswerable questions as their excuse for in-action in life. In reality, they are either afraid to live or just lazy, both lead to a missed destiny.

We read of Moses: *So the LORD spoke to Moses face to face, as a man speaks to his friend (Exodus 33:11)*. This friend of God would later share his understanding about the existence of God through the words of a Psalm: *Before the mountains were brought forth, or ever You had formed the earth and the world, Even from everlasting to everlasting, You are God (Psalm 90:2)*. I have always found it great comfort to know that God is eternal, solid, and unchanging as it is written; *Jesus Christ is the same yesterday, today, and forever (Hebrew 13:8)*.

Diving a bit deeper into the implications of God's name, it is through this name of God, LORD, that we discover the character of God. The Who and what of how God has chosen to be. We know from the scriptures that God is Holy and that He is a God who knows His people and wants His people to know Him. God also describes Himself as being kind in a particular way, described as loving-kindness. He is also just and has His heart set on what is right and uses His own name in telling us these things. *Thus says the LORD: "Let not the wise man glory in his wisdom, Let not the mighty man glory in his might, Nor let the rich man glory in his riches; But let him who glories glory in this, That he understands and knows Me, That I am the LORD, exercising lovingkindness, judgment, and righteousness in the earth. For in these I delight," says the LORD (Jeremiah 9:23-24).*

Have you ever stopped to consider that God was under no obligation to choose to be holy or just or loving or kind? There was no point in time when another suggested these things to Him. Each and every character quality and attribute of God was chosen by Himself. (See *Job 36:22-23, Isaiah 40:13-14, Romans 11:34-35.*) God could just as easily have chosen to be otherwise. I for one am grateful to find that my life is in the hands of the living eternal God, who loves me as Jesus said: *for the Father Himself loves you, because you have loved Me, and have believed that I came forth from God (John 16:27).*

God Himself revealed another level of His character and nature when He told the Israelites that if they follow Him they would not have to worry about their health, *for I am the LORD who heals you (Exodus 15:26).* Healing His people is part of God's chosen character, part of who God is.

On mount Moriah at God's rescue of Isaac, Abraham, the father of our faith and known as God's friend (see *Romans 4:11-12, James 2:23),* would learn that it is God's nature to provide for His people. *And Abraham called the name of the place, The-LORD-Will-Provide; as it is said to this day, "In the Mount of the LORD it shall be provided" (Genesis 22:14).*

At the first defeat of the Amalekite raiders, Moses, Aaron, and Hur would come to know that the LORD is a banner over His people. *And Moses built an altar and called its name, The-LORD-Is-My-Banner (Exodus 17:15).*

When Gideon realized that he had seen the Angel of the LORD face to face and still lived, *Gideon built an altar there to the LORD, and called it The-LORD-Is-Peace (Judges 6:24).*

Before he was king, David was a shepherd and the one thing he truly learned about God is expressed in his widely known *Psalm 23* which begins with: *The LORD is my shepherd; I shall not want (Psalm 23:1).*

In one of many prophecies of the first coming of Jesus, Jeremiah was used by God to affirm the nature of Christ. *"Behold, the days are coming," says the LORD, "That I will raise to David a Branch of righteousness; a King shall reign and prosper, and execute judgment and righteousness in the earth. In His days Judah will be saved, and Israel will dwell safely; now this is His name by which He will be called: THE LORD OUR RIGHTEOUSNESS" (Jeremiah 23:5-6).*

Ezekiel would end his prophetic book with a look at the Holy City coupling the name of God with God's presence, *and the name of the city from that day shall be: THE LORD IS THERE (Ezekiel 48:35).*

The main point and force of these and many other passages which reveal the character and nature of God is not that God will give you these as if they were things to be handed from one person to another. No, the power which is being expressed here is that God is: healing, provision, the banner, peace, your shepherd, righteous, and He Is There.

This same unfolding revelation continues right into the New Testament of Jesus Christ Who, as we have clearly seen, *is the image of the invisible God* and of Whom we read: *In the beginning was the Word, and the Word was with God, and the Word was God.*

We have also read that Joseph was told not to be afraid to marry his (oops, pregnant!) girl friend Mary. By the way, this was a much bigger deal in those days than it is now. The Hebrew law pretty much said that Joseph was to bring her to the town square to be stoned to death if she had cheated on him during their engagement. However, as we read *Matthew 1:18-24*, we find that Joseph was a just man who planned to put Mary away quietly. At this point the LORD sends Joseph a dream and tells him what the deal is and not to be afraid of the marriage. *But while he thought about these things, behold, an angel of the Lord appeared to him in a dream, saying, "Joseph, son of David, do not be afraid to take to you Mary your wife, for that which is conceived in her is of the Holy Spirit. And she will bring forth a Son, and you shall call His name JESUS, for He will save His people from their sins" (Matthew 1:20-21).*

What's in a name? Well, there is plenty in Jesus' name. Are you ready for a brain twister? Jesus is our English translation of the New Testament Greek name: Iesous, pronounced ee-ay-sooce, which is of Hebrew origin from the Old Testament Yehowshuwa`, pronounced yeh-ho-shoo'-ah, or as we have translated in English; Joshua.

Now why is that relevant? Well, Yehowshuwa` means: Yehovah saved, or Jehovah saved, in short the self-existent One has saved. *You shall call His name JESUS, for He will save His people from their sins.*

In many ways Jesus made it very clear that He was indeed God come to save us and one of His main methods for this communication was to let us know that He is 'I AM' who spoke to Moses from the burning bush.

And Jesus said to them, "I am the bread of life. He who comes to Me shall never hunger, and he who believes in Me shall never thirst" (John 6:35).

Then Jesus spoke to them again, saying, "I am the light of the world. He who follows Me shall not walk in darkness, but have the light of life" (John 8:12).

"I am the door. If anyone enters by Me, he will be saved, and will go in and out and find pasture" (John 10:9).

"I am the good shepherd; and I know My sheep, and am known by My own" (John 10:14).

Jesus said to her, "I am the resurrection and the life. He who believes in Me, though he may die, he shall live. And whoever lives and believes in Me shall never die. Do you believe this?" (John 11:25-26).

"You call Me Teacher and Lord, and you say well, for so I am" (John 13:13).

Jesus said to him, "I am the way, the truth, and the life. No one comes to the Father except through Me" (John 14:6).

"I am the vine, you are the branches. He who abides in Me, and I in him, bears much fruit; for without Me you can do nothing" (John 15:5-6).

The woman said to Him, "I know that Messiah is coming" (who is called Christ). "When He comes, He will tell us all things." Jesus said to her, "I who speak to you am He" (John 4:25-26).

Once again we are intended to understand the force and depth of power in these sayings. Jesus did not just come to give you light, a door, resurrection, truth, life, or to make a way insuring you get shepherded through life. Jesus Christ Himself is the light, the door, the resurrection and the life, the way the truth and the life, our Teacher, Lord, and that great Shepherd of the sheep. He is the branch to whom God intends to attach us and He is the promised Messiah, the Savior of the world.

Jesus spoke these things to His first followers and shortly thereafter He gave His life for ours and after three days, as fore-told, He rose from the dead. For anyone who remains skeptical regarding the truth of Jesus' resurrection the most powerful proof we have been given is that His followers went out and in only 300 years, turned the pagan world upside down.

Now perhaps we might find one person who believed some crazy story and spent their life telling others about it. In fact, that would not be hard to find in our day; there seem to be plenty of people who have 'lost it' wandering about. But where would you find eleven men, later joined by one more, who were so convinced of what they had seen and heard, and knew that they had met with the risen Christ, that they spent their lives preaching His message in hostile times with all but one being put to death for what they taught and believed?

Not just the Apostles but literally hundreds of thousands of souls across the Roman Empire experienced the power of God through the seed of their preaching and their actions and believed. In the first 300 years thousands of the members of Jesus' early church would stand firm in their faith being martyred by the Roman government, and the rest were typically familiar with persecution for their beliefs. Indeed although major segments of the future church would become mere religious shadows of what God in Christ had intended, there have always been areas of the world where true followers of Jesus suffer and even die for their faith, we just don't see it very often in our western news media.

Jesus had firmly established His church, cleansed by His own blood and sealed by His Holy Spirit. Near the end of the Apostle John's life, when John himself was in exile for the sake of the Gospel, Jesus appeared to him. Jesus commanded John to write, which resulted in creation of the last Book of the Bible known as Revelation. In that Book, Jesus puts the crowning touch on His I AM sayings, certainly affirming His identity for His church in no uncertain terms.

John records this encounter with Jesus Christ at the beginning of the Book: *And when I saw Him, I fell at His feet as dead. But He laid His right hand on me, saying to me, "Do not be afraid; I am the First and the Last. I am He who lives, and was dead, and behold, I am alive forevermore. Amen. And*

*I have the keys of Hades and of Death. Write the things which
you have seen, and the things which are, and the things which
will take place after this" (Revelation 1:17-19).*

In closing the Book of Revelation, Jesus would speak
these words: *"And behold, I am coming quickly, and My
reward is with Me, to give to every one according to his
work. I am the Alpha and the Omega, the Beginning and the
End, the First and the Last." Blessed are those who do His
commandments, that they may have the right to the tree of life,
and may enter through the gates into the city. But outside are
dogs and sorcerers and sexually immoral and murderers and
idolaters, and whoever loves and practices a lie. "I, Jesus, have
sent My angel to testify to you these things in the churches.
I am the Root and the Offspring of David, the Bright and
Morning Star." And the Spirit and the bride say, "Come!" And
let him who hears say, "Come!" And let him who thirsts come.
Whoever desires, let him take the water of life freely (Revelation
22:12-17).*

At the beginning of this chapter I did say that we were
diving into the subject of who God is and what God is
like. Do you feel wet yet? By now you should understand
more about the one God Who reveals Himself in three
persons: Father, Son, and Holy Spirit. We will be taking a
much deeper look at God the Holy Spirit in a later chapter.
However at this time let's ask ourselves why God decided
to reveal Himself in this way to mankind. After all, in
the same manner as His other attributes and the rest of
His personality, being one God eternally existent in three
persons is something which God chose for Himself and,
from what we know, we can bet that this was done with
purpose. We don't know whether this was chosen just for
our benefit or to serve a higher purpose. But as we will
see in our next chapter, where we consider what it means
to us that we have been created in God's image, it is not
really that strange and is actually highly relevant for us.

In examining God's triple personhood on the surface and in relationship to ourselves there are a few things to be grasped.

First of all, in God we will find a true Father. The main role of our earthly fathers was originally intended as a pointer to our Heavenly Father, to be a means of connecting us as children to God. Perhaps your father did a great job of this, perhaps he failed miserably; regardless we have a true Father in God who knows us better than we know ourselves and yet with all of our faults He loves us. Jesus reminds us once again: *for the Father Himself loves you, because you have loved Me, and have believed that I came forth from God (John 16:27).* While this describes a special love for those who believe, God's love did not begin at that point. *But God demonstrates His own love toward us, in that while we were still sinners, Christ died for us (Romans 5:8). For God so loved the world that He gave His only begotten Son, that whoever believes in Him should not perish but have everlasting life (John 3:16).*

We have read that Jesus Christ is the very Word of God. He was with God in the beginning and indeed is God. The Father sent the Son on His mission to seek and save that which is lost by placing Him into our world as a man, the Son of God. *Let this mind be in you which was also in Christ Jesus, who, being in the form of God, did not consider it robbery to be equal with God, but made Himself of no reputation, taking the form of a bondservant, and coming in the likeness of men. And being found in appearance as a man, He humbled Himself and became obedient to the point of death, even the death of the cross. Therefore God also has highly exalted Him and given Him the name which is above every name, that at the name of Jesus every knee should bow, of those in heaven, and of those on earth, and of those under the earth, and that every tongue should confess that Jesus Christ is Lord, to the glory of God the Father (Philippians 2:5-11).*

Christ is not actually Jesus' last name. In His day, what passed for a last name was the place you were from or your father's name. Jesus gave Simon the new name of Cephas or Peter, both meaning a stone or rock (see *John 1:42*). He was originally called: Simon bar Jonah, meaning Simon the son of Jonah (see *John 21:15*). We do read of Jesus of Nazareth, which is where Jesus was from. We never read of Him being Jesus bar Joseph, the son of Joseph. We do read of Jesus being the Son of God. In *Matthew*, we have Jesus' question and Peter's response: *He said to them, "But who do you say that I am?" Simon Peter answered and said, "You are the Christ, the Son of the living God" (Matthew 16:15-16).* The Greek word used is Christos meaning the anointed, from the Greek word chrio: to smear or rub with oil, which also implies the act of consecrating someone for their mission in life.

We come to know Jesus Christ as our Savior, our Lord, and our Master, however it is His intent that we also come to find Him as our closest friend, the older brother of the new family into which our Heavenly Father has called us. The scriptures give us a hint about what Jesus' friendship is to be like, *"A man who has friends must himself be friendly, But there is a friend who sticks closer than a brother" (Proverbs 18:24).* Jesus is the friend who will stick closer than a brother, a friend who understands us, knows us, and is not afraid to tell us the truth about ourselves. He is a friend with whom we can be open and honest, bringing our deepest problems and fears to Him for help. It is an awesome thing that the living God, whom we do need to respect and are called to obey, desires that we come to know Him, sharing in His love and friendship.

Before Jesus departed from His original disciples He made them a promise. *"These things I have spoken to you while being present with you. But the Helper, the Holy Spirit, whom the Father will send in My name, He will teach you all things, and bring to your remembrance all things that I said to you" (John 14:25-26).* We need God to be this level of present reality in our lives, where He is actually with us and we can learn from and be guided by Him on a daily basis. Jesus made it very clear that the Holy Spirit of God was not separate from Himself and the Father, but rather a distinct representation of God toward us in this manner of being able to live within our spirit. Jesus indicates this very directly, *Jesus answered and said to him, "If anyone loves Me, he will keep My word; and My Father will love him, and We will come to him and make Our home with him" (John 14:23).* There is much to learn about God the Holy Spirit and I have devoted a full chapter to this further on.

Beloved, let us love one another, for love is of God; and everyone who loves is born of God and knows God. He who does not love does not know God, for God is love. In this the love of God was manifested toward us, that God has sent His only begotten Son into the world, that we might live through Him. In this is love, not that we loved God, but that He loved us and sent His Son to be the propitiation for our sins. Beloved, if God so loved us, we also ought to love one another (1 John 4:7-11). Everything we have looked at so far with regard to who God is and what God is like comes together in John's writing: *God is love.* God has been incredibly gracious and patient with mankind and with you and me in particular. He sacrificed His own Self, Jesus, to pay the price for our violation of His holiness that we might have a way back to Him.

Lastly, let us take a look at what might be considered the flip side of God: jealousy, anger, and wrath.

In the same manner as ourselves, the Israelites lived in a day and age when the world was filled with false gods. People are far more readily drawn to worship the creation rather than the creator, give their love to material things, worship pleasure, one another, and even their own selves. How must that make God feel? It is not in the fallen nature of mankind to seek the LORD, which is why He is seeking us and calling us to become those who seek Him that we might find Him. God feels deeply about this. He is not just jealous about our worship of the creation, He is that jealousy. *Take heed to yourself, lest you make a covenant with the inhabitants of the land where you are going, lest it be a snare in your midst. But you shall destroy their altars, break their sacred pillars, and cut down their wooden images (for you shall worship no other god, for the LORD, whose name is Jealous , is a jealous God), lest you make a covenant with the inhabitants of the land, and they play the harlot with their gods and make sacrifice to their gods, and one of them invites you and you eat of his sacrifice, and you take of his daughters for your sons, and his daughters play the harlot with their gods and make your sons play the harlot with their gods (Exodus 34:12-16).*

Your greatest creation goes astray, how would you feel? You want them back; in fact you are jealous for them. The Hebrew word used means just that. The self-existent One is: qanna', pronounced kan-naw', meaning jealous. It comes from the prime root word qana', pronounced kaw-naw', which means to be zealous, mostly found in use in the Bible where God or someone was zealous for God's cause, having a deeply felt desire for the outcome that God desires. You see, God is very intent on His mission of seeking and saving that which was lost, (us).

Is God an angry God? Is He a God of wrath? This is a common accusation which we hear from people. It is usually part of an excuse for why they don't seek God. Those who tread lightly through the Bible without seeking much depth or those who take the words of others without exploring God for themselves often end up with this conclusion, that God is angry and wrathful. That God is the proverbial kid with the magnifying glass tormenting the poor human ants with the heat of the sun's rays. We live as if God neither exists nor matters until difficulty or disaster strikes and then we bring Him into the equation. Where was God? Why did God let this happen? The fact is that God is often angry about what goes on down here. *God is a just judge, and God is angry with the wicked every day (Psalm 7:11).* God has also acted in wrath on many occasions, which we can read about and see though history. We learn of God's wrath in its current form from *Romans Chapter 1:18-32.* I will not print the entire selection here, as you can read it from the Bible, but it does tell us that from God's viewpoint He has revealed Himself to mankind and for the most part they want to follow their passions and not be bothered with His truth. His 'wrath' has been to give mankind up to their own uncleanness, passions, and debased ways of thinking and behavior. It starts like this: *For the wrath of God is revealed from heaven against all ungodliness and unrighteousness of men, who suppress the truth in unrighteousness (Romans 1:18).*

In effect God lets people reap the fruit of whatever kind of seed they choose to plant. It is important even for those of us who are actively seeking God and following Him daily to understand that all of us 'reap what we sow'. It is one of God's great natural laws as sure as the law of gravity. There are a number of places in the scriptures which cover this principal of God's creation but few say it better than the Apostle Paul: *Do not be deceived, God is not mocked; for whatever a man sows, that he will also reap. For he who sows to his flesh will of the flesh reap corruption, but he who sows to the Spirit will of the Spirit reap everlasting life (Galatians 6:7-8).*

Even in His wrath of giving man up to man's own devices we find that God has merely created another tool for assisting us in finding Him. When do people seek the

Lord? Do they usually turn to God when everything is
going well, or when their lives are a mess and out of control? When do people usually cry out for salvation or at
least seek to know whether there is a God who cares? The
old army saying is usually true: there are no atheists in
foxholes. God has more patience than we do and His actions versus our actions show that He definitely values
our souls much more highly than we do and so makes
every opportunity to connect with us. There is a point after which it is too late to be saved, too late to seek God,
too late to turn one's life around. The day of the Lord will
come and indeed comes for each of us at death. *But, beloved, do not forget this one thing, that with the Lord one day is
as a thousand years, and a thousand years as one day. The Lord
is not slack concerning His promise, as some count slackness,
but is longsuffering toward us, not willing that any should perish but that all should come to repentance (2 Peter 3:8-9).*

Notice that there is never any connection between
God being angry or God being wrathful and the name
of God. We don't read that: I the LORD am angry or am
wrathful. In all the occasions and ways we have covered
in which God has revealed 'who' He is and 'what' He is
like we have not found Him to reveal Himself as having a
character or nature that 'is' anger or 'is' wrath.

Humans should live in a proper fear of God. This fear
includes the respect due to Him and the knowledge of
what will result for those who insist on lives of disobedience and neglect of God. Being afraid of God is not the
same thing as having a healthy fear of God. Those who
are afraid of God are either misguided and in need of instruction or are specifically guilty and in need of repentance.

Would you like to look into the very heart of God and
see what is really there? How does He really feel? Because if my creation went south on me I would definitely

have some strong feelings. Well, let's jump back into the scriptures and find out.

Do you know why God chose to bring the great flood in the days of Noah, leaving only Noah and his family alive? It could not have been an easy choice to make but basically God just could not take the pain any more. If you have ever experienced grief of heart then try and imagine it on the scale of God's experience. *Then the LORD saw that the wickedness of man was great in the earth, and that every intent of the thoughts of his heart was only evil continually. And the LORD was sorry that He had made man on the earth, and He was grieved in His heart (Genesis 6:5-6).*

For another peek into the very heart of God we turn to that moment just after God had given Moses the Ten Commandments. The children of Israel were a nation newly freed by God after 400 years of slavery. God had brought them out of bondage and was beginning to establish them as a nation with guidelines, laws, worship, etc. In *Deuteronomy Chapter 5* the people send their leaders to Moses to tell him that they heard the words of God, the Ten Commandments, and that they are afraid and don't want to hear God's voice anymore. They want Moses to go listen to God for them and then tell them what God says.

Note that this is not the heart of a seeker of God. God has called each of us to seek Him and not to hide behind a 'holy' man.

God's response to what the people tell Moses reveals His heart and what would have been His desire for them. He knows it is true that they are afraid but He desires a life of depth and peace for them. *"Then the LORD heard the voice of your words when you spoke to me, and the LORD said to me: 'I have heard the voice of the words of this people which they have spoken to you. They are right in all that they have spoken. Oh, that they had such a heart in them that they would fear Me and always keep all My commandments, that it might be well with them and with their children forever!'" (Deuteronomy 5:28-29).*

Putting It into Practice:

Everything we have just covered about Who God is and what He is like indicates that God is intensely interested in calling us into a peaceful relationship with Himself. Indeed the Living God has gone out of His way in promises, actions, influence of historical events, and a level of graciousness which we humans do not deserve. God has done this in order to call us to Himself as those who seek Him, find Him, and follow Him into the blessing such a relationship will bring.

Do yourself the ultimate favor and make time on a daily regular basis to respond to God, Who is intently interested and has gone out of His way to offer this relationship to you. Be sure that some of your time spent with God includes simply seeking Him for Who He is.

Ask God to reveal Himself more and more to you. Learn to get in tune with His Spirit through waiting on Him in a listening mode.

If we need more then there is more for many of the truths about our Creator are revealed to us through His creation. We have read that: *In the beginning God created the heavens and the earth (Genesis 1:1)* and that: *All things were created through Him and for Him. And He is before all things, and in Him all things consist (Colossians 1:15-17).* King David proclaimed: *The heavens declare the glory of God; and the firmament shows His handiwork. Day unto day utters speech, and night unto night reveals knowledge. There is no speech nor language where their voice is not heard. Their line has gone out through all the earth, and their words to the end of the world (Psalm 19:1-4).*

Putting this all together, the Apostle Paul, in speaking of those who refuse to know God wrote: *because what may be known of God is manifest in them, for God has shown it to them. For since the creation of the world His invisible attributes are clearly seen, being understood by the things that are made, even His eternal power and Godhead, so that they are without excuse (Romans 1:19-20).*

Everything created has something to tell us about the one who created it. If at all possible consider taking the time to get yourself out into nature, a local park, or out under the stars at night. If this is not possible for you due to confinement or situation, then perhaps pictures from books, magazines, or even the television may help. As a last resort use your God given imagination.

Consider the universe, geology, plant, animal, and ocean life which surround us. Begin to ask God to show you what these reveal about His invisible attributes, eternal power, and Godhead.

Of all that is involved in becoming one who seeks God for daily living and destiny, your direct relationship with God, based on your understanding of Who God is and what God is like, is the most important and foundational. *Thus says the LORD: "Let not the wise man glory in his wisdom, let not the mighty man glory in his might, nor let the rich man glory in his riches; but let him who glories glory in this, that he understands and knows Me, that I am the LORD, exercising lovingkindness, judgment, and righteousness in the earth. For in these I delight," says the LORD (Jeremiah 9:23-24).*

There is one facet of God's creation which on surface examination can provide far more confusion than understanding. That facet is mankind. In the next chapter we will explore our own creation, how we became such poor representatives of our creator, and more of

God's plan to lead us back into a true life of peace and righteousness. Armed with what we have learned in this chapter and what we will learn in the next, we will then be ready to truly step into seeking God for daily living and destiny.

Chapter Four

In the Image of God

Now that we have some basis for knowing about God let's take a closer look at ourselves, in fact a deep look into what it means to be created in the image of God. The thoughts and behavior of humans throughout history has truly provided a point of confusion in understanding God and interpreting the world in which we live. Any study of human history reveals that in general humans are violent, selfish, and untrustworthy. There have been many exceptions but on the whole the history of mankind has been a history of war with the stronger taking advantage of, and even preying upon, the weaker.

Some would blame God as a deficient creator. Others would claim it as proof that God does not really exist and that man is after all just a higher form of animal evolved through chance. Over the centuries the greater percentage of mankind has chosen to seek, serve, or reach out to 'God' or 'gods' through various forms of religion. In many cases, mankind has made gods of the things they can see around them or even worshiped those things which they experience like love, war, or sexuality. In our modern western world we are no different with our daily focus on materialism, outward appearance, and prestige to name a few.

Immediately after God's initial creation of this world and mankind, we were given the inside scoop on His thoughts about it. *Then God saw everything that He had made, and indeed it was very good (Genesis 1:31).* We can easily see what God was thinking when we get ourselves out into areas of the earth that are untouched by the cities and pollutions of mankind. We may also behold some of the wonders of creation and think: wow this is very good! But then we remember, oh yeah, mankind!

How did mankind in general become such poor representatives of the God who created us? Just how did all of the selfishness of sin enter in to spoil our race? What truly happens to change a person for the better when they receive Jesus Christ into their life as Lord and Savior?

Pulling back the curtain for a peek behind the scenes we find both the scriptures and human experience teaching that we are created in the image of God. This is a foundational truth which has great bearing on understanding who we are, why we are here, and what path God would have us follow to go forward.

Do you talk to yourself? That's a ridiculous question, of course you talk to yourself, everyone does. Who are you talking to when you are alone, perhaps driving alone in your car? Why, yourself of course. Who else? And why do we talk to ourselves? I am sure that there are volumes written somewhere on this subject but basically we talk to ourselves as a means of sorting out our thoughts and working out our plans. Picking any given subject, we turn it over within ourselves to determine how we think and feel about it and whether or not we plan to take any action.

Do we know of any other person or persons who talk to their self like we do? Indeed, we find that God, whom we have explored as being a trinity of Father, Son, and Holy Spirit, talks to Himself and the first example we have of this is immediately before He created us. *Then God said, "Let Us make man in Our image, according to Our likeness; let them have dominion over the fish of the sea, over the birds of the air, and over the cattle, over all the earth and over every creeping thing that creeps on the earth" (Genesis 1:26).*

How do we know that God was talking to Himself (Father, Son, and Holy Spirit) and not to angels or someone else who was 'like' God? We know because the very next passage confirms to us just who God meant when He said *'Us'*. It clearly states that we are not made in the likeness of angels or any other being, but in the likeness of God Himself. *So God created man in His own image; in the image of God He created him; male and female He created them (Genesis 1:27).*

What is the significance of being created in the image of God? What can we observe about the nature of our creation, our fall into sin, and the potential of our redemption through Jesus Christ, which will help us understand and move forward in both daily living and long-term destiny?

I will be using an analogy along with a diagram to take us through these concepts and it needs to be said that no analogy is going to be perfect. However, as intended, it should be helpful as an aide in beginning to understand this subject.

First of all, like God we are a trinity, we have a physical body, a soul, and a spirit. These parts of our whole are mentioned many times in scripture and they are part of every human being's experience. Paul's prayer sums them up. *Now may the God of peace Himself sanctify you completely; and may your whole spirit, soul, and body be preserved blameless at the coming of our Lord Jesus Christ (1 Thessalonians 5:23).*

Our soul also contains a recognizable trinity of: Mind, Will, and Emotions. From our human experience in general we know that the condition of our soul greatly affects our body. Sickness or health of the body is greatly affected by the levels of stress, depression, joy, and other conditions of our thoughts and emotions. At times these are enhanced or aggravated by the choices we make in regard to what we will or will not do.

In the scriptures we find many references to our conscience or heart which seem to indicate that these are the parts of our spirit which communicate with our soul. The conscience is perhaps descriptive of the link between our spirit and mind, the heart between spirit and emotions. It is mainly with our spirit that we seek God, connect with God, and live toward God. Therefore if we have hardened our heart or closed our conscience then communication with God does not function as intended by His design. *While it is said: "Today, if you will hear His voice, do not harden your hearts as in the rebellion" (Hebrews 3:15). Now the Spirit expressly says that in latter times some will depart from the faith, giving heed to deceiving spirits and doctrines of demons, speaking lies in hypocrisy, having their own conscience seared with a hot iron (1 Timothy 4:1-2).*

Picturing these aspects of our creation in God's image might look like the following diagram:

Now let's explore the three states of mankind (another trinity) and some of the affect of each state on these different parts of our whole being. The first state is the purity of our creation in God's image. The second is our separation from God though sin. Last, we will explore the state of being reconciled to God through Jesus Christ.

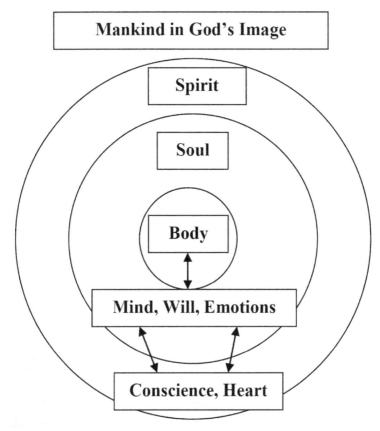

Created:

What were Adam and Eve like based on their original creation in the image and likeness of the holy and perfect God?

And the LORD God formed man of the dust of the ground, and breathed into his nostrils the breath of life; and man became a living being (Genesis 2:7).

The LORD God planted a garden eastward in Eden, and there He put the man whom He had formed. And out of the ground the LORD God made every tree grow that is pleasant to the sight and good for food. The tree of life was also in the midst of the garden, and the tree of the knowledge of good and evil (Genesis 2:8-9).

If you have ever been to a funeral where the body was on display then you know that it is one thing for a body to exist and quite another for there to be life within that body. It is an amazing thing to ponder because the body of that person whom you know is still there but that person is no longer to be found anywhere on earth. Their 'soul' and 'spirit' have departed.

Playing this in reverse, God first formed man's body and then God installed man's soul and spirit and as the passage says: *man became a living being.*

Created in the very image of God the spirit of man was fully awake and fully alive. The soul of man: mind, will, and emotions were clean and clear, as yet no sin had fouled them in any way. Man's conscience or heart was in open communication with his spirit relaying the truths of God to the soul and returning the matters of the soul back to the spirit to share with God. Man's body provided the physical interface into his soul through the five senses: hearing, seeing, feeling, tasting, and smelling within a God provided garden setting.

Then the LORD God took the man and put him in the Garden of Eden to tend and keep it. And the LORD God commanded the man, saying, "Of every tree of the garden you may freely eat; but of the tree of the knowledge of good and evil you shall not eat, for in the day that you eat of it you shall surely die" (Genesis 2:15-17).

The world's oldest profession is actually gardening. God knew that it would be of little value for man to be created in His image if man had no purpose for existing. God's creation of earth was and still is magnificent in many ways, having every potential to glorify God. Creation's every aspect calls out to us to notice the Creator. We do well to follow Adam's original example in taking care of the earth, this great spaceship which God has given us and from which we and our children's children are sustained. Isn't seeking God for daily living and destiny all about finding and understanding our God given purpose in this world so that we may find fulfillment in bringing glory to God? It is, isn't it?

Now in this first garden there was a tree which God had put 'off limits' to man. We might speculate that it was the one thing in the garden which God had reserved for himself alone. Picture telling your children: 'the gumdrops and ice cream are for you but the Belgian chocolate is only for me.' Or we might speculate that God had a future purpose for the tree of the knowledge of good and evil which was to be revealed at a point when man was ready for it. Then again, perhaps it was a test to see if man would choose to follow God or go his own way. No doubt that to be created in the image of God man would have to be free to choose as God has always been free to choose. If God had sheltered man in such a manner that only beneficial and good things could be chosen, that would not really be a true definition of freedom.

And the LORD God said, "It is not good that man should be alone; I will make him a helper comparable to him"
(Genesis 2:18).

This is the first time in creation that we hear of God saying that something is *'not good'*. The man had God and the man had all of creation. There were animals, birds, and sea creatures to interact with but there was no one like man. Man was not an animal and although man was like God man was not God. In a real and tangible way man was experiencing what it meant to be alone and God saw that it was *'not good'* and in His over the top way God did something remarkable about it in creating woman.

And the LORD God caused a deep sleep to fall on Adam, and he slept; and He took one of his ribs, and closed up the flesh in its place. Then the rib which the LORD God had taken from man He made into a woman, and He brought her to the man

(Genesis 2:21-22). And they were both naked, the man and his wife, and were not ashamed (Genesis 2:25).

Like God, the man and woman were alive in spirit and spiritually alive toward one another and God. Their consciences and hearts functioned as intended. Their minds were studious, clear, and useful, without evil thought. Their emotions were peaceful being capable of grasping and holding onto such things as love and joy and being devoid of such things as bitterness and rage. Their wills, being led by their mind and emotions and governed by their spirit, were in tune with the purpose and creativity of the One who formed them. Lastly their bodies were healthy and strong reaping the benefits of souls at peace.

Like God there were no boundaries to inhibit the freedom of mankind's spiritual interaction with God. There was nothing to be afraid of and nothing to feel ashamed about. The man and woman knew God. They were free, together, and truly alive. Any choice was theirs to make and any experience was theirs to enjoy. God had placed one and only one thing 'off limits' to Adam and Eve. As we shall see they were even free to choose that one thing if they wanted to, however that choice would be a game changer.

Separated:

What were the effects of mankind's decision to sin and what was added to or marred regarding the image of God now that mankind was separated from Him by sin?

Now the serpent was more cunning than any beast of the field which the LORD God had made. And he said to the woman, "Has God indeed said, 'You shall not eat of every tree of the garden'?"

And the woman said to the serpent, "We may eat the fruit of the trees of the garden; but of the fruit of the tree which is in the midst of the garden, God has said, 'You shall not eat it, nor shall you touch it, lest you die.'"

Then the serpent said to the woman, "You will not surely die. For God knows that in the day you eat of it your eyes will be opened, and you will be like God, knowing good and evil" *(Genesis 3:1-13).*

The scene is the Garden of Eden. Eve may or may not be out by herself but this creature, the serpent, chooses to address her directly. Who is this person and what does he want? The Bible has quite a bit to say about the devil or Satan, or by name Lucifer, and we will touch a bit more on that subject in future chapters. For the moment what we need to understand is that Lucifer is indicated as one of God's highest angels who became dissatisfied with his God appointed station and chose to rebel against God in a bid to take Heaven's throne for himself. You can read about this in *Isaiah 14:12-15.*

There are indications in Bible prophecy that he lead as many as one-third of all angels in this rebellion. The name Satan means the accuser, and in the Old Testament, *Job 1:6-11,* we read of Satan interacting with God in accusation of Job. At that time the devil seemed to be free to wander the earth and visit heaven.

We know that in the time of Jesus, Satan's gang of disobeyers were defeated and cast out of Heaven down to the earth. *And war broke out in heaven: Michael and his angels fought with the dragon; and the dragon and his angels fought, but they did not prevail, nor was a place found for them in heaven any longer. So the great dragon was cast out, that serpent of old, called the Devil and Satan, who deceives the whole world; he was cast to the earth, and his angels were cast out with him (Revelation 12:7-9).*

This serpent of old is the one and same serpent that tempted our ancestor Eve to rebel against God. The devil and his angels, now known as demons, are unseen beings who inhabit this earth with us. The very presence of Jesus seems to have exposed them for what they are. As we read throughout the first four Gospel books of the New Testament we see how Jesus confronted and cast demons out.

Pondering God's full purpose, in having allowed such a person as the devil to be in the garden with Adam and Eve and to continue to live among mankind to this day, we might conclude once again that without the ability for us to choose to do evil we are not truly free.

What does the serpent want? Well, he probably still wants the throne of God for himself but he cannot have that. Choosing second best he wants as many of God's creatures as he can get, whether angels or humans, to follow and worship him instead of God. We know this to be the case as we listen in on part of his temptation of Jesus.

Again, the devil took Him up on an exceedingly high mountain, and showed Him all the kingdoms of the world and their glory. And he said to Him, "All these things I will give You if You will fall down and worship me."

Then Jesus said to him, "Away with you, Satan! For it is written, 'You shall worship the LORD your God, and Him only you shall serve'" (Matthew 4:8-10).

The serpent wants Adam and Eve, the very crown of God's creation, to join his camp, the camp of those who disobey God. The devil goes about this by first putting a slight twist on God's word: *"Has God indeed said, 'You shall not eat of every tree of the garden'?"* When Eve corrects him then he comes out with a direct lie: *"You will not surely die. For God knows that in the day you eat of it your eyes will be opened, and you will be like God, knowing good and evil".* Whoa Eve, stop, wait, don't! God has said you will surely die. You are already created in the image of God. You are already like God. Your eyes are already open. If God wants you to know more about good and evil then trust Him to teach you in His own time!

So when the woman saw that the tree was good for food, that it was pleasant to the eyes, and a tree desirable to make one wise, she took of its fruit and ate. She also gave to her husband with her, and he ate. Then the eyes of both of them were opened, and they knew that they were naked; and they sewed fig leaves together and made themselves coverings (Genesis 3:6-7).

Eve did not listen to whatever warnings were going off inside of her did she? This is what it means to be deceived and there is only one thing worse for us than choosing to walk in deception and that is when we do what Adam seems to have done and walk right into sin by direct choice. Adam did not fall into transgression like Eve did. Adam walked in on his own two feet. *And Adam was not deceived, but the woman being deceived, fell into transgression (1 Timothy 2:14).*

Oh, the devil was true to the half-truth of his promise, their eyes were opened, but it did not make them more like God. They had already been like God with the exception of knowing evil. Adam and Eve had stepped across the line, of which God had clearly warned them that if they did so they would die. By their choice and actions they had joined the camp of those who disobey and live in rebellion against God. In God's camp Adam and Eve had been the rulers of the earth, but this new camp already had a ruler and it was not them, it was Satan.

And they heard the sound of the LORD God walking in the garden in the cool of the day, and Adam and his wife hid themselves from the presence of the LORD God among the trees of the garden.

Then the LORD God called to Adam and said to him, "Where are you?" So he said, "I heard Your voice in the garden, and I was afraid because I was naked; and I hid myself." And He said, "Who told you that you were naked? Have you eaten from the tree of which I commanded you that you should not eat?"

Then the man said, "The woman whom You gave to be with me, she gave me of the tree, and I ate."And the LORD God said to the woman, "What is this you have done?" The woman said, "The serpent deceived me, and I ate" (Genesis 3:8-13).

What is the first thing that sinful mankind does as a reaction to the exposed feeling of their own sin? Hide! Especially from God and his presence, this is of course the exact opposite of being one who seeks God.

The story we are reviewing is known as the fall of mankind. Man is now fallen from the position of grace and unity with God which was our birthright. Hiding is now engrained deeply within the fallen and now self-focused sinful nature of man. If you read *Isaiah 14:12-15* remember Satan's focus on himself in wanting God's throne?

Along with hiding we see another function coming into play which also becomes ingrained within this fallen nature of man and that is the function of blaming. Does God ask Adam *'where are you?'* because God does not know that Adam is hiding behind the tree? Or does God ask because God wants Adam to realize where Adam is? This would have been a great time for Adam to repent of his decision to sin and ask God for mercy but instead Adam blames the whole business on Eve and on God. *"The woman whom You gave to be with me, she gave me of the tree, and I ate."* Eve does not shine either; she blames the whole business on the serpent. *"The serpent deceived me, and I ate"*.

Hiding and blaming are the first scars to appear on those who were created in the image of God. Feel free to test this out at any time because there are two very simple ways to check and see that these scars are present both in your fellow man and yourself. In the first test, read the newspaper or watch the evening news. Without doubt someone will be hiding by deflecting blame from their self and placing blame on someone else. Our politicians do it every day and it is openly published as if it were normal to do so. The second test can be performed on yourself. Take notice the very next time that it is presumed by another that you are at fault about anything big or small. Note your own reaction, if you don't instantly move to protect and justify yourself with words you will at least be tempted to do so.

Then the LORD God said, "Behold, the man has become like one of Us, to know good and evil. And now, lest he put out his hand and take also of the tree of life, and eat, and live forever" — therefore the LORD God sent him out of the garden of Eden to till the ground from which he was taken. So He drove out the man; and He placed cherubim at the east of the garden of Eden, and a flaming sword which turned every way, to guard the way to the tree of life (Genesis 3:22-24).

Like the devil being cast out of Heaven, Adam and Eve are now cast out of Eden. They have their new friend Satan but where is he to be found when you need something? They now live lives of hiding and blaming. They are excluded from fellowship with God since they left His camp for another. Their bodies are now subject to a new force known as death. The devil is an ever present factor, sowing lies and mistrust among mankind. Next we find that of Adam and Eve's first two sons, one murders the other out of jealousy.

Reading further in Genesis we find man in cities with walls. Walls have a few purposes but chiefly they are meant to hide behind, either for protection from others or for protection of self after having done others wrong. Mankind as a whole is now lost in this world, alone and without God no longer being members of His eternal family. We have come to know and in general accept all of these things as part of what is 'natural' or even 'human', because they fit naturally with our fallen sinful nature, but in the context of what God had created these things are not normal.

Just a few chapters further in Genesis we find the passage mentioned in the last chapter where we looked at the heart of God. Then *the LORD saw that the wickedness of man was great in the earth, and that every intent of the thoughts of his heart was only evil continually. And the LORD was sorry that He had made man on the earth, and He was grieved in His heart (Genesis 6:5-6).*

The sinful choices and actions of Adam and Eve have truly passed on through them to all of mankind. *Therefore, just as through one man sin entered the world, and death through sin, and thus death spread to all men, because all sinned (Romans 5:12).*

God had warned them, *in the day that you eat of it you shall surely die.* Their bodies now subject to death began to age and decay, something we are all familiar with or will be. Their souls: mind, will, and emotions were now the home of many new things. One of the lists from the Bible, though not exhaustive, exposes many of these: *being filled with all unrighteousness, sexual immorality, wickedness, covetousness, maliciousness; full of envy, murder, strife, deceit, evil-mindedness; they are whisperers, backbiters, haters of God, violent, proud, boasters, inventors of evil things, disobedient to parents, undiscerning, untrustworthy, unloving, unforgiving, unmerciful (Romans 1:29-31).* Most importantly the spirit of man was now dead because of the departure of God's Spirit who only remains as long as there is a Father to child relationship between ourselves and God.

In the next section we will be looking at reconciliation and the affect of being born again in which we receive the Spirit of God into our spirit through Jesus. Suffice for the moment to mention that mankind no longer naturally functions as intended by original design. Instead of receiving direction for our lives from God's Spirit within our spirit and basing our thoughts, feelings, and decisions upon God's truth, our conscience is now closed and our hearts are hardened, removing the path of communication between soul and spirit. In our fallen state we take direction from our soul and our lives are governed by what we think and believe with our minds, whether right or wrong, how we emotionally feel in the moment, typically based on how we think and believe, and the strength or weakness of our own will. Think about this and you will see that it is true; this is why God is calling us back into being seekers of Him. This is why He is intent on our coming to salvation through Jesus, in which the Spirit of God can be restored into our spirit, and as His seekers the pathways of our conscience and heart begin to open directing our lives through the daily revelation of God Himself who is truth.

God's creation, mankind, is incredibly marred and spoiled by the decision to sin. It is amazing that God values us as highly as He does in His quest to seek and save us. Everyone exists but existence is not life. Jesus has told us: *"It is written, 'Man shall not live by bread alone, but by every word that proceeds from the mouth of God'"* (Matthew 4:4). In our fallen state we cannot hear and receive the regular guiding word of God, which is intended to lead us in life, because we are dead.

Reconciled:
What does being 'born again' bring back into our lives and how does this help us to move back toward being people who reflect the true image and likeness of God?

After listening to Adam and Eve's excuses, God curses the serpent, including within the curse the first of what will be many prophecies foreshadowing the coming of

Jesus Christ. Speaking of the seed of the woman, God tells the serpent: *He shall bruise your head, and you shall bruise His heel" (Genesis 3:15)*. God does not directly curse Adam and Eve. But He does curse the ground for their sakes. Pain and difficulties will be their lot in life from this point forward. *In the sweat of your face you shall eat bread till you return to the ground, for out of it you were taken; for dust you are, and to dust you shall return" (Genesis 3:19)*.

In the very first act of redemption, creating a picture of the sacrifice Jesus would make for all of us; God insures that the naked Adam and Eve would not die from exposure to the elements outside of the garden. *Also for Adam and his wife the LORD God made tunics of skin, and clothed them (Genesis 3:21)*. This is the first recorded act picturing salvation. Death was a newcomer on the scene, having been welcomed in by Adam and Eve's decision. They had just died spiritually and now for the first time their choices have affected other living things, in this case animals. God Himself sacrificed the innocent creatures so that sinful man may be kept warm in their skins and live.

In Chapter Two 'Taking the Biggest Step' we thoroughly covered our need for and response to God's offer of salvation toward us. My presumption is that you have taken that step or are in the process of seeking God about doing so, bringing your questions to Him and asking Him to reveal Himself to you more and more.

We are all familiar with what it means to have a store coupon, a gift card, or a ticket. Each of these has the potential to gain us something when we take them to the appropriate store or event and 'redeem' them by exchanging them for the goods and services for which they were intended. Redemption from our sinful state or to be redeemed by God is similar in that He offers us that gift card good for one salvation and backed by the sacrifice for our sins and the resurrection power of God through the Son Jesus Christ. Two actions have to take place. First we have to receive this gift card from God and next we have to take it to the 'event' and actually cash it in.

When we do so we become 'reconciled', that is reconnected, with God. It is a fresh start so profound and so potentially life changing that Jesus called it being 'born again'. *Jesus answered and said to him, "Most assuredly, I say to you, unless one is born again, he cannot see the kingdom of God" (John 3:3).*

Of Jesus and those who become His we read: *He was in the world, and the world was made through Him, and the world did not know Him. He came to His own, and His own did not receive Him. But as many as received Him, to them He gave the right to become children of God, to those who believe in His name: who were born, not of blood, nor of the will of the flesh, nor of the will of man, but of God (John 1:10-13).*

God supplies the ticket; it is available to us through Jesus. We must receive it from Him or else how can we use it if we will not take it from His hand? Having received, we must take it to the event which is done by believing. Our common use of the English word for believe can carry a meaning of mere mental choice or of assent to an idea and in that sense we are warned by James: *You believe that there is one God. You do well. Even the demons believe – and tremble! (James 2:19).* However, in the original Greek the word believe is pisteuo, pronounced pist-yoo'-o, and carries a firm connection to actions within the soul which go beyond mere mental assent to an idea. Pisteuo means: to have faith, to entrust ourselves, to believe, to commit, to put ourselves in trust with. It is in faith, in this committing of ourselves to God that we gain the right to become children of God, born as the passage says: *of God.*

And you He made alive, who were dead in trespasses and sins, in which you once walked according to the course of this world, according to the prince of the power of the air, the spirit who now works in the sons of disobedience, among whom also we all once conducted ourselves in the lusts of our flesh, fulfilling the desires of the flesh and of the mind, and were by nature children of wrath, just as the others.

But God, who is rich in mercy, because of His great love with which He loved us, even when we were dead in trespasses, made us alive together with Christ (by grace you have been saved) (Ephesians 2:1-5).

Returning to our diagram we can examine the changes which initially result from this born again experience. These changes reveal the path for following Jesus and where that path leads.

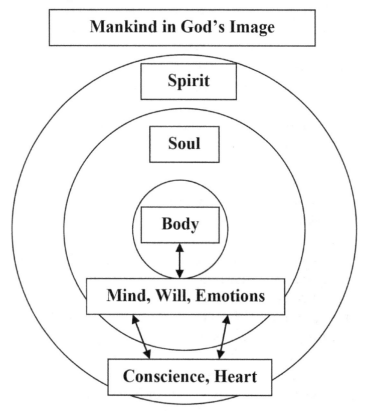

Mankind in God's Image

Spirit

Soul

Body

Mind, Will, Emotions

Conscience, Heart

Receiving God's gift of life through Jesus Christ and believing in His Name, we are restored as children of God. The first and most profound change which happens is the reintegration of God's Spirit into our spirit. *And you He made alive, who were dead in trespasses and sins. God, who is rich in mercy, because of His great love with which He loved us, even when we were dead in trespasses, made us alive together with Christ (by grace you have been saved)* (from *Ephesians 2:1-5)*. It is by this grace, meaning 'undeserved favor', that God once again takes up residence within the human spirit and it is by this grace that, even though the clean-up process will be messy, God chooses to remain.

Colossians 1:27 calls this: *Christ in you, the hope of glory.* In 2 *Corinthians 1:21-22* we read: *Now He who establishes us with you in Christ and has anointed us is God, who also has sealed us and given us the Spirit in our hearts as a guarantee.*

Then Peter said to them, "Repent, and let every one of you be baptized in the name of Jesus Christ for the remission of sins; and you shall receive the gift of the Holy Spirit. For the promise is to you and to your children, and to all who are afar off, as many as the Lord our God will call" (Acts 2:38-39). It is this act of repentance, which simply means to turn and go the other way, taking the new path of receiving and believing, that gains us the result of this promise, God's Spirit within our spirit, born again from the dead.

Now those parts of our spirit which communicate with our souls are re-enabled to awaken. The things of the Spirit of God begin to flow from His Spirit through our spirit and into the mind, will, and emotions of our soul. It is called new birth because we start anew like babes. It will take time and effort for our conscience and heart to come fully awake and time and effort for our soul to purge its old ways and exchange them for those of a seeker who daily listens to the Spirit of God within and comes to an ease in trusting God's governance as guidance for daily living. It is learning to hear, speak, feel, taste, touch, perceive, walk, and talk all over again in what is indeed a brand new way.

Having been given *the right to become children of God* we are to understand that no parent wants their child be remain infantile or immature, least of all God. His goal is for us to grow into and fulfill the destiny for which He purposefully planted each one of us. The restored communication between our spirit and soul is intended to bring His light and truth into our lives and call us more clearly to full reformation.

We who are saved are led by God to put away evil thoughts, plans, and selfish patterns from our minds, replacing them with the love and selflessness which Jesus so clearly revealed. *And do not be conformed to this world, but be transformed by the renewing of your mind, that you may prove what is that good and acceptable and perfect will of God (Romans 12:2).*

As followers of Christ our mind and emotions need complete restoration to turn them from such things as hatred, envy, and lust. *Therefore, laying aside all malice, all deceit, hypocrisy, envy, and all evil speaking, as newborn babes, desire the pure milk of the word, that you may grow thereby, if indeed you have tasted that the Lord is gracious (1 Peter 2:1-3).*

Through Jesus we begin to learn what true fulfillment means as we discover that in seeking God's will instead of our own we actually achieve the true desires of our heart. *"Therefore do not worry, saying, 'What shall we eat?' or 'What shall we drink?' or 'What shall we wear?' For after all these things the Gentiles seek. For your heavenly Father knows that you need all these things. But seek first the kingdom of God and His righteousness, and all these things shall be added to you (Matthew 6:31-33).*

It is also God's intent that our bodies benefit from this new relationship of being reconciled to Him. Worry, fear, and anxiety related stress which promote sickness are slated for demolition in God's new construction project with our souls. Depression which easily overcomes our inner motivations and makes our bodies weak and sick is to be challenged to leave by the Spirit of God within us. We are called to: *Be anxious for nothing, but in everything by prayer and supplication, with thanksgiving, let your requests be made known to God; and the peace of God, which surpasses all understanding, will guard your hearts and minds through Christ Jesus (Philippians 4:6-7).* Ultimately, God will heal every part of our bodies when we are either caught up with Christ at His return or resurrected to spend eternity with Him. *So also is the resurrection of the dead. The body is sown in corruption, it is raised in incorruption. It is sown in dishonor, it is raised in glory. It is sown in weakness, it is raised in power. It is sown a natural body, it is raised a spiritual body (1 Corinthians 15:42-44). And the dead in Christ will rise first. Then we who are alive and remain shall be caught up together with them in the clouds to meet the Lord in the air. And thus we shall always be with the Lord (1 Thessalonians 4:16-17).*

In reconciliation, our spirit, soul, and even bodies are now on the path of Jesus Christ and the more and sooner that we open up and follow Him, the faster our maturity in Him will progress. With God in the lead, doubt about destination is removed. We will definitely get to where He is trying to take us as long as we continue to follow. This is what seeking God for daily living and destiny is all about.

God's ultimate goal for His children is Christ likeness, a total restoration for everyone who will hear His voice, take His hand, and let their self be pulled from the raging ocean of the lost into the security of God's ship and the fellowship of His crew. *And we know that all things work together for good to those who love God, to those who are the called according to His purpose. For whom He foreknew, He*

also predestined to be conformed to the image of His Son, that
He might be the firstborn among many brethren. Moreover
whom He predestined, these He also called; whom He called,
these He also justified; and whom He justified, these He also
glorified (Romans 8:28-30).

Tying It all Together:
   Notice the radical contrast between mankind's
original creation in the image of God and the depths to
which we have fallen in sin.
   We were intended for perfection, to be holy just as He
is holy. Our spirits were meant to freely commune with
His. Our souls and bodies were meant to be an expression
of His blessing and goodness and power in all things. In
all ways, we were intended to affect and bless the world
and community of other souls around us.
   We have become depraved and decidedly unholy.
Attested to by our own history, mankind is so steeped
in our own sin and deceived by false beliefs that our
selfishness and self-absorption is to a point where even
when we do good it is all about ourselves wrapped in
how we feel or think.
   Notice again the radical contrast between our fallen
estate and the newness of life which God gives us in
salvation through Jesus Christ. There is every potential
of restoration and the path of holiness is again laid before
us. On this side of heaven will you and I take it as far as
God intends for it to go? Will you and I truly and eagerly:
put off , concerning your former conduct, the old man which
grows corrupt according to the deceitful lusts, and be renewed
in the spirit of your mind, and that you put on the new man
which was created according to God, in true righteousness and
holiness (Ephesians 4:22-24). Will we become those who:
seek first the kingdom of God and His righteousness (Matthew
6:33). Will the Lord God be able to look on this span of

history into which He has placed you and me and take delight that we not only received Him but went the whole distance in allowing Him to have His way?

By all rights God should be able to say that His investments of creation, love, sacrifice, and grace bore good fruit through our lives and that He was free to use us as His ambassadors and agents of change in our moment under the sun. We all would say that we want to fulfill our God given purpose and destiny. We have been told this may be hard and have even experienced that the way can be difficult, but difficult is not impossible. The walls may be high but with King David we can say: *By my God I can leap over a wall (Psalm 18:29).* The things God calls us to face and do may be challenging but as it is written: *I can do all things through Christ who strengthens me (Philippians 4:13).*

The Context of Life:

And so we arrive again at the context of life. God has made choices for you and me, in many cases choices which on examination we would not have made for ourselves.

God chose our family of origin or other circumstances of our nurture and, as much of a blessing or as difficult as that ended up being, it was God who chose to plant your soul into that family.

God also chose the circumstances of environment into which we would be inserted where so many of the events external to family have shaped and molded our lives. Was it a time of war or a time of peace? In America our current time is one in which there is much uncertainty about the future. Both in politics and in the mystical rumblings within every soul, there is an unrest that can be felt and is very influential.

Finally God chose that point of history into which He decided you and I would best be placed. From His perspective, which we have been reviewing, God's intention is to lead us into our own restoration and use us as His ambassadors and agents of change, bringing the life of His Son Jesus into our day and age through us. Somehow in selecting who He should send into this task God chose us and here we are, hopefully ready to be outfitted and equipped for what lies ahead.

Putting It into Practice:
Faith, as the world understands it, is more akin to hope. Sometimes you will hear people talk of faith and having faith when they really mean, 'I hope so'.

In many cases those unfamiliar with Biblical faith will claim that they find it impossible to just blindly trust in God or anyone. However, Biblical faith is not just hope and really has nothing to do with blindly trusting that God might come through for us or that something is so.

Faith, as spoken of in the New Testament of the Bible, is summarized in the following verse in which we come to understand the deep connection between pleasing God and the action of seeking: *But without faith it is impossible to please Him, for he who comes to God must believe that He is, and that He is a rewarder of those who diligently seek Him (Hebrews 11:6).*

The Greek word for faith in the New Testament is closely related to the word for believe. It is Pistis, pronounced pis'-tis, and meaning: persuasion, assurance, belief, faith, 'a belief based on knowing that I have heard' i.e., I am persuaded, I am assured and having the quality of knowing, not just hoping, that thus and such is indeed true.

Where can we get such faith, how can the faith we have be strengthened, and how much faith do we need?

Romans 10:17 tells us: *So then faith comes by hearing, and hearing by the word of God.* This tells us where faith comes from and puts an action and responsibility of hearing squarely on us. We are called once again to be seekers of God. The Bible does not put a limit on the *'word of God'* in the sense of only what is on the written page of the Bible, instead in many words of the Bible we are instructed on how to interact with God's Holy Spirit to gain the *'word of God'* which we need for daily living. We will explore this to a greater depth in the next chapter.

Regarding the amount of faith, Jesus taught His first followers that it is not the size but rather that we put faith into practice. *So the Lord said, "If you have faith as a mustard seed, you can say to this mulberry tree, 'Be pulled up by the roots and be planted in the sea,' and it would obey you (Luke 17:6). Then He said, "To what shall we liken the kingdom of God? Or with what parable shall we picture it? It is like a mustard seed which, when it is sown on the ground, is smaller than all the seeds on earth; but when it is sown, it grows up and becomes greater than all herbs, and shoots out large branches, so that the birds of the air may nest under its shade" (Mark 4:30-32).*

By this time my hope is that you are becoming one who seeks God. Hopefully you are getting beyond some of your initial questions about Him and for Him and beginning to ask His direction in those things which concern daily life and destiny. I encourage you to keep walking, keep following. Get back up when you stumble, dust yourself off and get moving again. Are you letting God get down into the details of how you do business within your soul? Are you experiencing the beginnings or continuation of His Spirit making things clear to you via conscience and heart? Is Jesus becoming more and more the Master of your life in actual practice and beyond just mental belief?

Put your faith into practice as small or great as it may seem to be. God is: *a rewarder of those who diligently seek*

Him. There is high adventure to be had for those who will take God at His word and press on to experience what *'rewarder'* really means.

Chapter Five
Interacting with His In-dwelling Spirit

But all things that are exposed are made manifest by the light, for whatever makes manifest is light. Therefore He says: "Awake, you who sleep, arise from the dead, and Christ will give you light" (Ephesians 5:13-14).

For as many as are led by the Spirit of God, these are sons of God (Romans 8:14). But the natural man does not receive the things of the Spirit of God, for they are foolishness to him; nor can he know them, because they are spiritually discerned (1 Corinthians 2:14).

At this point in the journey we come to a bit of a dividing line. Everything we have covered so far should have served to awaken you to the true source for satisfying that inner hunger for significance: beginning to know who you are, why you are here, what this world is all about, and where you are going. We have clearly reviewed who God is, the meaning of our own creation, and what it means to come to Jesus for salvation and begin to follow Him as the Lord of all life.

If you are still working with God to sort this out and have not yet taken that biggest step of asking God's pardon for your sinful life, surrendering yourself to God's mercy, and asking Jesus Christ to come into your life and save you, then you are not ready to start looking any further into seeking God for daily living and destiny.

Simply put, Jesus is the door to salvation through which the Spirit of God is restored to His rightful place within your spirit. *I am the door. If anyone enters by Me, he will be saved, and will go in and out and find pasture (John 10:9).* Jesus also stands at the door of your heart and knocks in hope that you will let Him in. *Behold, I stand at the door and knock. If anyone hears My voice and opens the door, I will come in to him and dine with him, and he with Me (Revelation 3:20).*

The rest of this book presumes that you have made the decision both to enter the door of Christ and to open your life up to Him. Without this you are still on the outside looking in and will not be able to *receive the things of the Spirit of God.* If that is truly the case then I encourage you to continue in the challenges already given, reading and studying His word, bringing your questions to God, asking the Lord to reveal Himself to you, until such time as you are satisfied that He is the way. Then by all means open your heart, enter His door, and we will see you again at that point.

The Road Goes On From Here:

Picking up my own testimony from where I left off. I was 18 years old, had just received the Lord into my life and I had a new best friend, Jesus. The total sum of my understanding about godliness would not have filled a thimble. How could such a person begin to walk a path that he knew little or nothing about? How would he even know what signposts were valid guides along the way? The miracle here is that God knows and His Spirit within us is completely capable of leading us out of the blackest darkness and into His marvelous light.

In those first few months I read the New Testament rather quickly and in bits and snatches as I worked or rested. It was a bit dry the first time through, probably because I had no background to understand the context of the people and events I was reading about and no one to explain anything.

I started to seek the Lord about my chief concern at that time: I was lonely and I hoped very much for someone who could love me and whom I could love in return. Loneliness is definitely the result for a person who had shut themselves off from others for as many years as I had. Now that I was open it was one of the first things that I sensed. Perhaps it goes back to God's first 'not good' statement in the Garden of Eden where He said: *it is not good that man should be alone.*

Unknown to me but not to the Spirit of God, He had been preparing my wife through His work in her life. I had ended up at that particular Army post by what seemed to be total chance. I now know there is no such thing as luck or chance when God is in the driver's seat. Petra grew up in Giessen, West Germany, where I was stationed. She had received the Lord with joy as a child after hearing the preaching at a Lutheran tent mission. She had continued in the faith until her mid teens when her mother was tragically taken by cancer. Petra had prayed that her mother would not die but this was not God's plan. With her young heart disillusioned about God she turned from Him and, like me, she began to destroy her life.

How did God react? Did He turn His back and give up on her as a lost cause? No indeed, He did what God alone does and started the long process of guiding our lives together with the intent of shaping the image of Christ out of that which was broken and unholy.

I proposed one month after meeting her and we were married just 6 months into our relationship. I was 19 and she had just turned 20. This year we celebrated our 35th anniversary, but back in those days we were very raw as believers, hardly recognizable as followers of Christ and fellow drug addicts to boot.

It is dark in here who knows the way out? Jesus does. Fast forward just a few years and God had let matters go from bad to worse. This is often how the Spirit of God handles major dominating issues in our lives when we are too ignorant or unwilling to change. I was coming up on age 21. I was an acting sergeant in the U.S. Army, on duty in charge of a crew manning a NATO missile base, and on the side I was a hopeless heroin addict.

Petra and I were entrapped and had tried numerous times in our own strength to quit but had failed. I sat down alone on the edge of a gutter in Frankfurt, Germany. I had just finished one of my three injections for the day and was waiting for my wife to finish hers. A German man walked past. As he did, he straightened up his shoulders and looked down the end of his nose at me. In decent English with a harsh voice he asked "Isn't it dirty for you down there?" and walked off.

I jumped to my feet ready to punch that guy but the message rang true and I began to lift my eyes to heaven. I knew Who was speaking to me and yes, it was dirty down there. Help me Lord, I want out and cannot find the way by myself. I had never really asked the Lord in that manner before. Jesus and His word had kind of fallen by the wayside the last few years as I climbed deeper and deeper into addiction. But now He had my attention and my heart was ready for change. What was going to happen next? What would be God's plan?

Some will call me nuts and say that God would never do this, but His instructions sort of rolled very clearly into my mind. I would never recommend this method to anyone who is addicted outside of their hearing it from God like I did. We had about one month to go before I was to take my wife home to California and the Lord told me to purchase a large quantity of heroin and to cut our doses in half each day until we left. He not only supplied the instructions but the power to do so and on that day when we boarded the plane we finished off a very small portion for each of us, tossed our works in the trash and departed. Not that life after that was not tough but we did not suffer withdrawals as we had so many times before when we had tried to quit.

Over those last two years and the next year, many we had known fell on our right hand and on our left. They fell into hopeless addiction, some died of overdose, one committed suicide, and others went to prison. But, even though deserved many times over, we escaped imprisonment and death by the grace of God. Why did He do this? God knows we were not likely candidates for redemption but then again each of us had received Jesus and the Spirit of God within us was jealous for His glory.

Lead on, Lord! We arrived in my home area of Marin County, California, and I promptly began wasting my Army money on buying things I had wanted but never had as a kid. We connected with my old friends and began to party on what for us was the light stuff of pot and booze. I remember driving over the hill from San Rafael one day, all my money gone, and I said to myself "You're married you idiot, get a job." Well, I got a job but the wages were too low to establish a home for us and so

I said to myself "Go to school you idiot!" Yes, the Lord works in mysterious ways.

I started a seven month program in San Francisco which would lead me into a solid career path that has lasted all these years and been a blessing to my family. I rode the bus to school an hour each way and as I was bored, I read a paperback about some sort of existential living. When I finished I remember tossing it and saying to myself "This is trash, I am going to read the Bible."

I started at Genesis and read on the bus daily, one hour each way. This was another miracle because from childhood to this day I cannot read more than a few lines in a moving vehicle without getting car sick. By the time I had read from Genesis to the middle of the New Testament I had begun to talk to God again and He was surely talking to me through those pages. We got to 1 Corinthians 12:12-31 and the Lord was showing me from this passage that I was supposed to be a member among many of His people, fellowshipping and working together for the glory of His Kingdom.

Well, I did not know what to do with that. Where would I go and who were these people? Lord, I don't know what to do and I don't know anything about religious people, but I am willing and if this is to happen then You will have to take care of it.

A day or so later a man sat next to me on the bus and pointing to my open Bible he said: "Hey, that's a neat book you are reading there". We talked and he had come out of religious Mormonism and become a follower of Jesus Christ. I shared my life with Ralph and told him about my dilemma of God wanting me to be part of His church. Ralph said: "We got a drive in church, we pull it up in the Rexall Drug Store parking lot, let down the stage, string the antennae and people drive in and hear us over the AM radio, you wanna come?"

Next Sunday, Petra and I arrived at what would be our first church together and the Lord had a surprise for me. For the last three years I had worked on a missile base as a radar operator. These radars and missile launchers were all on trailers with wheels, jacks to level them, and cables to connect them. They were pulled by trucks to whatever location we needed to set them up for combat. Here was my first church experience and it was a trailer with wheels, jacks to level it, cables to connect it, and a truck to pull it to its location. I remember thinking: "Hey I know that!"

More important than the trailer, the group of people welcomed us and provided the Lord's intent for connection with His people, His church. The pastor, Harold Hendricks, invested himself in working with me to understand what I was reading in the Bible and how to live it out in practical daily life. God bless him for that.

The old ways and patterns of belief and behavior began to change as we were drawn more and more into God's kingdom and influence through learning, action, and that unseen governance of God's Holy Spirit.

I had been hired right before graduation by a Silicon Valley company and had a commute of two hours. In the beginning it was typical for me to meet with Pastor Harold in his office on a Monday, then jump into my car, and perhaps smoke a joint of pot on the way to work. On the way home I had a favorite liquor store in San Francisco where I would get a tall beer for the ride home. But, as we learned more and more from the Lord, the Holy Spirit began to bring conviction about these and other practices. In the same week, Petra and I began to question whether there might be something wrong with getting high and so we began to ask God about it.

We each had a separate experience in how that answer came about but in the end we knew this was something we must drop and by God's grace we did. Even in our ignorance the Lord was intent on our reformation. God slowly separated us from filthy outward habits and then He began to work on the inside by challenging the reasons for why we had been doing those things in the first place.

God's plan to reform and train us up included parenting a large family. At least in our case there was no better way to instruct us as His followers, and in what it means to be part of God's forever family, than a family of our own. Parenting definitely provides a small taste of the joys and trials which God goes through as Father of the whole human race.

After the birth of our first son we moved into Silicon Valley to be near my work. By this time I had been regularly praying and worshipping during my two hour commutes. With a rental home not far from work this changed into time spent with God each morning studying His word and saying my prayers before anyone else in our house awoke. Saying my prayers was pretty much what it was because, as I understood it, prayer was where I talked and God listened. God was indeed a patient listener but I am sure He was thinking 'The boy is not yet getting it.'

One morning at prayer God spoke back. I had perceived His urgings within my heart before. I was familiar with inner convictions of knowing that something was right or wrong. But this was different, here was an inner voice telling me something very directly. It was obvious that God was speaking to me and He said: "I anoint you to preach My word." Just those few simple words but for a guy who was at this time very intent on living a life that pleased God it was big stuff. At first I was awed, then I began to question whether or not we are really supposed to be hearing from God in this way. I studied the scriptures to know if this was supposed to be common experience and found that it was. We will be looking at the role of God's Holy Spirit in more detail in this chapter.

This was a game changer for me. I was not disobedient to that first calling and soon began to preach and teach the word of God in church, life, and mission settings and have been doing so ever since.

I began to balance my times of prayer with an expectation of hearing from God. Over the years this has extended our relationship much deeper into my life in the sense that anytime and anyplace is the right time and place to ask the Lord a question or simply be available to receive direction from Him. Dedicated time spent with God at the beginning of each day also took on fuller meaning with the clear understanding of my own purpose in life. The Maker of the Universe had words and direction for me, even me. Seeking God with regard to the decisions of life and waiting on Him for direction and assignments became my new normal.

One morning at prayers I distinctly heard the Lord tell me to quit my job, give notice on our rental, and move back to Marin to re-engage and work with our first church. My response was something like; OK I will begin to look for work in Marin, to which the Lord said: "No, today." So I quit my job and told my landlord we would be out by the end of the month. I can still remember my feelings having packed my family and our worldly possessions into a U-haul truck and looking back at that small house and the living room where I had by this time for over two years met with God to listen and obey. I felt like a man with a sack full of treasure, so rich and so full, with not a care at all about where He might be taking us. Some parts of that future have been full of adventure and some parts have been extremely difficult. Most of it has been what anyone would consider normal day-to-day living; believe it or not God does do that as well.

For many years it has now been my practice to try to listen to God more than talk to God. I have been privileged to spend time listening to what God wants both privately and in the company of other dedicated followers. There is nothing wrong with bringing the issues of our lives to God but I have learned to bring them in question form expecting to hear from His Holy Spirit the things that pertain to daily living and destiny.

His In-Dwelling Spirit:
The role of God the Holy Spirit is without doubt far greater and more far reaching than we could imagine. The basic mechanics of His role as Christ in us are clearly laid out in the Bible. Truly grasping the significance of His role within our spirit requires us to embrace the fullness of who He is and to continue with determination on the daily path of seeking God and letting Him be the Lord and Master of our destiny.

Jesus Himself is our main instructor when it comes to gaining a correct understanding of what it is supposed to be like to interact with God's in-dwelling Spirit. Jesus had finished His earthly ministry and was heading toward His end game of laying down His life for our sins, rising from the dead, and returning to Heaven. He needed to make sure that His followers would understand how to be led by God and what to do when He was no longer around in physical form to guide them.

After all, being the physical Christ His influence had so far remained localized. But in His goal to reach the whole world for salvation, Jesus would need to be a bit more mobile. Filling each of His followers with His Spirit and turning them loose into the world was the next step in His strategy.

Turning to His words in the Book of John we begin to learn what that would be like. *"A little while longer and*

*the world will see Me no more, but you will see Me. Because
I live, you will live also. At that day you will know that I am
in My Father, and you in Me, and I in you. He who has My
commandments and keeps them, it is he who loves Me. And he
who loves Me will be loved by My Father, and I will love him
and manifest Myself to him" (John 14:19-21).*

The world may not see Jesus anymore but we who are
His know Him and live because of Him. Jesus describes
the normal flow of the life of His followers as one of
returning the love of God by keeping His commandments.
Though I did not deserve it, the living God has looked
for me and invited me into His life. He has shared His
great love with me. How can I show Him that I love
Him in return? In what way can I reflect my love back
to God who has so richly loved me? By doing what He
says. Wow! This is a very different motivation for keeping
God's commandments than the usual and futile religious
method of keeping a list of rules to try to make sure God
is not mad at me isn't it? Jesus clearly says that He and the
Father will manifest, meaning make their selves known,
to the one who walks with them in obedience.

In the very next verse a fair question is raised.
We should know by now that God is not afraid of our
questions and will certainly answer those which come
from the true heart of a seeker wanting to know. *Judas (not
Iscariot) said to Him, "Lord, how is it that You will manifest
Yourself to us, and not to the world?" (John 14:22).*

*Jesus answered and said to him, "If anyone loves Me, he
will keep My word; and My Father will love him, and We will
come to him and make Our home with him. He who does not
love Me does not keep My words; and the word which you hear
is not Mine but the Father's who sent Me. These things I have
spoken to you while being present with you. But the Helper, the
Holy Spirit, whom the Father will send in My name, He will
teach you all things, and bring to your remembrance all things
that I said to you" (John 14:23-26).*

Wow! OK, now we are getting somewhere. So we are indeed to expect that, as we bring our lives before God intending to follow His leadership, we can count on His help and His teaching to be delivered right inside of our spirit by His Spirit. The Spirit of God will: *teach you all things.* Jesus and the Father in the form of the Holy Spirit: *will come to* (you and me) *and make* (their) *home with* (us).

Won't that make us a bit odd and perhaps put us at odds with the world in which we live? Yes, it will. But who is odd, those who have allowed the Savior to pull them into the safety of His ship or those who deny the hand of rescue being outstretched to them? True oddity is found in not knowing who you are or why you are here. It is not the found who are odd but rather those who are still lost.

The next words Jesus has to say about the Holy Spirit within us cannot be separated from the conflict which God and those who follow God experience in this world. Jesus speaks of this in *John 15:18-25*, summarizing we read: *Remember the word that I said to you, 'A servant is not greater than his master.' If they persecuted Me, they will also persecute you (John 15:20).* Jesus follows this with both a promise and a task. *"But when the Helper comes, whom I shall send to you from the Father, the Spirit of truth who proceeds from the Father, He will testify of Me. And you also will bear witness, because you have been with Me from the beginning" (John 15:26-27).* Jesus promises that the Holy Spirit will work at making Him known. Also, Jesus lets us know that we are to bear witness of what we know and have experienced in cooperation with the Holy Spirit and, yes, it might indeed lead to misunderstandings and persecution.

There are two main views which Christians commonly hold of Jesus and of which you will hear people speak when they either share why they follow Him or justify why they do not. We need to take care that our understanding of Him is built on truth because His Spirit within us is very expressly named *the Spirit of truth*.

In the first view we see Jesus as God Almighty, so high above ourselves that there should be no thought or pretense of any link between His words and actions and ours. In this view, the works that He did while He was here were evidently done because He is God. In this view we are to have no aspirations of being like Him or doing the things which He did. Certainly a review of major portions of Christian history between 350AD to 1960AD reveals that the established churches often kept their members ignorant and controlled, with a clergy that was 'above' the common man and the scriptures needing 'interpretation'. Sadly, even with the changes God has been making in established Christian denominations over the last 50 years, some form of this viewpoint can still be heard from the mouths of believers. The belief is that I could not possibly do anything out of the ordinary and God would not expect me to because I am not Him.

The second view has been held by those who have followed Jesus since the day He launched His ministry until this present time. They have not always been in the majority and have often been found to be marginalized by society and even at times by the 'established' church. This view, supported by scriptures, teaches that although Jesus is the perfect and sinless Son of God and God the Son, His ministry flowed from a daily walk with the Father from which Jesus learned what He was to do. In short, the man Christ Jesus is our perfect example having modeled for us how to live in daily relationship with God. There are many passages which directly teach and indicate this to us, none more strongly than Jesus own words. *Then Jesus answered and said to them, "Most assuredly, I say to you, the Son can do nothing of Himself, but what He sees the Father do;*

for whatever He does, the Son also does in like manner. For the Father loves the Son, and shows Him all things that He Himself does; and He will show Him greater works than these, that you may marvel" (John 5:19-20).

A good example of Jesus seeking God the Father for daily living and destiny is found in His selection of the Twelve Apostles. *Now it came to pass in those days that He went out to the mountain to pray, and continued all night in prayer to God. And when it was day, He called His disciples to Himself; and from them He chose twelve whom He also named apostles (Luke 6:12-13).* How did Jesus know which twelve to choose for this historically important task? He *continued all night in prayer to God.*

Continuing to examine Jesus' words regarding the Holy Spirit we learn more of His intentions to affect the entire human race which Jesus speaks of as the world. *Nevertheless I tell you the truth. It is to your advantage that I go away; for if I do not go away, the Helper will not come to you; but if I depart, I will send Him to you. And when He has come, He will convict the world of sin, and of righteousness, and of judgment: of sin, because they do not believe in Me; of righteousness, because I go to My Father and you see Me no more; of judgment, because the ruler of this world is judged (John 16:7-11).* Sending us His Holy Spirit, as the 'helper', provides the great and winning advantage in this life of following Jesus. Our relationship with God can be far closer with His Spirit on the inside and it plants us in the greater context of His world wide family of followers who all have this same Spirit. Notice the emphasis Jesus puts on the Spirit's role of bringing conviction. I have learned that conviction from the Holy Spirit plays a large part in directing us to walk in God's ways. I have been a member of various Spirit filled leadership groups and I have been a member of various leadership groups related to the works of the world. The difference between these is like night and day in the manner in which business is conducted and decisions are made. It is refreshing to work with a group of people who are all motivated by the same Holy Spirit and are interested in God's glory rather than their own egos. In such groups decisions can be made by openness and consensus after seeking the Lord. As it is said: *Now the Lord is the Spirit; and where the Spirit of the Lord is, there is liberty (2 Corinthians 3:17)*. In groups that are not led by the Spirit there are often conflicting loyalties and ambitions which get in the way of true progress. Instead of consensus many of our employers and political groups typically expect their members to arrive at compromise as a means to make progress.

It is not uncommon to encounter people in our culture who find it easy and even automatic to use the name of Jesus when they get excited, scared, or just to make a point as part of what they are saying. It is also not uncommon to notice how many people bristle or get uncomfortable when we speak of Jesus as if He were a normal part of everyday life. However, during an acute natural disaster or in times when their lives or livelihood are threatened these same people will try prayer in a form of bargaining with God. God, if you will just get me out of this trouble, I promise to do such and such. This is further evidence that the Holy Spirit is indeed at work convicting *the world of sin, and of righteousness, and of judgment.*

"I still have many things to say to you, but you cannot bear them now. However, when He, the Spirit of truth, has come, He will guide you into all truth; for He will not speak on His own authority, but whatever He hears He will speak; and He will tell you things to come. He will glorify Me, for He will take of what is Mine and declare it to you. All things that the Father has are Mine. Therefore I said that He will take of Mine and declare it to you" (John 16:12-15).

This final passage of Jesus' direct teachings about the Holy Spirit in the Book of John confirms for us the Trinity which is God: Father, Jesus, Holy Spirit, and the unity in which the triune God speaks from a single mind and with one voice. It also focuses in on God's fulfillment of the goal which He has planted in the heart of everyone who builds a lifestyle of seeking Him. Remember that God has called us to seek Him. *And you will seek Me and find Me, when you search for Me with all your heart. I will be found by you, says the LORD (Jeremiah 29:13-14).* And, in the passage we are examining, we come across this statement about the Holy Spirit: *He will guide you into all truth.* It is an affirmative statement made by Jesus and declaring to us that this will indeed happen, that those who receive Him will have full access to 'all' truth.

Picture it like this; two friends get together around a picnic table to meet and talk and learn of each other. When they are earnest and engaged in their interaction then learning happens. When either of them begins to wander in thought or become otherwise distracted and disengaged while his friend is talking (you married people know exactly what I am talking about here) then learning does not happen.

God is at the table. As the people of God who are supposed to seek Him for daily living and destiny, the more regularly we come to the table and give God our undivided attention the more the truth from the Holy Spirit of God will actually be understood by us.

Can God's plans be blocked? In the Bible we see that at times God's ultimate plans get delayed by those who choose not to follow His directions. However we also see that His plans do not ultimately get blocked because God will go around those who won't follow and will use someone else. A good example of this would be from the book of *1 Samuel* where God rejected Saul as King of Israel and went around Saul to establish David as King.

Now the word of the LORD came to Samuel, saying, "I greatly regret that I have set up Saul as king, for he has turned back from following Me, and has not performed My commandments." And it grieved Samuel, and he cried out to the LORD all night (1 Samuel 15:10-11).

Now the LORD said to Samuel, "How long will you mourn for Saul, seeing I have rejected him from reigning over Israel? Fill your horn with oil, and go; I am sending you to Jesse the Bethlehemite. For I have provided Myself a king among his sons" (1 Samuel 16:1).

God's plans cannot and will not ultimately be blocked. However this is where you and I come in is as seekers of God and as those who learn to still ourselves and listen to His Holy Spirit. God's plan is for us to be His ambassadors and His agents of change toward the people living within the culture, environment, and point of history into which He has placed each of us.

Can the will of God be thwarted? Somewhat different from God's plans of 'what' He wants to accomplish is God's will of 'how' He wants to accomplish it. Using our example from *1 Samuel*, God intended for the King of Israel to live the life of an obedient seeker in order to accomplish His plans for Israel. God also intended for the King of Israel to model the life of an obedient seeker as a means of instructing the rest of the nation. God specifically chose Saul and this should have happened through Saul. David could have still been the next King and perhaps done a better job than Saul but God's will was thwarted because Saul was not an obedient seeker. Historically God still accomplished His plan, but God's will was not carried out during the reign of Saul. Will it be carried out during your reign? How about when the going gets tough? I have to say I have failed to carry out God's will many times. I have not had much of a problem with willingness but learning to listen has been a challenge. Remembering what I have heard so that I do it has also been a challenge. God knows this and, instead of 'fixing' me so that I always follow through on the instructions of His Holy Spirit, God's plan has been simple. Gordon, write down what you are hearing from my Spirit so that you will not forget to carry out my will. This has been my method for quite some time now because I know that if I don't write something down I will forget.

There is so much more to learn about interacting with His Holy Spirit. Most of what you learn will come from doing so. I would encourage you to read through *Romans Chapter 8* and *Galatians Chapter 5* to learn about the work of the Holy Spirit with regard to reforming our souls. Having been brought up in sin and apart from God our souls are used to the behaviors associated with not knowing Him. It feels, and is, more natural for us to let our lives be guided by our own thoughts and feelings rather than by His Spirit. Many of these things must be unlearned and replaced with the path of godliness and we will be digging further into this in the next chapter.

Interdependence of Those Filled With the Spirit:
In looking at our interaction with the Holy Spirit, it needs to be pointed out that none of us is an island unto our self. Jesus has from the beginning formed His world-wide followers into His church. On a local level we have churches which are supposed to be gatherings of those who follow Jesus and are also supposed to be structured in such a manner that those who are not His followers would be drawn in. In God's house they should be welcomed and befriended, and provided with the opportunity to get to know God, experience His Spirit, and learn what it means to serve Him.

Within these communities Jesus has purposely put different people with different motivations. His Spirit will communicate some plans that involve everyone and some plans which are more specific for one or few individuals.

How do you know which local church you should belong to? That answer should be obvious to a seeker, ask God. By inner words, urgings, or in some substantial way, the Holy Spirit can show you where He wants you to be and over time He can also show you what your purpose is in that context.

None of our churches are perfect because they are made up of ex-sinners in reform and sinners who are looking for God. If they were perfect then the moment you or I stepped into them they would become imperfect for the same reason. My advice here is to stop looking for the perfect church which will feed you in a perfect way. Rather, find out from God where He wants you to be and get busy with the Holy Spirit discovering and living out His will in that context for the benefit of others. This is part of the destiny for which you and I were created and we don't want to miss that by being self-focused and living as if life is all about us. You know what I am talking about because self-centeredness is one of the deeply rooted diseases of our present time.

Jesus had the Holy Spirit without measure. *For He whom God has sent speaks the words of God, for God does not give the Spirit by measure. The Father loves the Son, and has given all things into His hand (John 3:34-35).* The church in its fullness should also have the Spirit without measure. However to individual believers the Spirit is given by measure. *For as we have many members in one body, but all the members do not have the same function, so we, being many, are one body in Christ, and individually members of one another. Having then gifts differing according to the grace that is given to us, let us use them (Romans 12:4-6).*

Jesus' obvious purpose in doing this is to bind us together in mutual need of one another and mutual respect for the differences and importance of what He will bring to create the whole from each individual.

When we are engaged in seeking God for His purposes in daily living and destiny, then we should be too busy to be conceited about how God is showing us things others don't understand or using us in more important ways. If you find that happening as a result of seeking God then be sure that He is identifying your conceit with the intention of rooting it out of the garden of your life.

The least fellow member of the family of Christ is worthy of all of our love and respect. If we believe they are straying or in need of being built up further then we are to pray for them and ask God to show us what, if anything, we are to do about it. *But now indeed there are many members, yet one body. And the eye cannot say to the hand, "I have no need of you"; nor again the head to the feet, "I have no need of you." But God composed the body, having given greater honor to that part which lacks it, that there should be no schism in the body, but that the members should have the same care for one another. And if one member suffers, all the members suffer with it; or if one member is honored, all the members rejoice with it. Now you are the body of Christ, and members individually (1 Corinthians 12:20-21, 24-27).*

As we have reviewed, God has created His worldwide and local church, gatherings of followers, in such a way that none of us is independent from the others. For the business of His Kingdom to prosper, Jesus needs us to learn to be interdependent on one another. Interdependence goes particularly against the grain of the independent human spirit and often we must change the ways in which we behave in order to fully serve the Lord.

As with all things that are part of God's plan, if He finds that we will not do His will then His history will wait for those who will. What a poor day if we the saved stand before the Lord in heaven and God has to express sorrow that He was not able to do much in the day and age in which you and I were placed. Reading about Jesus' trip to His hometown of Nazareth we find such a sad story. *Now He did not do many mighty works there because of their unbelief (Matthew 13:58).*

The Giver of Gifts:

Digging further into our interdependence on one another as fellow members of the same Kingdom, we cannot neglect to review the intention of the gifts of the Holy Spirit. It is not my intention to review the purpose and function of each biblical gift in this chapter although we will cover spiritual gifts a bit more in Chapter Nine. There are many books written about the gifts of the Holy Spirit, some are of value and some perhaps not. The main book I can recommend for learning 'about' the gifts of the Spirit is the Bible. The main point I can offer you regarding 'experiencing' the gifts of the Holy Spirit in your own life is for you to seek the Lord. I encourage you to read the main passages of the Bible concerning these gifts and to work with the Lord to understand which one or ones He is calling you to walk in. Some of them may be more obvious based on the type of person He has created you to be. However in all cases, instead of making assumptions, listen to the Lord and then step out in obedience to what His Spirit shows you to do.

If you are new to this then be prepared to be surprised. You will be surprised by what does work and by what does not work and God will teach you through all of it. I can say that I want to drive from point A to point B and I can even get in the car, but to actually get there I have to put that car in gear and alternate the gas and brake pedals appropriately or I will never arrive. Those of us who drive are familiar with the experience of getting lost. What do you do when you are lost? Consult the map (Bible), ask directions (Prayer), follow the GPS (Holy Spirit) and try again.

The Apostle Paul is the most widely published example of a devoted follower of Christ. He spoke about the difference between what we have now through Jesus and what we will have when we depart this world. *For now we see in a mirror, dimly, but then face to face. Now I know in part, but then I shall know just as I also am known (1 Corinthians 13:12).* As clear as our experience with the Holy Spirit may seem at times, it is appropriately humbling to understand that we are limited and should not expect to bat 1000 every single time.

Speaking expressly about God's overall purpose in giving the gifts of the Holy Spirit we find the following passages. First, our particular gifting is to be used for the benefit of others. *As each one has received a gift, minister it to one another, as good stewards of the manifold grace of God (1 Peter 4:10).* Next, the gifts of the Spirit are not chosen by us but are distributed in the body of Christ by God's appointment. *There are diversities of gifts, but the same Spirit. There are differences of ministries, but the same Lord. And there are diversities of activities, but it is the same God who works all in all (1 Corinthians 12:4-6). And God has appointed these in the church: (1 Corinthians 12:28).*

For reference there are a number of New Testament passages which list the gifts of the Holy Spirit and you can find them there. *Romans 12:6-8, 1 Corinthians 12:4-11, 1 Corinthians 12:28, Ephesians 4:11-12, 1 Peter 4:10-11.*

Un-Hindering the Flow:
In the final section of this chapter we will cover various hindrances to the flow of God's Holy Spirit in our lives.

We have already discussed interdependence, the ability for local followers to trust and work with one another as God's chosen team to bring about His Kingdom. As a final word on that subject let us just say that refusing to become interdependent or insisting on being independent will limit what God can do through you. It can be tough to change but many of us need to do so for the sake of Jesus' Kingdom.

Another limiting mistake can be made through expecting our connection with God to have to somehow be mystical vs. being part of the regular, the every day, and the ordinary. *For we are His workmanship, created in Christ Jesus for good works, which God prepared beforehand that we should walk in them (Ephesians 2:10).* It is God who knows the works for which He created you. His word, the Bible, spends quite a bit of time on ordinary everyday instructions on how to love and how to treat one another. Without doubt many of the acts which God will have us participate in will be of the ordinary and everyday variety.

It is easier to stay on track with the Holy Spirit if we recognize that not everything that we hear from the Lord is going to lead where we think it will. *"For My thoughts are not your thoughts, nor are your ways My ways," says the LORD. "For as the heavens are higher than the earth, so are My ways higher than your ways, and My thoughts than your thoughts (Isaiah 55:8-9).* Reading the Bible we learn from the interaction of various people with God that they sometimes received short answers, and sometimes received long answers. There will be times when God wants you to do something which has a bigger purpose than is apparent at the moment. Also, God is under no obligation to explain to you or me all of the reasons for the choices He makes. If we remember that we are the servant and He is the Lord and not the other way around, and if we can get comfortable with not controlling an expected outcome as a result for what God asks us to do, then we will do well.

Keep your heart with all diligence, for out of it spring the issues of life (Proverbs 4:23). Keep watch over your own motivations because God at times will give us answers that fit both the questions we ask and the motivations with which we ask them. We are all sinners saved by the grace of God and we all have areas of our soul which are not yet lined up with God's Spirit. In those areas of motivation we can expect the Lord to discipline us as any worthy father would discipline his child. There will be times when Father God lets the child touch the flame if that is what the child insists on doing. *For whom the LORD loves He chastens, and scourges every son whom He receives (Hebrews 12:6).*

Next, how do I know that it is God speaking in my Spirit or revealing something to me rather than just my own voice and my own will? This is a great question which is worthy of the best answer I can offer.

We should pay attention to the examples and teaching we have in the Bible on this subject. These reveal the patience and other character qualities of God by which we can begin to recognize His voice.

In one example, Elijah learned this lesson while fleeing for his life from Queen Jezebel. Elijah hid himself in a cave on a mountain and had been crying out to God with the complaint that he was the only follower of God left in the land. *And behold, the LORD passed by, and a great and strong wind tore into the mountains and broke the rocks in pieces before the LORD, but the LORD was not in the wind; and after the wind an earthquake, but the LORD was not in the earthquake; and after the earthquake a fire, but the LORD was not in the fire; and after the fire a still small voice. So it was, when Elijah heard it, that he wrapped his face in his mantle and went out and stood in the entrance of the cave. Suddenly a voice came to him, and said, "What are you doing here, Elijah?" (1 Kings 19:11-13).*

From this we see and understand that God does not get frantic like we do about the things that go on. His voice is normally still and small and yes at times God will be the one asking the questions.

The still small voice of God is experienced in concert with what we learn about the gifts and fruit of His Holy Spirit. At times He sends: a word of wisdom, a word of knowledge, a prophecy for someone, discernment to understand a situation, in the proper situation the ability to understand or use other languages, an impression to employ our gifting. God's voice typically communicates these things in the context of the fruits of the Holy Spirit. *But the fruit of the Spirit is love, joy, peace, longsuffering, kindness, goodness, faithfulness, gentleness, self-control. Against such there is no law. And those who are Christ's have crucified the flesh with its passions and desires. If we live in the Spirit, let us also walk in the Spirit. Let us not become conceited, provoking one another, envying one another (Galatians 5:22-26).*

Recalling my early days as a follower of Christ, I had an experience which I have always referred to as 'the battle of the voices'. I was young in the Lord, very zealous, but my zeal and my willingness to obey did not yet match up. Many times in prayer I would get conflicting messages and I often spent quite a bit of time making sure that it was God speaking before I would obey. One day I was driving along, wrestling within my soul with something I had heard from God and with the conflicting inner voices of perhaps my will or the devil's. Of a sudden it hit me square in the soul. Wait a minute, stop! You are God in heaven and I am Your servant. God You are bigger than I am, so I will seek trusting You to make sure it is Your voice I hear, and I will make it my job to simply obey. That was a life changing moment as the 'battle of the voices' stopped right then and there. Since that time I have not really had much anxiety in hearing from God because the struggle of whether or not I would obey was for the most part removed. Would you like God to guard your heart and your mind? I encourage you to remove any anxiety you may have about whether or not you are hearing from God and just become a person who says 'Yes, Lord' and obeys. *Be anxious for nothing, but in everything by prayer and supplication, with thanksgiving, let your requests be made known to God; and the peace of God, which surpasses all understanding, will guard your hearts and minds through Christ Jesus (Philippians 4:6-7).*

Another great hindrance to the flow of God's Holy Spirit in our lives is a lack of self-acceptance. This is very common in our day and age being typically labeled as low self-esteem. It is true that Jesus' followers are not to think more highly of themselves than they ought and should be learning true humility. At the same time, God did not create us to be creatures of debilitating low self-esteem. Also, it is actually an insult to our Creator when we reject ourselves based on comparisons to others. *Jesus said to him, "'You shall love the LORD your God with all your heart, with all your soul, and with all your mind.' This is the first and great commandment. And the second is like it: 'You shall love your neighbor as yourself.' On these two commandments hang all the Law and the Prophets" (Matthew 22:37-40).* We may love God but we can hardly obey His second commandment to love our neighbor as our self if we do not love ourselves. It just won't work that way.

Do we take issue with God about our appearance, our character, or some other area in which we are not like others? *Or shall the thing formed say of him who formed it, "He has no understanding"? (Isaiah 29:16).* We know that: *the LORD does not see as man sees; for man looks at the outward appearance, but the LORD looks at the heart (1 Samuel 16:7).*

How does God see His followers? *But you were washed, but you were sanctified, but you were justified in the name of the Lord Jesus and by the Spirit of our God (1 Corinthians 6:11). But you are a chosen generation, a royal priesthood, a holy nation, His own special people, that you may proclaim the praises of Him who called you out of darkness into His marvelous light (1 Peter 2:9).*

I encourage you to receive the Lord's perspective and viewpoint about you. Stop looking at mere outward appearance. Accept the sense that you are washed and sanctified, that you are chosen, royal, holy, and special. Drop your low self-esteem and self-rejection at His feet in prayer on a regular basis and let Him re-make you into one who can proclaim His praises.

Refusal to deal with known sin in our lives is yet another area that will greatly hinder our progress in following Christ. *But your iniquities have separated you from your God; and your sins have hidden His face from you, so that He will not hear (Isaiah 59:2).* We will cover this subject more completely in the next chapter where we look at embracing maturity. It is one of the functions of the Holy Spirit to bring conviction of sin and He does so without partiality. We should expect this as part of God's loving discipline because we really do not fully perceive all of those things within us which need to be realigned with God. *And do not grieve the Holy Spirit of God, by whom you were sealed for the day of redemption (Ephesians 4:30).*

Lastly, it is very important for us to embrace the context into which God has placed us. I have seen both new and long term Christians who have not been taught about this or who just never got it. Their lives are typically lived in an un-purposeful manner, just taking things as they come. In short, they are not awake but asleep in the light, not perceiving God's plans and purpose. Hopefully they will awaken but be aware of this and be careful to check with God regarding your involvement with those who should be moving forward but are not.

God has placed you into this earth on purpose and in context. There is an individual context relevant to your life since God Himself chose to place you here. There is a historical context for your life based on what God has been doing over the centuries on behalf of mankind. There is a current context for your life based on what is happening in the Kingdom of God today. We are intended both to understand and be influenced in our decisions and actions by the context of these things.

Putting It into Practice:

For as many as are led by the Spirit of God, these are sons of God (Romans 8:14). This is the ultimate goal for every servant of God, to know that day by day we are being led of His Spirit. As we yield to Him in trust and obedience, Jesus will write history through us which is really His-story.

How big can you go? Are there any limits to what the Lord might want to accomplish through us by His in-dwelling Spirit? *Hebrews Chapter 11* is commonly called the faith hall of fame. In it the writer relates the faith and deeds of many of the Old Testament saints and concludes with these words: *And what more shall I say? For the time would fail me to tell of Gideon and Barak and Samson and Jephthah, also of David and Samuel and the prophets: who through faith subdued kingdoms, worked righteousness, obtained promises, stopped the mouths of lions, quenched the violence of fire, escaped the edge of the sword, out of weakness were made strong, became valiant in battle, turned to flight the armies of the aliens. Women received their dead raised to life again (Hebrews 11:32-35).* In short it should never be on our side of the table to limit what God wants to do. Let Him have His way as we pray: *Your kingdom come. Your will be done on earth as it is in heaven (Matthew 6:10).*

At the same time we must not underrate daily necessities. God is glorified in daily living as well as in what we presume to be big things. *I can do all things through Christ who strengthens me (Philippians 4:13)*.

Let us not be found seeking great things for ourselves. It must be God Who directs our lives and the size and scope of the results are His business. God alone is the one who sees beyond our horizons.

Lastly, come to the quiet making it your daily habit to spend time with the Lord. Renew your strength, start your prayers in silence drawing near to the Lord with your spirit before beginning to speak. You will be surprised to find that God really does reward those who diligently seek Him.

Even the youths shall faint and be weary, and the young men shall utterly fall, but those who wait on the LORD shall renew their strength; they shall mount up with wings like eagles, they shall run and not be weary, they shall walk and not faint. "Keep silence before Me, O coastlands, and let the people renew their strength! Let them come near, then let them speak; let us come near together for judgment" (Isaiah 40:30-41:1).

Chapter Six

Embracing Maturity

(Cleansed and Ready for the Masters use.)

Have you ever been job hunting? Most likely you have. When we are in need of a job we knock on doors, search the internet, and scour the want-ads. Here's one that sounds pretty good! They are looking for a CEO and from the looks of it I am qualified. Wait a minute, look at the requirements: must be willing to put up with an entire company of workers who are infantile and refuse to grow up. Yeah, thank you but no thanks. Next.

Of course we would be unlikely to even accept an interview for such a job. However, consider Jesus as the CEO, Chief Executive Officer, of His Kingdom. His goal for this corporation is that it seek out and rescue as many of those who are drowning in sin as possible. Perhaps beyond the understanding of those who work in His Company, CEO Jesus Christ knowing all and seeing all, has determined that the very best and most effective manner in which to accomplish this goal is to multiply Himself by living in and through His employees.

The plan and method of accomplishment are sound. However, to grow this company into a success the employees will not only need to be trained but will need to accept and embrace a step up in their maturity. As each generation passes through His-Story CEO Jesus is able to accomplish much or little based on whether His Kingdom's employees at that time in history decide to grow up or not.

Repentance leading to life change is the best indicator of whether a person is really in the faith or not. *From that time Jesus began to preach and to say, "Repent, for the kingdom of heaven is at hand" (Matthew 4:17).*

The New Testament Greek word for repent is metanoeo, pronounced met-an-o-eh'-o, meaning to think differently, to reconsider. It carries the moral quality of compunction, where we get that Holy Spirit provided nudge in our conscience, the sense of having done wrong that drives us to reconsider.

Repentance is the related word metanoia, pronounced met-an'-oy-ah, which puts the direct focus on our compunction for guilt as a driver that follows through to reformation. The implication of repentance is that we reverse our decision choosing to go the other way. One of the best explanations we have of the function of repentance was written by the Apostle Paul to the church in Corinth where he appropriately calls compunction godly sorrow. Paul shows us the function of godly sorrow which leads to life in contrast with the sorrow of the world, sorry I got caught, which leads to death. *For godly sorrow produces repentance leading to salvation, not to be regretted; but the sorrow of the world produces death (2 Corinthians 7:10).*

Very basically, repentance or to repent simply means to turn around based on the conviction that you were going the wrong way. Imagine driving a nighttime highway in thick fog. You're late and rushed so you are going as fast as you can. Not being sure if you are on the right track you are hoping for that next sign post to appear. There it is, you can barely make it out, wait a minute it says: Do Not Enter Wrong Way! Now just one thing remains before you end up in a terrible crash: how fast can you pull over and turn the heck around?

Not every change toward maturity which the Lord wants to bring into our lives will have this same urgency, but many will. As previously discussed, salvation through Jesus is certainly a starting point where we gain the right to become children of God. On the path with Jesus there will be some huge milestones of freedom and progress though I have never seen any child grow up without any difficulties in the process, have you?

I can remember being a young 20 something. Jesus had just brought me through a very significant breakthrough of revelation and life change. I remember thinking to myself: 'Praise God I am totally free of sin and my children will never be affected by any sin from my life!' Oh, to be sure the Lord let me have my joy that day but He knew something that I did not. Jesus knew that this event was just part of the tip of the iceberg.

It has been my experience that, in His mercy, God simply does not reveal everything that needs to be fixed or changed in our lives all at once. He gives His infant ones the challenges of infants, His child and teenagers the challenges appropriate to them and His young adults are called to yet greater and higher life change. This is God's mercy and the blessing of having Him as our true Father, *being confident of this very thing, that He who has begun a good work in you will complete it until the day of Jesus Christ (Philippians 1:6).*

Jesus said: *"I am the true vine, and My Father is the vinedresser, I am the vine, you are the branches"* *(John 15:1&5).* As an expert vinedresser we can expect certain activities on the part of Father God which will impact our individual lives and the life of the community of followers in our day and age.

We can expect Him to weed out those things in the garden which would hinder the growth of the entire vine. We can expect Him to fertilize, which provides the entire vine with the nutrients it needs to grow strong. We can expect Him to prune the branches removing areas of our individual lives which hinder growth. We can expect Him to provide support for the branches, moving them into the light where photosynthesis can take place, allowing us to grow strong and bear fruit.   Now of course this is an allegory and like all allegories it is meant for instruction. There is certainly a difference between us and the branches of a vine. We have something which the branches of a grape vine do not have. We have the ability to resist the efforts of the Vinedresser even though such resistance is to our own disadvantage.

We all know that we do at times resist what God seems to want. But why would we resist God's efforts to promote our maturity? We resist at different stages of our growth. Those newborn into Christ or who have advanced to childhood are fresh out of the world and still have so many areas of their soul which are more used to the ways of the world than the ways of God. As we become God's young men and young women He will start to challenge us to grow in ways that are counter-cultural to this world and this can be scary. Resistance to God's desired flow is natural because of these attachments and fears. In gaining maturity, we often have to fight our way through entrenched bad human qualities of indifference, laziness, petty emotions, hatreds, prejudices, and a hundred other things associated with the unrighteousness which we needed saving from in the first place.

Yet the Holy Spirit clearly works within us indicating through our conscience that we need to turn around first in this and then in that area of life. You were going in this direction which is away from God now start going in this direction toward God. It sounds like a simple enough act and it actually is. True repentance always starts in the soul where we receive and accept the conviction that we must indeed make a change. Repentance based on conviction from the Lord's Spirit calls us to change through the discovery of areas within that promote separation from God. We need to shed the false idea that God is somehow angry at having discovered sin within us. God already knew about everything within us before offering His salvation (see *Romans 5:8*). His actions in calling us to change are the loving actions of a true Father. Even a good earthly father guides his child through the process of resistance and only gets upset if the child digs in and absolutely refuses to cooperate.

Repentance and the need to repent extend far past the point of initial salvation and are intended by God as the means through which we mature. In every area of our lives where reform may be needed, in order to change that area back into the image of God, we are confronted with choices. Will I repent and work with God to make the change or will I choose not to look.

To be sure, some things are harder to change than others and in some cases change may take years rather than moments. But this is why we are talking about maturity. Again, no baby becomes a youth in one day and no youth grows into adulthood overnight. At times great leaps and bounds are made and at times progress is slow. What matters is that we continue to seek the Lord staying open to whatever He wants to bring. There is no expectation in scripture to indicate that God wants us to conduct a witch-hunt within our own lives to root out every last sin. Rather it is *the goodness of God* which *leads you to repentance* (from *Romans 2:4*) and in my experience that is a gradual work.

Nevertheless the solid foundation of God stands, having this seal: "The Lord knows those who are His," and, "Let everyone who names the name of Christ depart from iniquity." But in a great house there are not only vessels of gold and silver, but also of wood and clay, some for honor and some for dishonor. Therefore if anyone cleanses himself from the latter, he will be a vessel for honor, sanctified and useful for the Master, prepared for every good work. Flee also youthful lusts; but pursue righteousness, faith, love, peace with those who call on the Lord out of a pure heart (2 Timothy 2:19-22).

In a Great House:

Surely the Lord's house is the greatest house and His house contains many 'vessels'. These vessels are the human pots, pans, cups, pitchers, and basins of every shape size and material. Perhaps because of weakness or limitations in those who lead, many churches have gone astray from this human factor of faith through enforcing a cookie cutter approach to Christianity. 'If it does not look like this then it's not Christian!' However, as we reviewed in our chapter on interacting with His Holy Spirit, God in His wisdom has made us all a bit different for purposes of His own choosing.

The purpose of a vessel can be summed up in one word: stewardship. Good stewardship is the quality of faithfully carrying out the duties and purposes for which one has been equipped. Poor stewardship is found in those who neglect to carry out the duties and purposes for which they have been equipped. We all have our ideas of what it means to be rich but, in comparison; much of the world exists on the equivalent of less than one or two dollars a day. In that sense anyone who eats their fill each day and has spare change to spend on luxuries is rich. An example of poor stewardship would be for a 'rich' person to spend all of their wealth in the pursuit of pleasure with never a regard to how they might affect the abject poverty of others (see *Matthew 25:31-46*).

A vessel exists to be filled by its owner, then to contain its owner's contents until needed by the owner. A faithful vessel remains available for the owner at any time to extract or pour those contents out for whatever purpose the owner chooses. For the Lord's vessels to honor Him as good stewards two things are required. First we must be cleansed of dishonoring contents. Second we must be available to freely receive the contents of His choosing and freely dispense them at His desire. *Therefore if anyone cleanses himself from the latter, he will be a vessel for honor, sanctified and useful for the Master, prepared for every good work (2 Timothy 2:21).*

How do you react to the idea that you are supposed to be a vessel at the Lord's beck and call? In comparison to any other, Jesus will be the most wonderful, adoring, and attentive Master a vessel like us could ever have. However, every one of His followers must go through the scrubbing that removes our own ideas and pride about who we are, our perceived privileges, and about what we will or won't do. Ultimately Jesus Christ is Lord of all or of nothing. He may allow this concept to develop gently over time but it absolutely must if we are to be useful in His Kingdom and fulfill the daily deeds and destiny for which we were created. Do you know where you are in this process? How would you measure yourself in regard to ownership of things vs. all things being owned by the Lord with some of them being placed under your stewardship? Do you currently own things that you would find it difficult to share if the Lord required them of you?

But we have this treasure in earthen vessels, that the excellence of the power may be of God and not of us (2 Corinthians 4:7). It is truly of no real consequence whether God has chosen to make you and me from *gold and silver* or *wood and clay.* Ultimately all of these materials are *earthen* being founded from the common-place materials of earth. What matters is that we remain vessels cleansed and useful to our Master.

In any house some vessels get to hold the flowers and others the waste. In his passage to Timothy, Paul indicates that it is perfectly OK to be a different manner and material of vessel as long as we understand that no follower of Christ is to remain a vessel for dishonor. Whether I am an intricate golden basin or a simple clay pot is not the issue, what I contain should honor the Lord and not dishonor Him. We are to depart from iniquity, to cleanse ourselves from dishonor, so that we will be: *'sanctified and useful for the Master, prepared for every good work' (2 Timothy 2:21b).*

As the Lord continues to work on your life to make you into a vessel that is His very own, what methods is He using to get your attention about things that need to change and to secure your commitment to take them seriously enough to pursue cleansing? Are you remaining open to the still small voice of His Holy Spirit, or does God have to veritably knock your noggin with a two-by-four before you will listen? He is not planning to quit moving you in His direction and the more we identify those areas where we are resisting such progress, the easier it gets. One of the examples from my life where I was clearly a vessel for dishonor would have been the use of my big mouth. It just came naturally to me to insult people with casual comments and jokes made at their expense. It made me the funny guy and got a laugh from the crowd.

Needless to say the time came when this aspect of my life bubbled up to the top of the Lord's priority list. I had made a 'witty' comment in a group setting which clearly hurt another person's feelings and now God was not happy about it. I actually felt the pressure of conviction from the Holy Spirit Who clearly wanted me to apologize. I spent a bit of time wrestling over this where I knew that He knew that I knew that He knew that I was to apologize to that person. But you see, for pride's sake I did not want to apologize, so I struggled against myself. My memory being fuzzy on His exact words, finally the Lord put it to this effect: 'You hurt that person and you are going to apologize, in fact you are from now on going to apologize every time your big mouth hurts someone.' That was pretty clear and I understood that my continued walk with Jesus was at stake, we were going no further until I repented. So I pulled myself together, found that person and apologized for hurting their feelings. As a follow up I made it my policy to make myself apologize right away to anyone I realized I had inappropriately offended. The cleansing came as a byproduct of my obedience because in some mystical way, that only God knows, I simply don't make such big mouth casual comments anymore. Ah, the peace that comes from a bit of maturity.

The Pursuit of Righteousness, Faith, Love, and Peace:
Our passage from 2 *Timothy* concludes with these words: *Flee also youthful lusts; but pursue righteousness, faith, love, peace with those who call on the Lord out of a pure heart (2 Timothy 2:22).*

Righteousness is something which to we must awaken. In some ways, many of our modern churches have distanced themselves from the concept of righteousness. There are worries about the appearance of being saved by works vs. saved by grace as well as concerns about projecting a message that we are 'holier than thou'. In minimizing righteousness, which simply indicates that there are right ways to live, modern Christianity has become soft with regard to many sins. However we must by all means take heed to Paul's words written to the church at Corinth. *Do not be deceived:"Evil company corrupts good habits." Awake to righteousness, and do not sin; for some do not have the knowledge of God. I speak this to your shame (1 Corinthians 15:33-34).* Indeed understanding and cooperating with God's righteousness is a very large part of embracing maturity.

What would it look like for a person to be awake to righteousness? For a follower of Jesus to be comfortable in living out the works for which they have been created (see *Ephesians 2:10*) and yet holding all within the proper context of the grace of God? The arguments we still hear in the church regarding salvation by grace through faith and not by works of righteousness are age old. It is of course important to understand that there is no salvation nor are there any works of righteousness apart from the grace of God through Christ Jesus.

James, son of Mary and brother of our Lord, who became the pastor of the church in Jerusalem, was not trying to make a case for the righteousness of works over faith. Instead it is clear that James was attempting to settle this same argument by simply showing us that we cannot call something faith if it is not recognizable through righteous actions referred to as 'works'.

But someone will say, "You have faith, and I have works." Show me your faith without your works, and I will show you my faith by my works. You believe that there is one God. You do well. Even the demons believe — and tremble! But do you want to know, O foolish man, that faith without works is dead? Was not Abraham our father justified by works when he offered

Isaac his son on the altar? Do you see that faith was working together with his works, and by works faith was made perfect? And the Scripture was fulfilled which says, "Abraham believed God, and it was accounted to him for righteousness." And he was called the friend of God. You see then that a man is justified by works, and not by faith only (James 2:18-24).

Remember our discussion at the end of Chapter four? The Greek word for faith in the New Testament is Pistis, pronounced pis'-tis, and meaning: persuasion, assurance, belief, faith, <u>a belief based on knowing that I have heard</u> i.e. I am persuaded, I am assured and having the quality of knowing, not just hoping, that thus and such is indeed true.

Where can we get such faith upon which to act? How can the faith we have be strengthened? *Romans 10:17* tells us: *So then <u>faith comes by hearing</u>, and <u>hearing by the word of God</u>.*

Returning to James to cement this concept we read: *But be doers of the word, and not hearers only, deceiving yourselves. For if anyone is a hearer of the word and not a doer, he is like a man observing his natural face in a mirror; for he observes himself, goes away, and immediately forgets what kind of man he was. But he who looks into the perfect law of liberty and continues in it, and is not a forgetful hearer but a doer of the work, this one will be blessed in what he does (James 1:22-25).*

Clearly in embracing maturity we are challenged day by day to be a people whose belief in God couples with obedience to His word to produce an active faith, lived out through righteous works, which make a real difference in the world in which we live. The word of God as delivered to us in the Bible gives us God's general will, while specifics about His will are revealed as we seek God each day.

Between these two there really are no areas of life left uncovered within which an honest seeker would end up saying that there are no answers. At the same time it is important for us to respect God's timing. Even the Apostle Paul mentions that at times he was perplexed indicating the condition of not knowing what was going on (see *2 Corinthians 4:8*). Yet in the long run God always brought Paul through even the worst of times to fulfill his destiny.

It seems to have become a habit over the last 60 years for churches and Christians to teach that we don't need the Old Testament because after all we are New Testament believers. However, Jesus taught us respect for and the necessity of the law and prophets of the Old Testament and clearly indicated that the path of righteousness aligns with the laws of God. Jesus said: *"Do not think that I came to destroy the Law or the Prophets. I did not come to destroy but to fulfill. For assuredly, I say to you, till heaven and earth pass away, one jot or one tittle will by no means pass from the law till all is fulfilled. Whoever therefore breaks one of the least of these commandments, and teaches men so, shall be called least in the kingdom of heaven; but whoever does and teaches them, he shall be called great in the kingdom of heaven"* (*Matthew 5:17-19*).

As a side note, take notice that Jesus has fulfilled many of the laws we find in the Old Testament portion of the Bible. His sacrifice and our cleansing by His blood are what the sacrifices and cleansings of the Old Testament were pointing to. We no longer seek to obey the Old Testament laws concerning animal sacrifice or things that are clean or unclean because Jesus has fulfilled them. We also know that to enable our salvation God took His holy and perfect law and nailed it to the cross with Christ (see *Colossians 2:14*). In that effect the law of God which was meant to reveal man's sin (see *Romans 3:20*) no longer accuses those who have received the sacrifice of Jesus Christ. However, with regard to mature righteousness it would still be unrighteous and a great sin for any of us to break the basic commandments of God's law in commission of disrespect for God's name, murder, theft, adultery, etc.

To help us keep our balance, God has blessed us with direct means to break down and simplify this path of righteousness in Christ. *Then Jesus said to His disciples, "If anyone desires to come after Me, let him deny himself, and take up his cross, and follow Me" (Matthew 16:24).*

Denying oneself occurs in our daily choices where the necessities of the path of Christ vs. pleasing ourselves intersect. Also, there can be little confusion about Jesus' call of *'follow Me'*, that He is clearly wanting to take us somewhere. We do have various definitions of what Jesus means by taking up our cross, each of which has merit.

We would not be wrong in presuming that the cross speaks of our physical body; after all, stretch out your arms like Jesus did when He died and you have the shape of a cross.

We would also be correct in saying that Jesus is calling us to die to ourselves which couples directly with self-denial. The Apostle Paul put it like this: *I have been crucified with Christ; it is no longer I who live , but Christ lives in me; and the life which I now live in the flesh I live by faith in the Son of God, who loved me and gave Himself for me (Galatians 2:20).*

Others rightly teach that the cross is an instrument of suffering. It is incorrect to understand Christian suffering as a form of paying for ones own sins because Jesus paid for our sins once for all (see *Hebrews 10:10*). However many of Jesus' followers do suffer in many ways. The convict serving a sentence may come to Christ and yet continue to suffer the deprivations of his or her sentence. Many of the world's poor enter richly into the faith and yet their daily realities and lack of economic opportunity may not change much. Very many of our brothers and sisters in Christ through the ages have suffered and do suffer persecution for their faith from unjust governments and their own countrymen just as Jesus promised it would be (see *Matthew 10:21-26*). God even appoints certain of His followers to suffer for His name (see *Acts 9:15-16*). With regard to embracing maturity in the Lord, whether we suffer or not has never been the issue. At times suffering will come to all of us. The issue of maturing is one of embracing the abundant life which Jesus has promised to us at all times, even in the midst of suffering. *The thief does not come except to steal, and to kill, and to destroy. I have come that they may have life, and that they may have it more abundantly (John 10:10).*

There remains one more aspect of taking up our cross which God has provided to simplify the path of righteousness in Christ and this is where the laws and commandments of God come into play. *Then one of them, a lawyer, asked Him a question, testing Him, and saying, "Teacher, which is the great commandment in the law?" Jesus said to him, "'You shall love the LORD your God with all your heart, with all your soul, and with all your mind.' This is the first and great commandment. And the second is like it: 'You shall love your neighbor as yourself.' On these two commandments hang all the Law and the Prophets" (Matthew 22:35-40).*

Love the Lord your God and Love your neighbor as yourself. Jesus said that these two commandments are the foundation for the rest of the law and all that the prophets spoke.

Without a doubt this is one part of taking up our cross which cannot be overlooked if we are to truly follow Jesus. Reiterating His call at a different time, Jesus adds an operative word to it which is the word 'daily'. *Then He said to them all, "If anyone desires to come after Me, let him deny himself, and take up his cross daily, and follow Me (Luke 9:23).*

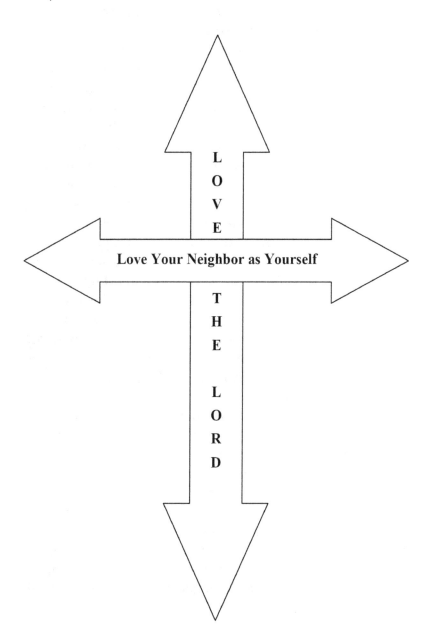

Daily we are meant to take up the vertical post of relationship and *love the LORD your God with all your heart, with all your soul, and with all your mind.* And daily we are meant to take up the corresponding horizontal cross beam and *love your neighbor as yourself.* Notice that the cross beam has no support without the post. Therefore, love for God is first and love for neighbor second, because without a love for God there is neither any point, nor anything real, to offer in loving one's neighbor.

Love fulfills the righteousness of God's law and is itself the law of Christ (see *John 13:34*). There are many in our world who have hearts of gold but who do not know God and may even say they have no use for Jesus Christ. Some of these are religious and some are not. We hear it said from time to time that 'so and so' is a good person and in all honesty, by comparison to others whom we know, they are. Mainly this comes from good upbringing in a loving home and, in our day and age, for the most part loving homes are found in cultures which have their foundations in Christian heritage. Surely there are societies without Christian heritage which are built upon honor and respect systems. I would suggest that one does not have to study much history or current events to understand that equity among mankind, where both men and women find acceptance and respect within societies, occurs within the context of Christian heritage. Examine our world and you will find that where honoring of Christ has either been currently or previously established there women and girls are valued and in other cultures that lack Christ they are thought of as less than furniture. Once again, many may seem to be good persons and by comparison to others perhaps they are, however goodness does not save our souls; only the grace of God through Jesus can do that.

In our passage from *Galatians 2* Paul talks about *the Son of God, who loved me and gave Himself for me.* Now this Son of God, Jesus, calls us to take up our cross and follow Him, to give of ourselves as He gave Himself for us. How do we do that? By living out the righteousness of the first and the second commandments to love God and love our neighbor. These are foundational and all of the rest of God's law hangs on these. In the great 'love' chapter of the New Testament, *1 Corinthians 13,* Paul speaks of the pre-eminence of love. He lists great deeds and righteous acts but leaves us to understand that they are meaningless without love. If I do all those things *but have not love, I am nothing (1 Corinthians 13:2).*

Lest we imagine that the commandments of God are mainly restricted to the Old Testament, Jesus punctuated this call to love in ordaining His new commandment. He also revealed that it is really the flow of love from His followers as witnessed by the world which would be the greatest tool in providing the lost with a correct picture of who we really are. *A new commandment I give to you, that you love one another; as I have loved you, that you also love one another. By this all will know that you are My disciples, if you have love for one another (John 13:34-35).*

Coupling Jesus' command to take up this cross and follow Him with our need to awake to righteousness and grow up into the fullness of Christ we read the following. *Owe no one anything except to love one another, for he who loves another has fulfilled the law. For the commandments, "You shall not commit adultery," "You shall not murder," "You shall not steal," "You shall not bear false witness," "You shall not covet," and if there is any other commandment, are all summed up in this saying, namely, "You shall love your neighbor as yourself." Love does no harm to a neighbor; therefore love is the fulfillment of the law (Romans 13:8-10).*

And do this, knowing the time, that now it is high time to awake out of sleep; for now our salvation is nearer than when we first believed. The night is far spent, the day is at hand. Therefore let us cast off the works of darkness, and let us put on the armor of light. Let us walk properly, as in the day, not in revelry and drunkenness, not in lewdness and lust, not in strife and envy. But put on the Lord Jesus Christ, and make no provision for the flesh, to fulfill its lusts (Romans 13:11-14).

Let Everyone who Names the Name of Christ Depart from Iniquity:

The beginning of our passage from 2 *Timothy* includes these words: "*Let everyone who names the name of Christ depart from iniquity.*"

While this directive is also echoed in the passage we just finished reading from Romans, we now come to the difficult part of embracing maturity: the struggle within.

Truly, we want the righteousness of God in every area of our lives. We want to be vessels of honor which are cleansed and ready for our Master's use. But there is a battle which rages within between how we really live and how we ought to live. This battle has two fronts. The first front is the war between our flesh and the Holy Spirit as the Lord works to move our souls from the darkness in which we had been living into the light of His image. The second battle front is the war between the Kingdom of God, of which we are now members, and that prince of the power of the air (see *Ephesians 2:2*) the devil or Satan who leads the camp we used to belong to.

Regarding our first battle front, the Apostle Paul was no stranger to this struggle and he also knew the ultimate answer, we learn this from the following selection of his words. *For I know that in me (that is, in my flesh) nothing good dwells; for to will is present with me, but how to perform what is good I do not find. For the good that I will to do, I do not do; but the evil I will not to do, that I practice. Now if I do what I will not to do, it is no longer I who do it, but sin that dwells in me. I find then a law, that evil is present with me, the one who wills to do good. For I delight in the law of God according to the inward man. But I see another law in my members, warring against the law of my mind, and bringing me into captivity to the law of sin which is in my members. O wretched man that I am! Who will deliver me from this body of death? I thank God — through Jesus Christ our Lord! (Romans 7:18-25).*

Paul's words have been used by many to justify their innocence regarding poor behavior. After all, they say, it is the sin which did it and not me. Without the need to debate this, I would merely point out that the rest of the force of scripture directly holds us accountable for our sin. Even our own lives bear witness that regardless of exactly how sin functions within us, it is we who suffer the consequences and continue in immaturity. There is only one deliverer as Paul has pointed out, Jesus Christ our Lord.

In his very next chapter *Romans 8* and also found in his writings, particularly *Galatians 5,* Paul lays out the path to victory in this war against our flesh and the sin which, as *Hebrews 12:1 says: so easily ensnares us.* It should come as no surprise that this path of victory is the path of the seeker, having everything to do with our daily walk with God's Holy Spirit.

But you are not in the flesh but in the Spirit, if indeed the Spirit of God dwells in you. Now if anyone does not have the Spirit of Christ, he is not His. And if Christ is in you, the body is dead because of sin, but the Spirit is life because of righteousness. But if the Spirit of Him who raised Jesus from the dead dwells in you, He who raised Christ from the dead will also give life to your mortal bodies through His Spirit who dwells in you (Romans 8:9-11). Who will deliver me from this body of death? *If Christ is in you.* It is through the in-dwelling Spirit of Christ that God will give us this victory of regeneration out of sin and into His image.

I say then: Walk in the Spirit, and you shall not fulfill the lust of the flesh. For the flesh lusts against the Spirit, and the Spirit against the flesh; and these are contrary to one another, so that you do not do the things that you wish. But if you are led by the Spirit, you are not under the law. Now the works of the flesh are evident, which are: adultery, fornication, uncleanness, lewdness, idolatry, sorcery, hatred, contentions, jealousies, outbursts of wrath, selfish ambitions, dissensions, heresies, envy, murders, drunkenness, revelries, and the like; of which I tell you beforehand, just as I also told you in time past, that those who practice such things will not inherit the kingdom of God. But the fruit of the Spirit is love, joy, peace, longsuffering, kindness, goodness, faithfulness, gentleness, self-control. Against such there is no law. And those who are Christ's have crucified the flesh with its passions and desires. If we live in the Spirit, let us also walk in the Spirit. Let us not become conceited, provoking one another, envying one another (Galatians 5:16-26). Our responsibility in this battle is very clear. By the grace of God we must regularly walk in the Spirit, crucifying our flesh with its natural deeds and letting the Holy Spirit bear His fruit through our lives without restriction. In short we must take the path of one who seeks God for daily living and destiny.

My own life has become a testimony of how this works on a real basis and that there is nothing too hard for God. To be sure after 36 years He is not done with me yet. Even as I write I am aware of some thorny issues that I am still working through with God in regard to how I relate to people. I am not entirely sure why I still get hung up at times with regard to the deep end of individual relationships but I still seek the Lord about this and little by little I am confident that improvements will be made with regard to the forming of His image in me.

My battles on this front did not start out with the finer points of relationships. When Jesus first introduced Himself and called me to salvation I was buried six feet deep and covered in muck. I can almost picture Him plucking me out by the scruff with thumb and forefinger and holding me up as He began to hose me off with the Holy Spirit.

As I related earlier, the Lord first let my ignorant condition of drug abuse get worse and worse until, triggered by His messenger, I was ready to be delivered and called to Him for help.

Also as previously mentioned, the Lord created a way out and gave my wife and me the strength to take it. First we were heroin free. Next, we were planted in Jesus' community of followers where good soil and the pure form of His light could help us start to grow. After this the Lord began to deliver us from most of the rest of our nasty outward habits: pot use and alcohol abuse, smoking with its impact on our health, profuse foul language, and a clutter of simply ungodly ways of thinking and living.

Jesus made a two pronged assault against the unrighteousness of our souls. He delivered us from many of these negative activities and associations and, at the same time, He also began to build into us the positive behaviors and thinking associated with being His followers. We learned to take the issues of our lives to the Lord in prayer. We learned to grow by saying 'yes' to His word. We learned to serve rather than be served. This was our spiritual childhood, the path from being newborn infants in the Lord into being young children of the Lord.

Although the memories of the good times I had with my own seven in their childhood are very dear to me, there is no way I would have wanted any of them to remain children forever. No serious father wants this and God, who invented fatherhood, is no different. The next phase of our maturity would move us forward into becoming a young man and young woman in the Lord and it had everything to do with departing from iniquity.

Now that we were rescued, generally cleaned off, clothed and in our right minds as it were, the Lord wanted us to start looking into the reasons why we had been so self-destructive in the first place. To be sure Petra's reasons were different than mine and she has her own story to tell. She had been the reckless one when it came to self-destruction whereas I had been the cautious and calculating one providing means and planning to insure that we were both destroyed in an organized and controlled fashion.

Remember God's question to Adam from Genesis? *Then the LORD God called to Adam and said to him, "Where are you?" (Genesis 3:9).* It was not because God did not know that Adam was hiding in fear behind the tree. It was that God wanted Adam to consider where Adam was. Gordon, where are you? Why were you engaging in behaviors and addictions which served to destroy My image within you? Do you understand what was happening? Let's take a look and see, because the underlying reasons for your sin must be dealt with if you are to move forward in maturity. In short, you must depart from iniquity.

Everyone's experience in this area will be different. The first step in maturing into a young man in the Lord came as I was dealing with issues of rage and anger that I seemed to have no ability to control. Oh, I would be sorry about my behaviors the next morning in prayer but that would do little to repair the damage such outbursts caused in my family. I know I sought the Lord's forgiveness but He had bigger plans. Through a clear teaching brought by a brother in the church I was confronted with the special link to wellness contained within the fifth commandment.

Here is how the Apostle Paul highlights it: *"Honor your father and mother," which is the first commandment with promise: "that it may be well with you and you may live long on the earth" (Ephesians 6:2-3).*

Needless to say, even if only considering my anger and rage, it was not well with me. I took this to heart and began to seek the Lord regarding my relationship toward mom and dad. In the end, it was me calling each of them to ask forgiveness for living a life that had dishonored them and requesting that our relationships be restored. To my delight they both received me and we did re-start relationships. My father had not let it develop into as close of a relationship as I would have liked and is gone now. My mother and I were able to get much closer and remain so to this day.   But something deeper within me was changed by taking this step of faith. I was healed and delivered down in the inner parts of my soul by the freedom of having obeyed the Lord and opened myself up to reconciliation. Somehow the Holy Spirit was then able to sweep away a major level of crud from within which was the iniquity driving the main parts of my anger and rage. This would be the first of many areas that the Lord would have me examine and take action on in this battle to break the chains of bondage which iniquity had on my soul.

Fifteen years into this process I first learned about the 12-step program. Now I had never been a 12-stepper and am still not. In my experience God has totally delivered me from my addictions and so I don't introduce myself as 'Gordon the heroin addict with 33 years sobriety' because I am not an addict any longer, not for 33 years. However I did discover that many of the steps which the Lord had me take were very similar to the steps of that program. So I do believe that, in general, 12-step programs can have merit but I also believe that they are not worth a nickel if they are not coupled directly with intentionally seeking God.

The seeker continues to work with the Lord and remains open to further life change. Our best examples of this come from King David who without doubt was one of the deepest persons with God whom we find in the Old or even New Testament. Listen to his words as He seeks the Lord, they can become a pattern for us.

Who can understand his errors? Cleanse me from secret faults. Keep back Your servant also from presumptuous sins; let them not have dominion over me. Then I shall be blameless, and I shall be innocent of great transgression. Let the words of my mouth and the meditation of my heart be acceptable in Your sight, O LORD, my strength and my Redeemer (Psalm 19:12-14).

Search me, O God, and know my heart; try me, and know my anxieties; and see if there is any wicked way in me, and lead me in the way everlasting (Psalm 139:23-24).

We can read of David's life and see how God was with David and used him to fulfill his destiny. David was able to confidently declare: *You enlarged my path under me, so my feet did not slip (Psalm 18:36).*

I have actually written an entire book about this subject with regard to departing from iniquity. It is based on my own life experiences and examines the role of Jesus as the Way of salvation, the Truth leading us out of patterns of sin, and the Life building the good things of God into us (see *John 14:6*). The title is: "Breaking the Cycle of Slavery to Sin" and I offer it here as a resource for those struggling to overcome repeating patterns of sin and wanting to build the good things of God into their lives.

Wrapping up our assault on this first battle front where we are called to depart from iniquity, it may be of value for us to understand the general nature of sin and what exactly is meant by iniquity.

Many modern English translations of the Bible have tended to lump the many facets of these important concepts under the umbrella of the word 'Sin'. However there are really four active words or concepts which we need to understand if we are to become vessels 'cleansed and ready for the Master's use'. By the way has anyone ever handed you a filthy cup to drink out of? Disgusting thought isn't it? Well, if we would not like it then how do you think God would feel about it?

Our first word is Sin which means to miss the mark. The Old Testament Hebrew word is chata', pronounced khaw-taw', meaning to miss. The New Testament Greek word is hamatano, pronounced ham-ar-tan'-o, meaning to miss the mark. *For all have sinned and fall short of the glory of God (Romans 3:23).* Falling short or missing the mark can happen intentionally or even unintentionally. Suppose my car skids on a wet street and I hit and injure another person. Cause of the accident? I didn't pay attention to the fact that my tire treads were worn down. That would be a sin on my part. The accident was unintentional but the fault is mine and there are consequences to be borne by the injured and probably by my wallet.

Trespass is a different form of what we would call sin. Different in that we clearly choose to go where we know we should not go or do what we know we should not do. Trespass includes the characteristic of rebellion. I know I am not supposed to but: 'I want to do what I want to do when I want to do it so I will.' The Old Testament Hebrew word is 'asham, pronounced aw-shawm', meaning to be guilty. The New Testament Greek word translated as trespass or trespasses is paraptoma, pronounced par-ap'-to-mah, meaning a side-slip, a deviation made willfully or unintentionally. Notice that making a conscious choice to trespass in the face of a clear no-trespassing sign is considerably more serious than discovering that we have missed the mark. Many of God's commandments represent no-trespassing signs: 'you shall not steal' is an example. It is possible to find that one has trespassed without intention but the main force of these words has to do with direct choice.

Another word we tend to equate with sin is transgression, which means to rebel. Transgression is where we shake our fist at God or other authority and say, 'No, I won't.' The Old Testament Hebrew word is pesha', pronounced peh'-shah, meaning to revolt. The New Testament Greek word is parabaino, pronounced par-ab-ah'-ee-no, meaning to go contrary to, i.e. violate a command. Judas Iscariot is said to have committed transgression in his betrayal of Jesus, see *Acts 1:25* where parabaino is used.

Finally we come to the word iniquity which is what our passage from *2 Timothy* is calling us to depart from. In the Old Testament the concept is called iniquity and the Hebrew word is 'avon, pronounced aw-vone', meaning perversity or moral evil. In the New Testament the same concept is carried by the Greek word adikia, pronounced ad-ee-kee'-ah, meaning the quality of injustice, morally wrongfulness of character, life, or act. Also by the Greek word anomia, pronounced an-om-ee'-ah, meaning wickedness and properly translated into English as either iniquity or lawlessness.

Notice that sin, trespass, and transgression, how-so-ever interrelated, are all things we either commit or intentionally choose to do. However iniquity, or lawlessness, is part of our character. It is part of who we are rather than what we choose to do. It is the character quality of iniquity, that drive or propensity (the moral evil) present within us that underlies many of the evil things we think, do, and say.

The creation of God has many things to teach us and in driving this concept home let's turn to the apple tree. I have one in my yard, the apples have never tasted very good but that is beside the point. I know that it is an apple tree regardless of whether it has apples or not. I can tell by its leaf or other characteristics. Let's say I don't like apples so I pick them all off. Is it still an apple tree? Yes, and even if I cut this tree off at the stump shoots will come up next year and if I let them grow there will eventually be more apples. It is not primarily an apple tree because of its fruit. Its identity as an apple tree is found in its root.

Sin, trespass, and transgression being things we do are like fruits. You can pick them off but in some form or another next season they will emerge again. Iniquities or lawlessness being qualities of our character in the form of moral evil or perversity are the roots which drive production of the fruits. In so many cases unless we remove the root, *depart from iniquity,* the fruit will continue to come.

Often, iniquity is first formed in us based on our having believed lies. For example: a father or mother tells their child that they are no good and will never amount to anything. Now, children are very susceptible to internalizing praise or condemnation from those they are supposed to look up to and can take such words to heart. A child may believe these statements down deep and that belief will color their choices as they go forward in life. One child, taking it to heart, internalizes that they are indeed no good and will never amount to anything and guess what, they don't. Another child internalizes the same message and their whole life revolves around desperate attempts to earn acceptance from their parents and others. Yet another child rebels in anger against that statement and the message of their life becomes: "I'll show you who is worthless!"

We all know or are people like this with various forms of the character flaws of iniquity driving many of the choices and actions of our lives. Make no mistake; God would have us root out such lies and other iniquities as unbecoming for His children. Small wonder then that we are called to *depart from iniquity.*

God is so intent at having us work through and pull these roots that, according to scripture; He visits these iniquities of our fathers to the third and fourth generation of those who hate him. *For I, the LORD your God, am a jealous God, visiting the iniquity of the fathers upon the children to the third and fourth generations of those who hate Me, but showing mercy to thousands, to those who love Me and keep My commandments (Exodus 20:5-6).*

The understanding of this concept has been a bit muddied by modern English translations which exchange the word iniquity for the word sin and the word for visiting for the word punishment. However the passage, being part of the Ten Commandments, specifically uses the word 'avon, iniquity (moral evil or perversity), and the word paqad, meaning to visit with friendly or hostile intent. The scriptures are clear in other areas that children are not punished by God for the deeds of their fathers. See *Ezekiel Chapter 18,* especially *verse 20* if this is a subject of further interest to you.

As an example: this is why we see things like alcoholism being repeated in families from generation to generation. Society and science can call it a disease but any real look at why someone would repeat the physical action of lifting too much liquor to their lips when it is destroying their lives will find that there are issues, iniquities, within the person which are the roots driving the fruit of this behavior.

God is in the business of salvation and redemption and He is looking for those who will step into His camp and mature through confronting and dealing with the damage that runs throughout their families' generations. In the words of Jesus: *But the hour is coming, and now is, when the true worshipers will worship the Father in spirit and truth; for the Father is seeking such to worship Him* (*John 4:23*). The Father's intention is also echoed by the Prophet Isaiah: *Those from among you shall build the old waste places; you shall raise up the foundations of many generations; and you shall be called the Repairer of the Breach, the Restorer of Streets to Dwell In (Isaiah 58:12).*

The Israelites of the Old Testament understood this very well. See *Leviticus 26:39-42* which reveals God's proclamation regarding what was to happen when the children of Israel rejected His ways. They would waste away in their iniquities and in their father's iniquities until they confessed and accepted their guilt for both theirs and their father's iniquities.

Examining the gospel of Jesus as foretold by Isaiah around 712 B.C. in snippets from Chapter 53 of his prophecy we find that the one foretold: *was wounded for our transgressions, He was bruised for our iniquities* and *the LORD has laid on Him the iniquity of us all. By His knowledge My righteous Servant shall justify many, For He shall bear their iniquities. And He bore the sin of many, and made intercession for the transgressors.* We are to understand that by His sacrifice Jesus has become the way of redemption for every area of sinful fruit and iniquitous root that may be found within us; first in welcoming us into eternal life and then in providing the power for victory over our fallen natures.

Arming yourself with these truths, pray along the lines we read from the prayers of King David as you approach the throne of God each day and be open to letting the

Lord show you what changes He wants to make and how He wants to make them.

Cleansing from Past Hurts:

Hand in hand with iniquities we often find many areas in our lives where we have built up protections based on past hurts. Remember that walls have two purposes. They are built by the wicked to hide behind after having done evil and they are also built from a felt need for protection by those who have been hurt before.

In essence and on examination it is not appropriate for those maturing in the ways of the Lord to continue to use walls to hide behind because of past hurts. This is another major area which I cover in "Breaking the Cycle of Slavery to Sin" so here I will be brief just to mention that Jesus is more than capable of assisting you in working through the decisional walls that you may have built based on past hurts.

As you recognize or as God confronts such areas in your life, Jesus has the power to remind you of what happened and reveal to you the ungodly wall building choices you may have made in the past. Then, He can show you how to renounce those choices and replace them with godly choices that build bridges instead of walls.

How can Jesus do that? Consider for a moment that time is also part of God's creation. We are bound within its limits but our God is not. As we reviewed, Jesus said many things identifying Himself as the great 'I AM'. What was the one thing which He said that made the Jewish people of His time so angry that they were about to stone Him to death?

Abraham, who lived some 1800 years before Jesus came to earth, is of course rightly considered the father of the Hebrew people and indeed as the Bible says the father of all who have faith in God. Jesus declared: *Your father Abraham rejoiced to see My day, and he saw it and was glad." Then the Jews said to Him, "You are not yet fifty years old, and have You seen Abraham?" Jesus said to them, "Most assuredly, I say to you, before Abraham was, I AM." Then they took up stones to throw at Him; but Jesus hid Himself and went out of the temple, going through the midst of them, and so passed by (John 8:56-59).* Before Abraham was, *I am.* Jesus is not bound by His creation of time as you and I are. He is free to review those periods we would call the past. It is easy for Jesus to review with you and remind you of the details of any event of your life when you take the time to seek Him, because, unlike ourselves, He is there. To borrow an analogy from one of my former pastors: we are like a kid watching a parade through a knot hole in a fence. We see the parade go by one small section at a time. God is high above the fence and can see the parade from start to finish all at the same time.

Through the fullness of the Gospel and the timelessness of God we understand the depth and power of Jesus Christ to save us from and then deliver us from every area of evil and sin that may be found within our lives. When you bump into the walls you have constructed in your life take them to Jesus in prayer. Ask Him to show you why that wall exists, what is it protecting? Let Jesus into those areas of your life where you are hurting and let Him show you how to replace the decisions to build those walls with godly decisions that will enable you to follow.

Dealing with Failure:

We are fallible and during this lifetime we are unlikely to experience anything close to full righteousness where we never think an evil thought or never say an evil word and never make regrettable errors. But we should be able to experience the holiness into which we have been called. In entering the door of Christ and opening the door of our life to Him, God sets us apart for Himself. That is the meaning of holiness: to be set apart. Part of this package of being God's holy people includes what to do when we fail. We get back up and we get going again (see *1 John 1:9*). The glory of the Kingdom belongs to the King. You and I have this treasure in earthen vessels for the purpose of bringing Him glory and making the same known to others.

Battle Front Number Two:

The second battle front is the war between the Kingdom of God, of which we are now members, and that prince of the power of the air (see *Ephesians 2:2*), the devil, or Satan who leads the camp we used to belong to.

The Apostle Peter wrote to make sure we would understand the reality of this front and how to address it. *Be sober, be vigilant; because your adversary the devil walks about like a roaring lion, seeking whom he may devour. Resist him, steadfast in the faith, knowing that the same sufferings are experienced by your brotherhood in the world. But may the God of all grace, who called us to His eternal glory by Christ Jesus, after you have suffered a while, perfect, establish, strengthen, and settle you. To Him be the glory and the dominion forever and ever. Amen (1 Peter 5:8-11).*

For His own purposes God has continued to allow this agent of evil, the devil or Satan, to continue in a role that seems contrary to the Kingdom of Heaven. We find the devil both in the Bible and in our personal experiences as one who is constantly working to tempt and deceive though we don't always recognize this. Peter tells us that sobriety, vigilance, and steadfastness in the faith are necessary to make our resistance successful. In short those who are mature will be the victors in this battle front.

Humans as a whole are lead about by Satan as if it were child's play. Even those of us who have been redeemed by the power of Christ can be very susceptible to the devil's deceptions if we are not mature. The reason for this is simple. As mentioned we were once members of his camp and our whole lives were walked out according to his plans. From God's perspective we were dead. *And you He made alive, who were dead in trespasses and sins, in which you once walked according to the course of this world, according to the prince of the power of the air, the spirit who now works in the sons of disobedience, among whom also we all once conducted ourselves in the lusts of our flesh, fulfilling the desires of the flesh and of the mind, and were by nature children of wrath, just as the others (Ephesians 2:1-3).* Eternal salvation comes in a moment when we receive Jesus Christ. Maturity, as we have covered, is a process of growing up and it always takes time and determination to change, even to change our souls from being used to darkness into being accustomed to light.

Putting our resistance into action requires that we know something of our adversary. One of the pages of that playbook reveals to us that Satan is the accuser of our brethren (see *Revelation 12:9-11*). In our chapter on interacting with God's Holy Spirit we learned that a major role of the Holy Spirit was to bring conviction. An important lesson of discernment for the seeker is being able to distinguish between the leading of the Holy Spirit and the promptings of the enemy. In maturity we learn to accept the rightful convictions and corrections which God's Holy Spirit may bring from time to time. However we should suspect the source if the messages we seem to be getting are coming in the form of accusations. At times we will have to say with Jesus: *"Away with you, Satan! For it is written, 'You shall worship the LORD your God, and Him only you shall serve'" (Matthew 4:10).*

Where does this second battle front against the devil cross over into the first battle front for the maturity of our souls between our fallen nature and the Spirit of God? The cross over points, and therefore the ability to counter them, can be clearly identified in the manner in which the deceiver operates. The devil always operates hand in hand with the selfish, fallen nature of our soul. It is man's fallen spirit of self which walks hand in hand with the devil to resist the plans and intentions of God's Holy Spirit. Notice the self-declarations made by Lucifer in the following passage.

"How you are fallen from heaven, O Lucifer, son of the morning! How you are cut down to the ground, you who weakened the nations! For you have said in your heart: 'I will ascend into heaven, I will exalt my throne above the stars of God; I will also sit on the mount of the congregation on the farthest sides of the north; I will ascend above the heights of the clouds, I will be like the Most High.' Yet you shall be brought down to Sheol, to the lowest depths of the Pit (Isaiah 14:12-15).

In this passage which outlines the fall and eventual destruction of the devil we clearly see the nature of his spirit. It is the spirit of self-centeredness which declares five times for itself above the wishes of God, 'I will!'

In the same manner, Satan does not visit you and me and introduce himself directly. 'Hi, I am Satan and I want you to commit this act of selfishness'. No indeed, rather as a true deceiver he whispers into our minds planting thoughts in the spirit of self directly into our minds and arriving disguised as our very own thoughts. Just put this to a simple test. The next time someone cuts you off in traffic and ask yourself where all the thoughts about wanting to choke the living daylights out of that person are coming from?

I learned this very clearly one day as I was driving over a hill on the freeway. I saw a Highway Patrolman driving up the other side and in my mind flashed a scene where I was blowing him away with big gun. Wow! Where did that come from I thought. Then the question struck me: I would never do such a thing so where did that thought come from? It was at that moment so many years ago that the Holy Spirit began to open my eyes about this manner of the devil's operation. What was the devil hoping to achieve by sowing such a thought? To be sure he was not expecting me to become a cop killer. Rather, he was simply trying in his usual way to upset my day so that I would be out of sorts with myself and not in step with the Lord. Have you not experienced days where you are so caught up in what is going on inside of you that you miss whatever God might have planned? It's time to begin to question where that comes from.

Walking counter to our flesh and the devil is a holy habit that needs to be established as part of embracing maturity. Nowhere is this more important than in our interpersonal relationships as we learn to 'love our neighbor as our self'. Love for neighbor wants the same grace of God for others that we have been privileged to enjoy for ourselves.

Interpersonal relationships definitely rank as among the most difficult of areas for any of us to keep our cool and walk in love. However this is what it takes to walk in the Spirit rejecting the tendencies of the flesh and the promptings of the devil. Any habit gets easier and more natural with exercise and so Paul calls his young disciple Timothy to this very same task. *And a servant of the Lord must not quarrel but be gentle to all, able to teach, patient, in humility correcting those who are in opposition, if God perhaps will grant them repentance, so that they may know the truth, and that they may come to their senses and escape the snare of the devil, having been taken captive by him to do his will (2 Timothy 2:24-26).*

Finally in order to win this battle we must be single-minded having renounced all other alliances outside of our devotion to God. *Then Samuel spoke to all the house of Israel, saying, "If you return to the LORD with all your hearts, then put away the foreign gods and the Ashtoreths from among you, and prepare your hearts for the LORD, and serve Him only; and He will deliver you from the hand of the Philistines." So the children of Israel put away the Baals and the Ashtoreths, and served the LORD only (1 Samuel 7:3-4).* Clearly there is no true return to God with all of our heart if we continue to hold onto alliances and allegiances to other deities which as Jesus adds, includes the materialism of mammon, meaning money or things. *"No one can serve two masters; for either he will hate the one and love the other, or else he will be loyal to the one and despise the other. You cannot serve God and mammon" (Matthew 6:24).*

Putting It into Practice:

By design children are meant to grow up. *That we should no longer be children, tossed to and fro and carried about with every wind of doctrine, by the trickery of men, in the cunning craftiness of deceitful plotting, but, speaking the truth in love, may grow up in all things into Him who is the head – Christ (Ephesians 4:14-15).*

I know that this chapter provides quite a bit of information and hopefully valuable insight. Of a certainty you have read this far because you have decided, or will decide, to embrace maturity and become a full grown man or woman of God. In doing so, God will gain a good return on His investment in you, allowing Him to be pleased that He placed you into your moment under the sun.

What is the next step forward? I would encourage you to take a number of the passages of scripture which have been reviewed in this chapter and use them in your weekly times with the Lord. Meditate on them before the Lord, opening yourself up by asking Him to reveal truth to you and to show you the next area or areas of maturity which He would have you work through. Ask the Lord to reveal to you any patterns of recurring sin in your life. What part of your character do these originate from? What iniquity needs to be addressed?

When the going gets tough, and most likely in certain areas it will, remember Who is the Builder and who is the building. *Unless the LORD builds the house, they labor in vain who build it (Psalm 127:1a).*

We seek the Lord because we are hungry. We are hungry to know Him and hungry to be used to make a difference in this world instead of just passing through. We cannot think it strange that a large part of the Lord's first response to our seeking is to call us into maturity so that we are indeed vessels cleansed and ready for His use.

The seeker must reject the world's path of hiding and blaming and come out into the light of Christ. We might echo the words of David: *'who can understand his errors?'* but we must not use that as an excuse to remain in the dark. *Then Jesus spoke to them again, saying, "I am the light of the world. He who follows Me shall not walk in darkness, but have the light of life" (John 8:12).*

The seeker must settle the question of who is serving who and make the choice to serve or not serve the Lord. *"And if it seems evil to you to serve the LORD, choose for yourselves this day whom you will serve, whether the gods which your fathers served that were on the other side of the River, or the gods of the Amorites, in whose land you dwell. But as for me and my house, we will serve the LORD" (Joshua 24:15).*

In our modern churches we hear a lot about passion. What is your passion? Are you following your passion? I understand the intention with which this is messaged.

Our pastors and leaders mean well and want us to embrace life. However, passions and desires are greatly over emphasized in this present generation and, in looking, we find that the way in which this is messaged from the church is often not different from the way it is being messaged in the world. The message is one of seeking self-fulfillment. The follower of Christ has better devotion to offer than merely seeking self-fulfillment. We have a God appointed destiny. *And those who are Christ's have crucified the flesh with its passions and desires. If we live in the Spirit, let us also walk in the Spirit (Galatians 5:24-25).*

Indeed our adversary the devil walks about like a roaring lion, seeking whom he may devour. What are the behaviors of a stalking lion? Do they not prey on the weak of the herd? The further you and I go into embracing maturity the less personally susceptible we are to the lion's attacks. As the devil can no longer fool us directly he turns his attention to the less mature members of our fellowships. His agenda becomes one of personally attacking them and through them stirring up strife within the church.

Maturity in the Church will and should always be a progressive matter. By nature our churches should be set up in such a manner that the least, the wounded, the broken, and the lost can find comfort, acceptance, and fellowship in our midst. They should be able to discover beginnings of purpose and be provided with the opportunity to meet with and get to know God. Because of the regular influx of new members who all need to grow up, church should always be a bit of a messy affair.

Lambs and sheep are messy creatures. Jesus' words to Peter were: *"Feed my lambs, tend my sheep, feed my sheep"* (see John 21:15-17). The mature seeker understands this and is able to take the issues of the church and the fellowship of believers to the Lord finding the best ways to address issues and the best means to build up both the weak and the strong. The mature seeker knows that it is the peace-maker not the peace-keeper who brings the will of God. *Blessed are the peacemakers, for they shall be called sons of God (Matthew 5:9).*

For if you live according to the flesh you will die; but if by the Spirit you put to death the deeds of the body, you will live. For as many as are led by the Spirit of God, these are sons of God. <u>For you did not receive the spirit of bondage again to fear, but you received the Spirit of adoption by whom we cry out,"Abba, Father." The Spirit Himself bears witness with our spirit that we are children of God, and if children, then heirs — heirs of God and joint heirs with Christ</u>, if indeed we suffer with Him, that we may also be glorified together (Romans 8:13-17).

Search me, O God, and know my heart; try me, and know my anxieties; and see if there is any wicked way in me, and lead me in the way everlasting (Psalm 139:23-24).

Chapter Seven

Becoming a Friend of God

It is noon-time at the well on a thirsty day. Jesus is actually alone and though we know He spent time alone with God at the start of each day it is a bit odd to find Him alone in the middle of the day. His disciples are off in a Samaritan town seeking food and a lone Samaritan woman arrives at the well to draw water. Perhaps she is disliked in the town and so comes to draw water in the heat of the day when the other women are not there. We do find out that her married life, for someone from a small town, has not been very stable. Perhaps something came up and she could not visit the well that morning or perhaps she just needed more water. Then again, perhaps it has to do with her destiny.

Jesus has nothing to draw water with and so asks her to give Him a drink. Instead she questions Jesus' motives pointing out the tension between their societies. You are a Jewish man and I a Samaritan women on both counts you are not supposed to even talk to me. In return Jesus tells her that He is able to offer her 'living water'.

During the course of their conversation, before the woman heads back to town to tell everyone that she thinks she has just met the promised Messiah, Jesus tells her something that should shout us out of any sleep we have been in.

Jesus said: *"But the hour is coming, and now is, when the true worshipers will worship the Father in spirit and truth; for the Father is seeking such to worship Him. God is Spirit, and those who worship Him must worship in spirit and truth"* (John 4:23-24).

Imagine that; God, Who has been calling us to seek Him, is Himself seeking us. We know from the scriptures that God's preference is salvation for all of mankind. He is: *not willing that any should perish but that all should come to repentance (2 Peter 3:9)*. But here we read that what God is actually looking for are those who will worship Him in the fullness of spirit and truth. These will be His true worshipers. In effect it will be how God recognizes His friends among the phonies.

We typically know a lot of people but are friends with fewer. Among those fewer we tend to count some as friends in general and perhaps others as 'true' friends whom we know we could call up and count on at any time. I hope you have at least one person in your life that is like that.

As humans our imperfect and limited souls tend to govern the number of friends we keep. Regarding imperfection, we may limit or even exclude close friends based on fears or past experiences. If such is your case I would suggest that getting past this is part of embracing maturity because it should be possible for us to be open to God bringing new people into our lives. Regarding reality, we may wisely limit the number of our friends based on how much real time we have to be a true friend in return. Thankfully, God does not have these same limitations. Being able to embrace an unlimited number of true friends has not been His problem. God's problem has been finding them and so, as Jesus says, He is still seeking for more.

Moving forward in the unfolding journey of being and becoming people who seek God for daily living and destiny, it should give great comfort to know that what we are really heading toward is the truest, closest, and most unlimited friendship that we can ever have.

Abraham is an example of a man whom God declared to be His friend and we would do well to study Abraham's life in the book of *Genesis*. Abraham withheld nothing from God once he knew it was what God wanted. Abraham boldly interceded in prayer when boldness was called for. Abraham lived, loved, and made mistakes all of which we can read about. Yet *Romans Chapter 4* calls Abraham: *the father of all those who believe. And the Scripture was fulfilled which says, "Abraham believed God, and it was accounted to him for righteousness." And he was called the friend of God (James 2:23).*

Moses is another man whose life speaks volumes and is worthy of study. He had a bit of a rough start at the burning bush (*Exodus Chapters 3 and 4*). However he came through as one of whom God said: *he is faithful in all My house (Numbers 12:7). So the LORD spoke to Moses face to face, as a man speaks to his friend (Exodus 33:11a).*

Jesus spoke to His disciples about the transition they had made from being His servants to being His friends. Notice that by this time they had been with Him for about three years.

You are My friends if you do whatever I command you. No longer do I call you servants, for a servant does not know what his master is doing; but I have called you friends, for all things that I heard from My Father I have made known to you (John 15:14-15).

It is worth noting that a fully trusting relationship had now been established for the disciples with Jesus. Like Moses, the initial fears were gone along with any concerns about what might happen if they did what Jesus was asking them to do. It takes time to reach this level of being able to trust the Lord fully but in return for the effort the seeker receives a welcome into the fullness of what the Master is doing.

I remember that in my own life this was something that dawned over time. In the early days I had a lot of questions about what I thought God was directing me to do through the Bible and in prayer time. It was typical for me to double check everything with God before I would be comfortable in stepping out. You know, I don't remember God getting angry about that. He was definitely angry with Moses at the burning bush when at the end Moses suggested that God find someone else to send to Egypt. Thinking back, the Lord was always patient with me and let me go through my need to double check as long as I ended up in obedience.

There were times when I missed windows of opportunity or when my fears led to missteps and mistakes. But over time my experience with the Lord changed me. I can't say when that happened but it just became easy for me to trust whatever I hear from Him and as easy to do it. I am sure that God could pull out something big at any time that would make me take a step back and want to double check, but at the same time I know that He knows that I will do whatever He makes clear to me.

This friendship did not happen overnight and I think this quality of being able to simply trust the Lord in whatever He asks us to do cannot be under stressed. Without it, we do not yet have the ability to act in simple childlike faith. With this level of trust, where we know that we know that God is good, we can move forward as His friend. Paul put it like this: *And we know that all things work together for good to those who love God, to those who are the called according to His purpose (Romans 8:28).*

Looking at Jesus' friends, His twelve disciples, Jesus always seemed to have the inner circle of Peter, James, and John who went with Him on special assignments such as into private healing sessions or up to the mount of transfiguration. No doubt Jesus knew he could count on those three as leaders and influencers of the others.

At times Jesus had to correct His disciples in their arguments about which of them was to be the greatest. At other times we have hints that there may have been some jealousy in those early days. However, Jesus' inner circle should not have been cause to make the other disciples jealous. Every one of us must take responsibility for our own life before God but not every one of us will be God's chosen leader in every situation. This is an important part of friendship with God that we need to understand and make peace with. It is very important to the success of the Kingdom of God among us that we learn to support rather than resist our fellow believers when God decides to use them in leadership.

Contrary to our current culture of individual independence, the Kingdom of God functions properly when we are interdependent on one another. As such we are called to: *Obey those who rule over you, and be submissive, for they watch out for your souls, as those who must give account. Let them do so with joy and not with grief, for that would be unprofitable for you (Hebrews 13:17).*

In this same vein, friendship with God also acknowledges that He has other close friends, and those in process of becoming so, who are just as important to Him as we are. Many are the warnings throughout the New Testament against passing judgment against others.

We are to judge situations and actions with true judgment and we are to judge ourselves (*1 Corinthians 11:31*) but we are not meant to pass judgment against others.

Our current culture is deeply entrenched in hiding and placing blame on others. It is easy for us to fall into that mode, but we are called to better things and to worship and serve God in spirit and truth without hiding and without the need to place blame. This also is a point of trust for us with God. Can we trust Him to be the righteous Judge which scripture says He is and that He will appropriately take care of justice? If we are honest, in many cases the 'justice' which we would have fall upon others are things where for ourselves we would want to find grace. *Who are you to judge another's servant? To his own master he stands or falls. Indeed, he will be made to stand, for God is able to make him stand (Romans 14:4).*

A true friend is able to hold a proper balance of love and fear in the sense of fear being respect as opposed to being afraid. In human relationships we understand that even our best friend has things that belong only to them and which we should fear to disrespect. If we violate that fear by coveting what belongs to our friend it may actually end that friendship.

It is not that much different in friendship with God. Throughout the Bible we read about people who either did or did not fear the Lord. In short, they had or did not have a proper respect for God and the potential consequences of crossing His boundaries. We know that: *The fear of the LORD is the beginning of knowledge, but fools despise wisdom and instruction (Proverbs 1:7).* As in human relationships and so with God, it is really very inappropriate for us to think that we can lean on the fact that we are loved as an excuse for violating the boundaries of a friend.

In our friendship with God, we still approach Him with the respect of which He is worthy, we don't take

God for granted, and we should be prepared for Him to want something done differently than it was always done before. It is important to always remember that God has an agenda of building His Kingdom. As one of those whom Jesus has pulled into His boat of safety we are intended to be part of the fulfillment of our own prayer: *Your kingdom come. Your will be done on earth as it is in heaven (Matthew 6:10).*

Sometimes the friends of Jesus failed Him. Peter is an example of a man who at times spoke out and struck out inappropriately. He swore he would stand by Jesus to the death but he fled with the others when Christ was arrested. When confronted about their friendship Peter lied, denying Jesus three times. *And the Lord turned and looked at Peter. Then Peter remembered the word of the Lord, how He had said to him, "Before the rooster crows, you will deny Me three times." So Peter went out and wept bitterly (Luke 22:61-62).*

Peter also out ran John on the way to Jesus' empty tomb. Then on the shores of Galilee, we see Jesus bringing Peter back into His friendship and tasking Peter with a main leadership role in caring for the others and those who would be added to their number in the future (*John 21:15-18*).

What about those times when with good intention we simply make a mistake? Looking in on another friend of God, Nathan the prophet made a mistake. From *1 Samuel Chapter 7,* it was in King David's heart to build a house for the Lord and Nathan with good intention told David to go ahead and do it for the Lord is with you. However God corrected Nathan that night and sent him back to David to let him know that David's son Solomon, rather than David, would build God's house. We have no record of God being angry with Nathan, simply of God correcting Nathan. Mistakes happen in friendships even with the best of intentions. We see God taking them in stride.

May we learn to treat those in whom we see the potential for friendship with as much grace when they fail us as we have seen Jesus do with Peter. Our current western culture is one which dumps friends and spouses who fail us like a hot rock. This is often done with all the huff of justification and generally with a rain of gossip just to make sure others know why we were in the right. *Out of the same mouth proceed blessing and cursing. My brethren, these things ought not to be so (James 3:10).* It should be clear to us, from these and many other behaviors, that the culture in which we live does not worship God in either spirit or truth.

God is looking for those who will worship Him in spirit and in truth. We have spent quite a bit of time looking at what it means to interact with God's in-dwelling Spirit. Starting with the biggest step of being born again so that our spirit is alive and filled with His Spirit and continuing in letting God's Spirit have his way in rooting out our iniquities and building in His truth. We have been studying and putting into practice what it means to be a seeker of God so that we are sensitive to His directions in this life. All of this is relevant so that the stream of our life may begin to run cleaner and clearer for God. The Lord can then take a drink from us as vessels cleansed and ready for the Master's use as well as being unashamed to offer a drink through us to others. In short, we become those who worship Him in spirit and in truth.

Where do you and I find a church that is worshiping God in spirit and truth? The North American, European, and even African and Asian churches I am familiar with seem to be a very mixed bag when it comes to spirit and truth. What I really want is to gather and work with a group of fellow believers whose leadership holds the word of God as sacred and does not limit the Holy Spirit, in short I want spirit AND truth not spirit OR truth.

Oftentimes what we find are different variations. One form of church allows what seems to be spiritual, 'God is love', to override the words of God from other parts of the scripture. Such churches end up welcoming practices that they should not in the name of love or because of some spiritual revelation. Among others, Jesus rebuked such churches in *Revelation Chapters 2 and 3*.

Another group of churches claim that the Bible is a closed book and that there is nothing more to be heard from the Spirit of God. In short, a limitation or denial of the role of the Holy Spirit with no revelation allowed and little reason to seek God for any answers that are not already written in the Book. Speaking of the Israelites we find it said: *Yes, again and again they tempted God, and limited the Holy One of Israel (Psalm 78:41)*.

We westerners are people of such extremes. You can find churches containing mixtures of both of these and other extremes in many places. What is a follower of Jesus to do? Sadly, I have seen the next generation of Christian youth and young people abandoning the church as irrelevant. Older folks too, who have done their time and put in their effort, are often leaving the western churches because they seem irrelevant to real life. What should the seeker do? Those whose lives are being shaped to seek God for daily living and destiny need to do two things.

First, we need to turn to the word of God and to Jesus who is the Truth (*John 14:*6) and rediscover Jesus' purpose for His church. Second, we need to turn to God in listening prayer and ask Him to show us by His Spirit what church He would have us engage with and what He would have us do as His servant within the context of that church.

Abraham and Moses were named friends of God and we have them as examples. However, they were different people than you and I and they served God in a different cultural context and under the different needs of the times in history into which they were placed. If we are going to fulfill the destiny for which God placed each of us into our cultural context and into our moment in history then we must seek Him and walk out what He shows us to do. In that context, this generation of believers is responsible before God, not for pointing out the faults of our present churches and their leadership, but for stepping in as God directs and working to make those churches He plants us in to become cities set upon a hill for all to see and which draw mankind to God instead of repelling them. Again contrary to our current western culture of individualism, Jesus was not talking to individuals but to His disciples collectively when He said: *"You are the light of the world. A city that is set on a hill cannot be hidden" (Matthew 5:14).*

This is a tough one for many of us. Do the churches have faults? Yes, they do. Are there shortcomings, even some serious ones among the leadership of some of our churches? Yes, there are. Is there real value to be gained by us pointing those out? No, there is not. Is there real value to be gained by us discovering with God what He wants each of us to do about it, rolling up our sleeves with God and getting to work? Yes, there is.

Perhaps He will have you work for Him in the context of the church you are now with or were with. Perhaps He will direct you to get to work with a different one or in a different way in the body of Christ. But it is important that we know that as friends of God we are not an island and the Kingdom of God is not about individualism but rather it is about the body of Christ, his worldwide family and locally His church in whatever form He has it take. *So we, being many, are one body in Christ, and individually members of one another. Having then gifts differing according to the grace that is given to us, let us use them (Romans 12:5-6a).*

We are God's ambassadors in this day and age, (see *2 Corinthians 5:20*). We are His agents of change in this world today. Discovering with God what He is trying to accomplish and build in this particular moment of history through His worldwide body of believers is our task as seekers. Learning from God the best ways to address Jesus into the culture and times into which we have been placed is crucial to success.

Some of the best examples in our modern time, in my opinion, can be found in two missionary books: Bruchko and Peace Child. These books record the experiences of their authors who entered primitive cultures and discovered with God the cues built into those cultures by which those people groups were then effectively brought to Christ. In more ancient times Patrick of Ireland, Saint Patrick, was called by God to become the first recorded missionary to leave the boundaries of the Roman Empire and go to live among the barbarians. He discovered the pagan Irish holding a specific mythos and an intense fear of death to which He was able to apply the trinity of God and the eternity of Jesus and bring almost the entire people group to Christ.

What cultural cues and mythos beliefs, which can be used to point people to Christ, lie undiscovered in the circles in which God has you travel? Well, for North Americans certainly the fear of death is there big time. Are there others? God knows, ask Him.

Don't become lackadaisical in your walk with Christ. This is our appointed moment under the sun with God and it will become and be recorded in God's history (His-Story) based on your friendship with God as you seek Him and based on what He leads you to do. God can be trusted to use those efforts we yield to Him in His own way in building the bigger picture. Our job is to walk with

Him in spirit and in truth as a trusted servant, friend, and good steward in the house of our God.

John knew who he was in the Lord. In his gospel he refers to himself in Chapters 13, 20, and 21 as: *the disciple whom Jesus loved.* You and I should be able to say the same and it should provide us with a firm foundation for our life in Christ.

We tend to think of Job as that guy who suffered tremendous loss and pain prior to his restoration. But behind the scenes it was not about Job at all. It was about God being delighted with one of His faithful servants and boasting the same to Satan. *Then the LORD said to Satan, "Have you considered My servant Job, that there is none like him on the earth, a blameless and upright man, one who fears God and shuns evil?" (Job 1:8).* It was only because of Satan's challenge that God allowed Job to go through intense trials and, in the end, God was proven right and Satan was proven wrong. I know, we all hope that we would not have to go through trials, but as God's friends it may need to be so.

God is building a house for His friends and using His friends as the materials to do so. His promises to David in *1 Chronicles 17:3-14* about David's son Solomon building God a house and establishing David's kingdom forever are not primarily about the temple in Jerusalem, which did not last. They are primarily about Jesus Christ, whom Father God placed on the throne of David and of Whose Kingdom there shall be no end (see *Luke 1:32-33*), and they are about the spiritual house which God is building using Jesus' followers including you and me. *Coming to Him as to a living stone, rejected indeed by men, but chosen by God and precious, you also, as living stones, are being built up a spiritual house, a holy priesthood, to offer up spiritual sacrifices acceptable to God through Jesus Christ (1 Peter 2:4-5).*

In *1 Chronicles 12* we read about those gathered to David in His early days as king, some of whom: *had understanding of the times, to know what Israel ought to do.* Each of us does have a personal role to play in God's Kingdom. At the same time, we should also recognize that God's role for us will also have to do with what ought to happen in these times and in regard to what the nation ought to do. In that light, an individual's mission should be in sync with the mission of that individual's nation and our nation is not of this world but is the Kingdom of God. Because of this, there will always be times when we don't get to see the bigger picture of why the Lord is asking us to do certain things. This is simply because the results God was seeking were about others and not about us.

Getting on the Same Page with God:

Like-mindedness, being of the same mind and in the same accord, is another quality of deep friendship and we are certainly called to it. *Therefore if there is any consolation in Christ, if any comfort of love, if any fellowship of the Spirit, if any affection and mercy, fulfill my joy by being like-minded, having the same love, being of one accord, of one mind (Philippians 2:1-2).*

Take a deep breath and slow yourself down, draw it in and let it out. Do it again if it helps. Relax the tensions of your body and let all the other thoughts of your mind go for a moment. Come to the quiet, you are before the Lord. *For David says concerning Him: 'I foresaw the LORD always before my face, for He is at my right hand, that I may not be shaken' (Acts 2:25).*

Open your spirit to the Lord right where you are at this moment. Sense the presence of His Holy Spirit Whom you received when you took the biggest step into salvation. Indeed He is there with you. *To them God willed to make known what are the riches of the glory of this mystery among the Gentiles: which is Christ in you, the hope of glory (Colossians 1:27).*

Sometimes it helps to lift my eyes to heaven. *Now when these things begin to happen, look up and lift up your heads, because your redemption draws near" (Luke 21:28).* Ah, there you are Lord! Yes, it is His presence that you sense.

Picture this in your mind and sense it within your soul. The Holy Spirit of God is communicating from His place in your redeemed spirit through your re-awakened conscience and into your mind within your soul. What might God have to say to you or reveal to you today?

You can also bring to the Lord the way you are feeling and let Him replace it with His peace. The Holy Spirit of God will communicate from His place in your redeemed spirit through your softened heart and into your emotions within your soul. This is what happens when we practice the promise of *Philippians 4:6-7.* I did this just yesterday when I was anxious at the start of a business meeting and the Lord swept in with His peace. *Be anxious for nothing, but in everything by prayer and supplication, with thanksgiving, let your requests be made known to God; and the peace of God, which surpasses all understanding, will guard your hearts and minds through Christ Jesus.*

Becoming like-minded and getting on the same page with God requires this sort of interaction between His Holy Spirit and our soul: mind, emotions, and will. We have just experienced His touch on our mind and talked about His effect on our emotions. Our will comes into play with the small but important word 'let'. In the beginning God said: *'Let there be light'.* The elements both existing and being created in that moment obeyed His word and there was light. We just read the passage from *Philippians Chapter 4* which said to us *'let your requests be made known to God'*. If we obey with our will and 'let' this happen then creation in the form of the fruit of this wonderful promise happens and: *the peace of God, which surpasses all understanding, will guard your hearts and minds through Christ Jesus.* If we do not 'let' then nothing happens.

What does this have to do with being like-minded with God? It has everything to do with it since He is the Creator and we are the creation. This brings us to our next 'let'.

Let this mind be in you which was also in Christ Jesus, who, being in the form of God, did not consider it robbery to be equal with God, but made Himself of no reputation, taking the form of a bondservant, and coming in the likeness of men. And being found in appearance as a man, He humbled Himself and became obedient to the point of death, even the death of the cross (Philippians 2:5-8).

Like Jesus we are now here on mission for God. We are to seek no reputation but rather be here as one who serves, becoming obedient to God to the last degree. Yes, we are called to die. We have covered this before; we are called to take up our cross daily in love with God and in love toward our fellow man. For this to happen we must open our will to God and 'let' this mind be in us as it was in Christ Jesus.

I beseech you therefore, brethren, by the mercies of God, that you present your bodies a living sacrifice, holy, acceptable to God, which is your reasonable service. And do not be conformed to this world, but be transformed by the renewing of your mind, that you may prove what is that good and acceptable and perfect will of God (Romans 12:1-2). Much could be written about this passage but in keeping our focus this portion of God's word calls us to be *transformed by the renewing of your mind.* As we have discussed in our chapter on Embracing Maturity, working with God to make the switch between the worldliness we have been part of into

the godliness into which we are called, is a process. Part
of that process is the renewing of our mind. In short God
wants to change the way we think so that as His friend
we can be on the same page with Him.

It is a simple process really. As a seeker, you go to
the Lord and begin to ask Him regularly to change the
way that you think. Lord, change how I perceive my
experiences in this world; please give to me the mind of
Christ. Lord, I know I reacted poorly in my conversation
with my neighbor yesterday, please show me where I
went wrong and what I should do next. Lord, I am very
concerned about my relative, please give me wisdom to
understand the situation and let me know how I can best
help. James put it like this, and it includes another let:
*My brethren, count it all joy when you fall into various trials,
knowing that the testing of your faith produces patience. But
let patience have its perfect work, that you may be perfect and
complete, lacking nothing. If any of you lacks wisdom, let him
ask of God, who gives to all liberally and without reproach, and
it will be given to him (James 1:2-5).*

The renewing of our minds, letting the mind of Christ
be in us, is not a minor change. Unless you grew up in
a strong Christ honoring household with loving parents
whose life focus was Jesus then it will be, and may still be,
a paradigm shift from the way you are used to thinking.
God knows there will always be more and He will tailor
this to be specific for you as you let Him do so but some
of the main areas of this shift are common to us all and I
will review some of them here.

First of all, God's friends know that He is good. The
world is too busy doubting His existence, testing God,
arguing with God, mistrusting God, and being afraid of
God to know this simple truth. Do you still share those
doubts? I have the iron clad sure-fire remedy and here it
is. *Oh, taste and see that the LORD is good; blessed is the man*

who trusts in Him! Oh, fear the LORD, you His saints! There is no want to those who fear Him. The young lions lack and suffer hunger; but those who seek the LORD shall not lack any good thing (Psalm 34:8-10).

Remember in the introduction I wrote that I could prove that God exists? Remember that the answer was His promise in *Jeremiah 29*; that if you do the work of seeking Him that you will find Him? *I will be found by you says the Lord.*

Learning that God is good is no different; you have to do the work of tasting and from our passage in *Psalm 34* we can see that it is coupled with seeking that we should lack no good thing. Get into your Bible and find the promises of God. You will see that, with the exception of His promise to Noah that God would not destroy the earth again by flood; every other promise including salvation is conditional. You do not get the results until you do your part. For example, salvation is extended to all but it is only given to those who believe (see *Mark 1:15 & 16:16 & Act 2:38*). Find the promises, do what they tell you to do, and you will experience that the Lord is good. *Philippians 4:6-7* is another great example of the typically conditional promises of God. I mentioned my experience with it just a few paragraphs back.

Second, God's friends trust Him completely and in everything and because of this He governs the paths of their lives. *Trust in the LORD with all your heart, and lean not on your own understanding; in all your ways acknowledge Him, and He shall direct your paths (Proverbs 3:5-6).*

This level of trust is always characterized by obedience. After all, we are members of the greatest Kingdom and we serve Jesus the greatest of Kings. Fulfillment of God's word to King David that David's heir would sit on the throne forever was again affirmed about Christ 700 years before Jesus was born into this world. Wouldn't the

King of such a Kingdom as this expect the loyalty of His subjects? Has Jesus earned your trust? *For unto us a Child is born, unto us a Son is given; and the government will be upon His shoulder. And His name will be called Wonderful, Counselor, Mighty God, Everlasting Father, Prince of Peace. Of the increase of His government and peace there will be no end, upon the throne of David and over His kingdom, to order it and establish it with judgment and justice from that time forward, even forever. The zeal of the Lord of hosts will perform this (Isaiah 9:6-7).*

Third, God's friends can come before Him without fear, knowing that God has accepted them. For me this acceptance is almost in the very air that I breathe, I sense it at all times and it brings such deep comfort. Perhaps that is because I felt so completely rejected before I met Jesus? I know that I have been adopted by God.

Blessed be the God and Father of our Lord Jesus Christ, who has blessed us with every spiritual blessing in the heavenly places in Christ, just as He chose us in Him before the foundation of the world, that we should be holy and without blame before Him in love, having predestined us to adoption as sons by Jesus Christ to Himself, according to the good pleasure of His will, to the praise of the glory of His grace, by which He made us accepted in the Beloved (Ephesians 1:3-6).

One of my grandsons is currently four years old and he stays with us about two days a week when his parents both have to work. Ever since he was old enough to walk he has appeared at our door, lunchbox in hand, giant smile, and ready to play. If it is a weekday, I try to make a point of coming home at lunchtime and he is always glad to see me. Why is that? It is because he knows that he is accepted by Grandpa and Grandma. He knows that he is always welcome in our house. Does he ever do something he should not and get disciplined? Of course, that is a normal part of life. Does that change his understanding and feelings of acceptance? No, it affirms that his grandparents love and care about him.

In this same way we too should be able to approach God freely. We have been adopted and accepted. The religions of man typically require that one do 'enough good' to balance out their evil and find out at the end if it was enough to be accepted. In Christ, we are accepted first, being cleansed by His blood and justified by His resurrection. It is after acceptance and adoption that Jesus helps us work out our issues and overcome our sinful nature. *Let us therefore come boldly to the throne of grace, that we may obtain mercy and find grace to help in time of need (Hebrews 4:16).*

Fourth, God's friends know that everything is about Jesus -- this world, the creatures and humans within it, our placement in nurture, environment, and history, that which God causes, that which God allows.

Even those things which God allows the devil to do or prevents him from doing. Everything, from the empty can in the garbage, to those persons in power, to the life of a suffering child is in some way all about Jesus. *He is the image of the invisible God, the firstborn over all creation. For by Him all things were created that are in heaven and that are on earth, visible and invisible, whether thrones or dominions or principalities or powers. All things were created through Him and for Him. And He is before all things, and in Him all things consist. And He is the head of the body, the church, who is the beginning, the firstborn from the dead, that in all things He may have the preeminence (Colossians 1:15-18).*

Why is this important? It is important because it shapes the mindset and manner in which the believer sees and perceives everything else. We chose not to put one of our sons on Ritalin, widely prescribed in America to assist boys in paying attention in school, and he turned out fine. My main concern was letting the Lord direct his life rather than forcing him into the world's mold. Discussing the same with another Christian parent who did have their son on the drug, they were worried that their son would not do well enough in school to go to college. My suggestion was that perhaps God had a different destiny for their son besides college. The mother replied to me: this is not about Jesus. All I could tell her was: everything is about Jesus. I am sad to say that things did not turn out well for him as a young man the last I had heard.

Fifth, God's friends understand that He is the potter and we are the clay. Regardless of outward appearances and the things that may seem right to men, the Kingdom of God is not built through our schemes and what we can manipulate. It is built by those who walk with God in faith to carry out His plans. *Hebrews 11*, the chapter known as the 'faith hall of fame' ends by saying that many others also lived by faith, *who through faith subdued kingdoms, worked righteousness, obtained promises, stopped the mouths of lions, quenched the violence of fire, escaped the edge of the sword, out of weakness were made strong, became valiant in battle, turned to flight the armies of the aliens. Women received their dead raised to life again (Hebrews 11:33-35).*

There is great joy to be found in God's ownership and governance over our lives. *Make a joyful shout to the LORD, all you lands! Serve the LORD with gladness; come before His presence with singing. Know that the LORD, He is God; it is He who has made us, and not we ourselves; we are His people and the sheep of His pasture. Enter into His gates with thanksgiving, and into His courts with praise. Be thankful to Him, and bless His name. For the LORD is good; His mercy is everlasting, and His truth endures to all generations (Psalm 100).*

Sixth, as friends of God we know that we are stewards and not owners of the things which God alone has provided. How many of us still want to win the lottery and be millionaires? Oh, the great things we say we would do with all that money. Yes, if the Lord would just make me rich I would do great things! News flash, you cannot get wealthier than being redeemed by the very blood of Jesus Christ, set apart by Him for eternal life through His resurrection, and filled with His Holy Spirit. Perhaps it is time we became benevolent with that?

This is about changing the way we think. Jesus told us: *"No one can serve two masters; for either he will hate the one and love the other, or else he will be loyal to the one and despise the other. You cannot serve God and mammon"* (Matthew 6:24).

We are stewards, governing what belongs to God under His direction until Jesus comes or we depart. In the midst of his misery, Job still understood this. *"Naked I came from my mother's womb, and naked shall I return there. The LORD gave, and the LORD has taken away; blessed be the name of the LORD"* (Job 1:21).

Is there an imbalance of wealth in our present world? Perhaps, but the better question is whether or not that imbalance should be our concern. If we focus on serving our true Master then He will take care of the rest. I find it sad that during my lifetime large segments of 'the church' have run toward doctrines of prosperity. Contrary to scripture, the general claim is that God intends for the faithful to be rich. However the scriptures tell us that it is the poor who are rich in faith and also call on the rich to share. *Listen, my beloved brethren: Has God not chosen the poor of this world to be rich in faith and heirs of the kingdom which He promised to those who love Him? But you have dishonored the poor man (James 2:5-6). Command those who are rich in this present age not to be haughty, nor to trust in uncertain riches but in the living God, who gives us richly all things to enjoy (1 Timothy 6:17).*

Seventh, we who are friends of God know that this world is passing away and that we await Jesus Who will restore all things.

Mankind is not going to save itself, much less save the planet, from the ravages of our own sin. There are many well-intentioned efforts in progress to protect the environment and by all rights we should respect and not destroy the gift of God's creation. I would advise caution with regard to involvement in those efforts but no more than with anything else. If these things are on your heart then perhaps they are there for a reason. Seek the Lord about what He would have you do and He will turn your efforts under His guidance into something that restores life.

We know from scripture that the very creation itself is sick and tired of its treatment at the hands of man. It groans to God for freedom from the pain of our sinfulness, *because the creation itself also will be delivered from the bondage of corruption into the glorious liberty of the children of God (Romans 8:21).*

We also know preserving our own earthly life is not the focus of our redemption. *When He had called the people to Himself, with His disciples also, He said to them, "Whoever desires to come after Me, let him deny himself, and take up his cross, and follow Me. For whoever desires to save his life will lose it, but whoever loses his life for My sake and the gospel's will save it. For what will it profit a man if he gains the whole world, and loses his own soul? Or what will a man give in exchange for his soul? For whoever is ashamed of Me and My words in this adulterous and sinful generation, of him the Son of Man also will be ashamed when He comes in the glory of His Father with the holy angels" (Mark 8:34-38).*

But the day of the Lord will come as a thief in the night, in which the heavens will pass away with a great noise, and the elements will melt with fervent heat; both the earth and the works that are in it will be burned up. Therefore, since all these things will be dissolved, what manner of persons ought you to be in holy conduct and godliness, looking for and hastening the coming of the day of God, because of which the heavens will be dissolved, being on fire, and the elements will melt with fervent heat? Nevertheless we, according to His promise, look for new heavens and a new earth in which righteousness dwells (2 Peter 3:10-13).

Lastly, God's friends know that eternal life is not primarily a ticket to 'heaven' but rather it is a relationship. John records one of Jesus' last prayers on the night before His arrest. In this prayer Jesus gives us the true definition of eternal life. *Jesus spoke these words, lifted up His eyes to heaven, and said: "Father, the hour has come. Glorify Your Son, that Your Son also may glorify You, as You have given Him authority over all flesh, that He should give eternal life to as many as You have given Him. <u>And this is eternal life, that they may know You, the only true God, and Jesus Christ whom You have sent</u> (John 17:1-3).*

Knowing God has been the pursuit of believers throughout all generations. It was the prayer of Moses. *Now therefore, I pray, if I have found grace in Your sight, <u>show me now Your way, that I may know You</u> and that I may find grace in Your sight. And consider that this nation is Your people." (Exodus 3:13).* It is also the desire of God: *Then I will give them a heart to know Me, that I am the LORD; and they shall be My people, and I will be their God, for they shall return to Me with their whole heart (Jeremiah 24:7).*

In like manner God's friends know that the way to God is more than a specific path, that God's truth is more than an abstract concept, and real life is greater than the sum of our daily experiences. Our minds reach beyond the surface perception of these as objects or things as we discover at last that Jesus IS. Then, all of a sudden it becomes clear that there really is no other approach to God. *Thomas said to Him, "Lord, we do not know where You are going, and how can we know the way?" Jesus said to him, "<u>I am</u> the way, the truth, and the life. No one comes to the Father except through Me (John 14:5-6).*

Take the time to get on the same page with God through the renewing of your mind. We know that God *is a rewarder of those who diligently seek Him (Hebrews 11:6).* As much as it is God Himself Who is that reward, the reward is mainly enjoyed this side of heaven by those who are on the same page with God.

Understanding Authority:

Returning to Jesus' prayer in John 17 we read again: *"Father, the hour has come. Glorify Your Son, that Your Son also may glorify You, as You have given Him authority over all flesh, that He should give eternal life to as many as You have given Him."*

You park your car and step out, a fellow citizen approaches and says, 'Hey buddy you ran that red light back there!' What is your reaction? Now presume that instead it is a member of the local police who is making that statement. What is your reaction now and why is there a difference? Don't do a two step, you know very well the difference is that the police have authority and can write you a pretty expensive ticket if they have a mind to. Yes, like the rest of us at that point, you will be playing nice.

Nobody has authority like Jesus who is over all flesh, the granter of eternal life. God's intention for His friends is that we also carry Jesus' authority wherever we go as ambassadors for Christ. This authority never belongs to us, it always belongs to Jesus, and it flows out of this submitted servant-friend relationship where we are in tune with and on the same page with God.

In Chapter 4 we covered the story of Adam and Eve. How, as the crown of God's creation, He gave them authority over the earth and its creatures. How they chose to leave the camp of those who obey God and join the camp of those who disobey. Part of the problem they most certainly did not think through was that this new camp already had a king and it was not either of them, it was Satan.

We find the devil on the scene again right after Jesus is baptized (*Luke 4:1-13*). Jesus is out in the wilderness fasting 40 days and nights in seeking God. The devil tries a number of angles to tempt Jesus into crossing the same line he was able to get Adam to cross. Join my camp, we are free from God and His ways and rules. Hungry? You're the son of God, command this stone to become bread. Jesus resisted the devil using the truth of scripture and eventually Satan departed.

One of the angles that the devil tried on Jesus had everything to do with understanding authority. *Then the devil, taking Him up on a high mountain, showed Him all the kingdoms of the world in a moment of time. And the devil said to Him, "All this authority I will give You, and their glory; for this has been delivered to me, and I give it to whomever I wish. Therefore, if You will worship before me, all will be Yours." And Jesus answered and said to him, "Get behind Me, Satan! For it is written, 'You shall worship the LORD your God, and Him only you shall serve'"* (Luke 4:5-8).

Was Satan lying? Indeed not, for through the abdication of Adam and Eve, the devil had indeed gained authority over all the kingdoms of the world and could have granted that to Jesus had Jesus, like Adam, chosen submission to Satan.

But the story does not end with Jesus' victory over temptation. It is finished through the cross and resurrection by which Jesus took back all authority from the devil. Listen to the words of the great commission which Jesus gave to His followers after He rose from the dead. In it He states: *"All authority has been given to Me in heaven and on earth. Go therefore and make disciples of all the nations, baptizing them in the name of the Father and of the*

Son and of the Holy Spirit, teaching them to observe all things that I have commanded you; and lo, I am with you always, even to the end of the age." Amen (Matt 28:18-20).

We read of Jesus: *that through death He might destroy him who had the power of death, that is, the devil, and release those who through fear of death were all their lifetime subject to bondage (Hebrews 2:14-15)*. And we read Jesus' reassuring words in the beginning of John's revelation: "*Do not be afraid; I am the First and the Last. I am He who lives, and was dead, and behold, I am alive forevermore. Amen. And I have the keys of Hades and of Death" (Revelation 1:17-18).*

We serve the unlimited King. With regard to heaven and earth, Jesus does not have some authority but all authority and we have been authorized by Him to carry out His mission of making and teaching disciples. Indeed the devil still holds sway and can claim legal ground over those areas of human lives which continue to be freely yielded to him. But, it is no longer the devil who holds authoritative sway over the nations nor over Hades or death, these squarely belong to Jesus.

In the beginning of His earthly ministry, Jesus encountered what seemed to be a simple and straight forward man who understood how authority was supposed to operate.

Now when Jesus had entered Capernaum, a centurion came to Him, pleading with Him, saying, "Lord, my servant is lying at home paralyzed, dreadfully tormented." And Jesus said to him, "I will come and heal him." The centurion answered and said, "Lord, I am not worthy that You should come under my roof. But only speak a word, and my servant will be healed. For I also am a man under authority, having soldiers under me. And I say to this one, 'Go,' and he goes; and to another, 'Come,' and he comes; and to my servant, 'Do this,' and he does it." When Jesus heard it, He marveled, and said to those who followed, "Assuredly, I say to you, I have not found such great faith, not even in Israel!" (Matthew 8:5-10).

In this passage we see that there is a direct relationship between understanding how authority operates and faith. Remember the seeker's connection between faith and hearing from God (from *Romans 10:17*)? Gaining God's direction through seeking is to gain faith. To act on God's direction under Jesus' authority is the work which completes our faith and produces God's intended fruit. Jesus marveled that this gentile believed in and received the operation of his earthly hierarchy of authority as a centurion in such a matter of fact, perhaps even child like manner. There is a challenge here to you and me to do the same in grasping and understanding the authority given us by God to act on His behalf. *Then Jesus said to the centurion, "Go your way; and as you have believed, so let it be done for you." And his servant was healed that same hour (Matthew 8:13).*

Clearly we also need to recognize that God has not only given each of us authority to act but has placed each one of us under various structures of authority for the greater benefit of all. Under God, we have parents, spouses, governments, employers, owners, and so forth. The opposite of walking in agreement with God's established authorities in our lives is not always outright rebellion. More typically it is the sin of presumption, where we presume or assume that we don't have to check with or agree with God or others but that our way is best. This was the sin we find in Israel in the days of the Judges. *In those days there was no king in Israel; everyone did what was right in his own eyes (Judges 21:25).* The remedy for this, which keeps us on the path with God, is to be a seeker of God for daily living and destiny.

When the typical westerner thinks of authority, it almost always comes with the baggage of power in the sense of being powerful over others. Certainly there is power in what God wants done but, as we know, God's ways and the world's ways are polar opposites. *But Jesus called them to Himself and said, "You know that the rulers of the Gentiles lord it over them, and those who are great exercise authority over them. Yet it shall not be so among you; but whoever desires to become great among you, let him be your servant. And whoever desires to be first among you, let him be your slave — just as the Son of Man did not come to be served, but to serve, and to give His life a ransom for many" (Matthew 20:25-28).*

We walk in agreement and like-mindedness with God when we exercise our God given authority from a servant's heart and when we submit ourselves to those God has put in authority over us.

Generosity Toward God:

Our last stop in becoming a friend of God is generosity. Jesus told a parable about a man who found himself rich and who made plans to service his own pleasure and needs. The man was deemed a fool for having so little regard to his eternal future and was told that his life would be required by God that very night. Jesus ended by saying: *"So is he who lays up treasure for himself, and is not rich toward God" (Luke 12:21).*

In my observation, western believers in our day and age are more hung up in their walk with God by the simple thing we call money than by anything else. It seems we will worship, pray, study, maybe even witness but just don't ask us for any of 'our' money. Money and personal possessions are without a doubt the great idolatry of our times.

Remember Adam and Eve hiding behind those trees and blaming others for their sin? Often the mask that is hidden behind in this case is to blame the church. 'The church is always after my money. Yep, that is why I don't give!' If you really belong to a church where the actions of leadership show they care for nothing but money then you should seriously evaluate with the Lord if that is the right place for you. In all honesty, and by scripture, it is not the church asking you for your money. It is God directing you, in Father to child instruction, how to trust. Money is simply a tool by which God can easily measure your trust.

I could give you all the reasons why I believe in and practice tithing but I will not. I could roll you through the testimony of my inability to out-give God and how He has always provided, but again it will be of no value. Until a person squares with God regarding generosity and the real underlying issue of their fears and inability to simply trust Father, they will never be convinced by words.

Call it tithing, which means giving a tenth, or if the general arguments about whether that is valid for today bother you, then call it giving. Either way you will struggle in your friendship with God until you learn how to: *Honor the LORD with your possessions, and with the firstfruits of all your increase; so your barns will be filled with plenty, and your vats will overflow with new wine (Proverbs 3:9-10).*

This is another one of those fundamental promises of God and if this is an issue for you then I encourage you to *'taste and see that the Lord is good'*. Walk in the requirement of the promise and see if you don't experience what it is like to have your barns filled with plenty and your vats overflow. Divorce yourself from the 'instant gratification' mindset of our present world and *'let patience have its perfect work'* investing in this area of your life. Be prepared for that plenty and that overflow to be of a different nature than what the world judges as wealth and you will be blessed. What value would you put on Joy or Peace?

Remember that God has *'chosen the poor of this world to be rich in faith'* and that: *everyone to whom much is given, from him much will be required* (from *Luke 12:48*).

The Apostle Paul, who wrote much of the New Testament, told us that he had learned how to live before the Lord during times of both want and of abundance (see *Philippians 4:10-13*). With regard to giving, Paul lets us know that when our hearts are in the right place and we are on the same page with God, then God will see to our needs. *So let each one give as he purposes in his heart, not grudgingly or of necessity; for God loves a cheerful giver. And God is able to make all grace abound toward you, that you, always having all sufficiency in all things, may have an abundance for every good work (2 Corinthians 9:7-8).*

Putting It into Practice:

It is not uncommon to hear someone say regarding their spouse or close friend, 'I am working on my relationship.' Friendship with God is not different in that respect, you have to put work into the relationship from your end if the friendship is to flourish. Do I really have to watch what I eat and exercise regularly in order to be in shape? Well, that all depends. How interested are you in being in shape? Yeah, there is no get rich quick scheme or instant diet pill that will boost your friendship with God either. You do have one thing working in your favor: God loves you and He is ready for the friendship to begin and become strong. Clearly the next steps to be taken are on your side of the table.

Having read this far, and hopefully put into motion what has been covered, you should have the knowledge and enough experience under your belt to take you the rest of the way.

Are you drawing near to the Lord regularly and finding that He draws near to you? Do you regularly bring your questions about life and the decisions you need to make before the Lord, asking, seeking, knocking on His door for direction and answers? What has been your experience thus far in hearing from or receiving direction from God? Are you noticing the still small voice of God? Are you experiencing His ability to somehow, for lack of a better term, drop understanding into your mind? Perhaps He is showing you things in dreams or even visions (I rarely get dreams from God and have never had visions but I know some who have).

Take a moment before the Lord to think about this very primary area of your life called friendship with God. If you sense that you are not making progress or could make better progress then what do you think the specific hindrances are? Spend some time with the Lord, what does He point out to you as your next step in friendship with Him?

Put on a different set of shoes and step outside of your own walk with God for a moment. Imagine that you are ministering to a person who has shared with you details about the flatness of their walk with God (perhaps someone actually has shared this with you). What questions can you ask that will help them to draw conclusions they can do something about?

Life can be tough and the last thing we want to do is set up a fantasy where we pretend that it isn't. Take some time alone with God to think about your daily life and its attendant struggles. Are you finding it a joy to count yourself a servant of the Lord or are you still regularly battling with choices between God and sin and whether or not you are going to do what you know He wants you to do?

Do you feel better connected with God than before you began to look into this subject? Do you sense yourself becoming more equipped as a seeker of God for understanding daily living and discerning your destiny than before? If so, then in what ways? If not, then why?

In these last few paragraphs I have purposefully asked you a number of questions which deserve more than a passing answer and I hope you will spend an appropriate amount of your time on them. That is why this section is called: putting it into practice. Muscles respond to exercise; they are challenged and strengthened by proper efforts well spent. The spiritual muscles involved in your friendship toward God behave the same way.

Chapter Eight

Waiting on the Lord

And you will seek Me and find Me, when you search for Me with all your heart. I will be found by you, says the LORD (Jeremiah 29:13-14).

We both know that unless we take the time and spend the effort to train ourselves as doers of the word, we will be hearers only, even forgetful hearers. *But be doers of the word, and not hearers only, deceiving yourselves. For if anyone is a hearer of the word and not a doer, he is like a man observing his natural face in a mirror; for he observes himself, goes away, and immediately forgets what kind of man he was. But he who looks into the perfect law of liberty and continues in it, and is not a forgetful hearer but a doer of the work, this one will be blessed in what he does (James 1:22-25).*

With this chapter I challenge you to roll up your sleeves and embrace the work. After all, we are working with God on our interface with Himself which will guide us through a lifetime and set our destiny. Fully embrace this process of seeking, add your own words and prayers as you work through the sections that follow. Spend an appropriate amount of time with The Lord on these areas and be prepared to follow through on what He shows you.

I can tell you that this would probably take me anywhere from a few days to a few weeks to work through, depending on how it goes. The intention is to assist you in assimilating and internalizing much of what we have learned. Most likely you will need to return to the material in these sections over again until they become instilled in you as the good habits of a seeker.

The best scenario will be to review the following sections, one at a time, alone with God in a manner that does not let: *the cares of this world and the deceitfulness of riches choke the word (Matthew 13:22).*

Most assuredly, I say to you, whatever you ask the Father in My name He will give you. Until now you have asked nothing in My name. Ask, and you will receive, that your joy may be full (Jesus - John 16:23-24).

Before the Throne of Grace: (Setting the stage)
We can cry out to God with any need and at any time, but we also need to create a regular space and time where we come just to connect with God. Much of what flows into us from His Spirit will happen during dedicated times of prayer. In Jesus' words: *But you, when you pray, go into your room, and when you have shut your door, pray to your Father who is in the secret place; and your Father who sees in secret will reward you openly (Matthew 6:6).*

Be purposeful about this. Where will that place be for you? When will that time occur? This is going to be life changing.

Consider your secret place, how can you remove from it those things which will distract you from being with God? My main secret place is my living room and the distractions are removed by being there before anyone else in the house awakes. There is a private room where I work, if I was to use that then it would be best if I leave my cell phone at my desk. It is good to have a few secret places. One of my favorite is being alone in the car. Quite a bit can get worked out with God on a long car ride: connection, worship, listening prayer. We also have a prayer room at our church which I take advantage of at times.

I go to plenty of business meetings and I see quite a few people sit through them without taking notes. If I were their boss I would want to box their ears because I know they cannot remember half of what was asked of them. For me, I do not show up before the CEO of the universe without something to take notes with. I have found that I will forget what God had to say and He will let me forget it. It is a lesson I had to learn the hard way as opportunities were missed.

Enter your secret place. Make it a practice to take the time to clear both your mind and your heart of all distractions. This is your time with God and this is God's time where you need to show up ready.

If you cannot clear your heart and mind then find out why not. Are you anxious about something? If so practice *Philippians 4:6-7* letting God lead you through the anxiety to His peace. Are you having a problem with somebody? Practice *Matthew 18:35* and forgive that person from your heart, likely God will not want to talk to you until you do. Is someone rightfully having a problem with you? God sees you both and loves you both, practice *Matthew 5:23-24* leaving your gift to God at the altar and going first to be reconciled with that person, then return to seek God.

Your mind and heart now clear, eyes open or eyes closed, mostly I leave mine open, breath in and out, and let your spirit draw near to God. If He brings anything else to mind that seems to be preventing the meeting, then confess it and give it to Him. *Draw near to God and He will draw near to you. Cleanse your hands, you sinners; and purify your hearts, you double-minded (James 4:8).*

Don't get discouraged in drawing near to God. Give it the time and perhaps the days it deserves to learn how to do this well. If you are used to worldly practices or outright sinning, then drawing near to God will alter your life as you look forward to meet with God regularly. It will start to dawn on you that worldliness and sinning are gumming up the works between you and God. Also, remember what I said early on about a city dweller going out into nature. No one moves from the noisy city into the country and is immediately able to perceive all of the small sounds of quiet nature. The same is true when we choose to move from the noise of our daily lives into that space where we can hear from God. Have patience and in due time you will learn to perceive the: *still small voice (1 Kings 19:12).*

No Other Reason but God:

In your quiet place once again take the time to draw near to God in heart, mind, and spirit. Picture yourself putting the vehicle's shift lever in neutral so that it is not wanting to go either forward or backward. Take your feet off of the pedals so that you are not controlling whether to stop or go. Take your hands off the steering wheel; it is God's turn to drive.

You are before God in this moment for no other reason than God Himself. There isn't anything in life or in this world that is not about Jesus. Begin to seek Him just for Who He is. 'Lord I want to know You more deeply than I do.' 'Father please reveal more of yourself to me today.' 'Open my eyes Lord that I may see and understand from Your perspective.'

Add your own prayers as the Spirit of God moves you during this time. Let each prayer hang out there and soak between you and God letting Him answer as He sees fit. Have the patience to wait. God knows what you need each day, if you insist on defining what that is then you will miss it. Learn to yield your will to Him during these times. *I would have lost heart, unless I had believed that I would see the goodness of the LORD in the land of the living. Wait on the LORD; be of good courage, and He shall strengthen your heart; Wait, I say, on the LORD! (Psalm 27:13-14).*

Addressing Doubts and Questions with God:

You are back in your secret place. You have taken the time to draw near to God. You have given Him space to define what this time with Him will be about. You have some doubts, perhaps some fears, and definitely some questions for which it would be good to receive some answers.

Sadly, some of our churches have developed into places where it is not OK to have any doubts or any questions about 'truth'. The old saying was: God said it, I believe it, that settles it. Perhaps the saying has some merit but not if it leaves us nowhere to go with the stuff that challenges us from within. Be assured that your Father in heaven is not afraid of your doubts and questions and prefers to welcome and answer them for you when you bring them in honesty.

Your job is to be sure that you really want to know the answers because the answers will no doubt call you to action and change. *If any of you lacks wisdom, let him ask of God, who gives to all liberally and without reproach, and it will be given to him. But let him ask in faith, with no doubting, for he who doubts is like a wave of the sea driven and tossed by the wind. For let not that man suppose that he will* _receive anything from the Lord; he is a double-minded man, unstable in all his ways (James 1:5-8)._ Putting away double-mindedness when you bring your honest doubts and questions to the Lord is done by wanting what He wants and being willing to change to get it.

Think about your question, maybe even write it down. Search within yourself a bit; does the question really address what you need to know? Turn the tables around, if you were being asked that question would you deem it a fair and honest question?

Draw near now before the Throne of Grace, ask your question and listen. Does asking whirl other things up in your soul? Does the answer do the same? Or, what does the Spirit of God seem to be saying or indicating? No answer? Don't despair; leave the question with God, ask it again another time. I have had times when I left a question with God and perhaps some days later will be walking down the street when the answer rolls into my mind as clear as day. Again, God knows what we need; we really don't know what we need or when we need it.

In regard to addressing doubts and questions with God, one other area stands out which many of us need to examine. Waiting, not whining, this is a very important thing to understand. We can get so intimate with God that there really is no limit to how deep and familiar we can be. But don't make God into the person you cry your bucket of tears to every single time you get together.

There are plenty of times to cry about something before and with the Lord. So many things break His heart also. But would you really enjoy a relationship where your friend shows up with a never ending weeping about their situation, their troubles and issues, the others in their life, and their unsolvable fears? Come on now, we all have had that relative or friend whom we love dearly who whines and moans on the other end of the phone to where you just want to hold the phone away from your ear until they are done. Don't do that to God.

If we get honest we will see that whining is really a method of avoiding real and substantial progress. We whine because we are dishonest at heart and hesitant to bring our true questions and doubts before the Lord; challenge that within yourself and you will do well.

Exodus Chapter 14, the people of Israel are at the Red Sea, God is leading them out of Egypt and 400 years of slavery. He has done this in a display of immense power and with a mighty outstretched arm. His glory guards their camp in a pillar of cloud by day and in a pillar of fire by night. One of their biggest problems is that they still have the mindset of a slave.

Here comes the Egyptian army ready to maim, kill, and re-enslave them. The people of Israel blame Moses: 'Didn't we tell you to leave us alone in our slavery, why have you brought us out here to die?' What does God say to that? *And the LORD said to Moses, "Why do you cry to Me? Tell the children of Israel to go forward (Exodus 14:15).* Let's admit that at times we are no different than they were, yet what we really need is to listen to God to find the way forward. He parted the Red Sea for the Israelites and drowned their enemies, the Egyptian Army, in it after Israel had crossed. What will He do for you if you do as Moses had said? *And Moses said to the people, "Do not be afraid. Stand still, and see the salvation of the LORD, which He will accomplish for you today. For the Egyptians whom you see today, you shall see again no more forever. The LORD will fight for you, and you shall hold your peace" (Exodus 14:13-14).*

Checking in with God Daily:

It is human nature to let even the most important things slide. I'll get to that, yeah, I am going to do that, and see there it is on my list of things to do. Things to do: check in with God daily. Hmm, that one should never get crossed out.

Through the LORD's mercies we are not consumed, because His compassions fail not. They are new every morning; great is Your faithfulness. "The LORD is my portion," says my soul, "therefore I hope in Him!" (Lamentations 3:22-24).

A prayer from our secret place: 'Lord I look for your mercies and compassions today, what do I need to know about this day so that I can live it in the light of your presence?' Listen for His Spirit, write down the impressions and words you receive to help insure that you follow through. Perhaps spend some time before the Lord to internalize them. This should not become a broken record that just plays the same tune each day, let your spirit flow with His Spirit and see where God takes you. The main intention is to have that daily meeting to get centered with God and His guidance.

Joshua and the elders of Israel missed this at least once that we know about and it cost them big time (see *Joshua Chapter 9*). The inhabitants of Gibeon were in great fear of the God of Israel. The day of reckoning for their sins had come to their land and Israel was sweeping away one wicked kingdom after another. The Gibeonites hatched a plan to save their skins. Dressing up in worn clothes and taking moldy provisions with them they came to Joshua and the elders with a story about being from a far off country and wanting to make peace with God's people. *Then the men of Israel took some of their provisions; but they did not ask counsel of the LORD. So Joshua made peace with them, and made a covenant with them to let them live; and the rulers of the congregation swore to them (Joshua 9:14-15).*

God had strictly charged Joshua and Israel not to let any of the idolatrous kingdoms remain in the promised land because their ways would become a stumbling block for Israel. (This did happen in the near future.) Joshua learned of his mistake in not seeking the Lord and was wise enough to know that, regardless of the commandment, God would be very unhappy if they broke their oath to the Gibeonites. *Then Joshua called for them, and he spoke to them, saying, "Why have you deceived us, saying, 'We are very far from you,' when you dwell near us? Now therefore, you are cursed, and none of you shall be freed from being slaves — woodcutters and water carriers for the house of my God." So they answered Joshua and said, "Because your servants were clearly told that the LORD your God commanded His servant Moses to give you all the land, and to destroy all the inhabitants of the land from before you; therefore we were very much afraid for our lives because of you, and have done this thing" (Joshua 9:22-24).*

Be careful about the decisions you make in life. And do not make any oaths (see *Matthew 5:33-37*). We have the benefit of protection for our lives in the Lord Jesus Christ but it works both ways. If we neglect to check in with God regarding the issues of our lives, we may end up making decisions outside His will and those decisions can be costly.

Seeking God for my own daily living and destiny for a number of years, I made it a habit to have a yearly review of my life and priorities with God. Everything went on the table. It still does. Should I still work for this employer? Are there any changes You would have me make at work? Am I pursuing the right ministries? What changes need to be made to conform to Your will? A general review of each of my relationships, what do I need to know about or do to make each successful? Completing this sort of comprehensive review of every area of my life with God somehow grounds me and establishes that inner sense of being set on a firm foundation. I highly recommend this practice.

Break up your daily routine by choosing some special times to spend with the Lord or setting aside some extended times. If possible, perhaps get out into nature: under the stars, on a mountaintop, beside a lake, stream, or ocean. You will be surprised at how a change of venue can bring change in perspective.

Meditating on the Words of God:

I have more understanding than all my teachers, for Your testimonies are my meditation (Psalm 119:99).

Choosing or letting God choose passages of scripture to meditate on should be a regular part of your quiet time with God. We must never forget that God's will for us is always expressed without contradiction in both His written word and with specifics for our situation at times provided by His Holy Spirit.

Don't neglect the Bible; it is God's word to you which He has preserved throughout the centuries. Nothing can begin to hold a candle to the validation and preservation of the scriptures. God's word is confirmed as authentic in thousands of manuscripts, portions, and inclusion in writings over the ages. It is validated by the express fulfillment of its own prophecies, and, not to say the least, our individual experiences of how God has changed our lives with His words.

In case you are wondering at this point: how am I going to maintain a quiet time with God that includes seeking Him for who He is, asking questions, looking for His direction, and now meditating on His word? That's a valid question. I do it by being comfortable in letting God's Spirit chose the activity for each day's quiet time rather than trying to work it all in.

In particular, meditation on God's word is the one activity that works best for me outside of my regular time with God. I can be sitting out in nature, taking a walk, driving somewhere. I read the passage of scripture and then just sort of turn myself and my thoughts off and place it out there before God with an openness to learn. It is truly an amazing experience to see what the Lord unfolds from His word during those times. *It is the Spirit who gives life; the flesh profits nothing. The words that I speak to you are spirit, and they are life (Jesus - John 6:63).*

Following are five passages along with a few words to get you started. Each passage focuses on an aspect of who you are in Christ because helping you to get a solid grasp of your identity in the Lord has been a fundamental purpose of this book.

Find the situation in which you will meet with God in meditation and take these passages one at a time before Him to see what the Lord wants you to learn. This may take a few days to work through. It is never a 'been there, done that' experience for me. God has been showing me new things year after year from passages I have read dozens of times because He tailors His revelations to what I need in the moment.

The word of God says that through Jesus I am His child and He is my heavenly Father. Take the following passage of scripture before the Lord for a time of learning through meditation: *Then Jesus called a little child to Him, set him in the midst of them, and said, "Assuredly, I say to you, unless you are converted and become as little children, you will by no means enter the kingdom of heaven. Therefore whoever humbles himself as this little child is the greatest in the kingdom of heaven. Whoever receives one little child like this in My name receives Me (Matthew 18:2-5).*

The scriptures direct us to always remember Whom we serve. Take the following passage to God for meditation. How does it apply to your life right now? *But Jesus called them to Himself and said to them, "You know that those who are considered rulers over the Gentiles lord it over them, and their great ones exercise authority over them. Yet it shall not be so among you; but whoever desires to become great among you shall be your servant. And whoever of you desires to be first shall be slave of all. For even the Son of Man did not come to be served, but to serve, and to give His life a ransom for many"* (Mark 10:42-45).

The word of God creates an awareness within us of being God's soldiers engaged in a war for the souls of our fellow men. Waging that war will be the subject of our next chapter. Focusing on your identity as a soldier for Christ is the subject of this paragraph for meditation before God: *You therefore, my son, be strong in the grace that is in Christ Jesus. And the things that you have heard from me among many witnesses, commit these to faithful men who will be able to teach others also. You therefore must endure hardship as a good soldier of Jesus Christ. No one engaged in warfare entangles himself with the affairs of this life, that he may please him who enlisted him as a soldier* (2 Timothy 2:1-4).

Meditate on your identity as one whom God would consider calling 'friend'. Think back on what we learned about becoming a friend of God and take this passage before the Lord to see what He may show you. *Greater love has no one than this, than to lay down one's life for his friends. You are My friends if you do whatever I command you. No longer do I call you servants, for a servant does not know what his master is doing; but I have called you friends, for all things that I heard from My Father I have made known to you* (John 15:13-15).

Finally we will meditate on an important aspect of our identity in Christ: self-acceptance. This is an area of struggle for many because we often don't like ourselves. The major downside is that it is hard to *'love your neighbor as yourself'* if you don't love yourself. Take the following passage before the Lord, open yourself up, and listen to what God may have to say about how He sees you. *For*

You formed my inward parts; You covered me in my mother's womb. I will praise You, for I am fearfully and wonderfully made; marvelous are Your works, and that my soul knows very well. My frame was not hidden from You, when I was made in secret, and skillfully wrought in the lowest parts of the earth. Your eyes saw my substance, being yet unformed. And in Your book they all were written, the days fashioned for me, when as yet there were none of them (Psalm 139:13-16).

I hope you enjoyed these times of meditation on the word of God and with God. Again, if you did not seem to gain much, then give it time and the practice will grow on you. Doubtless meditation will stir up questions, good thing that you already know what to do with those, right? I know you will find meditation upon God's word an invaluable part of seeking God.

Asking, Seeking, Knocking:

In *Luke Chapter 11* Jesus' disciples come with a request: *"Lord, teach us to pray, as John also taught his disciples" (Luke 11:1).* Jesus' immediate answer in *verses 2-4* is to teach them what we call 'The Lord's Prayer'. In verses 5-8 Jesus follows the prayer with a short story about persistence where in the right circumstances even a friend will send you away unless you are persistent.

The Greek word in *Luke 11:8* for persistence is

Anaideia, pronounced an-ah'-ee-die-ah', meaning impudence and by implication importunity. Impudence is the quality of offensively bold behavior. Importunity means to place an insistent or pressing demand.

All words are subject to the context in which they are used. In the context of Jesus' story, where a person is coming at midnight to ask his friend for a loaf of bread, the person is not trying to 'offend' his friend. Rather think of it as going on the offense in a battle rather than being on the defense and remember that Jesus is talking about prayer.

It is from this idea of bold behavior and insistence that we come to the modern English word 'persistence'. To be persistent means: continuing firmly or obstinately in a course of action in spite of difficulty or opposition. Jesus ends the passage with these words: *I say to you, though he will not rise and give to him because he is his friend, yet because of his persistence he will rise and give him as many as he needs* (Luke 11:8).

Let's keep that idea of persistence, a combination of impudence and importunity, right there in our back pocket as we cover asking, seeking, and knocking. If we are to do this Jesus' way then we have to recognize that there is a reason why He sandwiches the story about persistence between the Lord's Prayer and these next verses.

"So I say to you, ask, and it will be given to you; seek, and you will find; knock, and it will be opened to you. For everyone who asks receives, and he who seeks finds, and to him who knocks it will be opened. If a son asks for bread from any father among you, will he give him a stone? Or if he asks for a fish, will he give him a serpent instead of a fish? Or if he asks for an egg, will he offer him a scorpion? If you then, being evil, know how to give good gifts to your children, how much more will your heavenly Father give the Holy Spirit to those who ask Him!" (Luke 11:9-13).

Ask is the Greek word aiteo, pronounced ahee-teh'-o, and meaning simply to ask. Aiteo is used in context within the New Testament as: ask, beg, call for, crave, desire, require. Jesus' promise is that if we ask we will receive. We know from James that at times we do not receive: *because you ask amiss, that you may spend it on your pleasures* (James 4:3). Also from *James* we have read that we cannot expect to receive if we are double-minded. Context is always king when we are trying to understand something from the Bible and so it is important to notice that Jesus has used a story where a person is coming to their 'friend' and, from His words in our passage above, He likens it to a 'son' approaching a 'father'. Relationship is everything when it comes to asking. The asking may be persistent like a soldier on the offense but it should respect the relationship. When we remember how the Lord's Prayer starts: *Your kingdom come. Your will be done (Luke 11:2)* then our asking will be in line with proper purpose and relationship toward God and we can cling to the promise which tells us that our persistence will be rewarded.

Seek is the Greek word zeteo, pronounced dzay-teh'-o, and meaning to seek after or for and especially in the sense of worshipping God which is the context in which Jesus uses it. Jesus' promise in these verses is that if we will seek we will find. I find great comfort in knowing that the full force of this promise from my King stands behind the effort I will make in worshipping my God through the act of seeking Him for my daily living and destiny.

Knock is the Greek word krouo, pronounced kroo'-o, and means to rap, to knock. What a simplistic activity this seems to be. Just imagine this promise, given in context of prayer, is that if I will knock it shall be opened to me. Well, wasn't that the reason I was knocking for in the first place? Friends, sometimes we have to check ourselves. Are we praying to God because we are supposed to? Or are we at His door because we know that it simply must open if we are to go forward?

Jesus Himself is no stranger to this process or how it works: He asks, He seeks, and He knocks. His mission is to: *seek and to save that which was lost (Luke 19:10).* Jesus stands at the door of the sinners soul and is seeking to enter. *Behold, I stand at the door and knock. If anyone hears My voice and opens the door, I will come in to him and dine with him, and he with Me (Revelation 3:20).*

In another story Jesus tells us of a persistent widow who absolutely needed a local judge to grant her request (see *Luke 18:1-8*). It ends well for her and Jesus ends His story by asking: *"when the Son of Man comes, will He really find faith on the earth?" (Luke 18:8)*. Roll up your sleeves and get to work: ask, seek, knock because Jesus is actually supposed to find faith in you during your time on this earth. How have you been doing at this? What has been working best for you in spending regular time with God? What have your experiences been in following through with the things He is making clear to you?

Don't back away from God when answers seem thin or few and far between. Is God testing you during those times? Well, what if He is? It is the job of the teacher to put their students to the test. It is the role of a Father to teach and train and then step back and see what the kid has learned. Struggle strengthens and testing discovers, mainly for our benefit, what we are really made of.

You and I can always expect the Lord to do things in our lives which challenge us to grow so don't let difficulties master you, instead persist. *For you have need of endurance, so that after you have done the will of God, you may receive the promise: "For yet a little while, and He who is coming will come and will not tarry. Now the just shall live by faith; but if anyone draws back, My soul has no pleasure in him." But we are not of those who draw back to perdition, but of those who believe to the saving of the soul (Hebrews 10:36-39)*. Consider King David who, as a teenager, received God's promise that he would be King of Israel. When did David become King? He was 30 years old when he actually became King. David endured and David received the promise, now it is our turn.

I would never want to leave the impression that God always makes us struggle for every scrap. I find that most of the time the Holy Spirit readily answers prayer with insight, action, or both especially when it comes to day-to-day living.

But are there not things in our lives that are worth struggling for? Are there not things worth fighting for if indeed we are God's history makers in this present day and age? How many things have been surrendered to the world and the enemy un-challenged and un-fought just because the going got rough or the way was hard. *"Enter by the narrow gate; for wide is the gate and broad is the way that leads to destruction, and there are many who go in by it. Because narrow is the gate and difficult is the way which leads to life, and there are few who find it"* (Jesus - Matthew 7:13-14).

Children ask childish questions and good parents, like God, entertain those questions in a way that is appropriate to the child's age. As I have mentioned, one of my grandsons is currently four years old and comes over regularly. As children do, when he was old enough he began asking dozens of questions and at first I would answer them. However now, even at four, he has reached an age where I no longer answer questions for which the answers are obvious or are such that he should be able to discern them himself. Picking up a ball from the pool table he asks, 'Grandpa what kind of ball is this?' And I respond, 'What kind of ball is it?' Of course he brightens up and says, 'It's a pool table ball Grandpa.' To which I answer: 'You're right it's a pool table ball.'

I learned this lesson for myself early on from God. At one point I just had to ask Him, 'God why am I not receiving any answer from you to my questions in prayer?' Can you guess what He said? It went something like this, 'I am not going to give you answers in prayer to those questions for which you already know the answer or for which the answer has already been clearly given in My word the Bible.' To which my response was, 'Oh, OK.'

God does stretch us to make us grow and then God does expect us to act our age. You can count on that happening for you.

Now take these fundamentals of asking, seeking, knocking and persistence into your secret place with God. Spend some time before Him to let this soak in. I offer these prayers to get you started but I am sure that by now you can come up with your own prayers: 'Lord show me where I am when it comes to persistence and teach me what it will take for me to persist.' 'Lord show me where the battle is that I may set myself to ask, seek, and knock until your answers become clear and the way is opened to me.'

Meeting the Lord with Thanksgiving and Praise:
Picture the Old Testament temple in Jerusalem. The sun is rising on a Sabbath morning. The priests and Levites are all at their stations and ready to go. The city has awakened and the people are on their way to worship. For the regular residents of the area it is a place they come to every week. For others it is far from home; they usually worship in a local gathering but in obedience to God they travel and appear before Him at the temple at least three times a year.

The people bring tithe and sacrifice from their livelihood. The appointed singers and musicians begin their round, encouraging the people to action with their psalm: *Enter into His gates with thanksgiving, and into His courts with praise. Be thankful to Him, and bless His name (Psalm 100:4).*

To this day, thanksgiving and praise remain as methods by which we enter God's gates and the courts of our King. Unlike the common Israelite of those days, all who now follow Jesus are welcomed all the way in, even behind the torn veil and into the most holy place. *Let us therefore come boldly to the throne of grace, that we may obtain mercy and find grace to help in time of need (Hebrews 4:16).*

Learn to worship the Lord. I know believers typically gather for worship and many of us listen to and even sing quite a bit of contemporary Christian radio music. But as you may know there is a difference between singing and actually training yourself to worship.

In your secret place or other time alone with God, with all distractions removed, take the time to connect with His Spirit, then: *enter into His gates with thanksgiving, and into His courts with praise. Be thankful to Him, and bless His name.* Open your spirit and let it stretch out to God. Sing a song to the Lord. Perhaps start by reading a passage from the *Book of Psalms* they were written for this purpose.

Make up a love song for the Lord in that moment, become that *joyful shout* (see *Psalm 100:1*) and just let it flow. Your skill level at music doesn't matter to the Lord and no one else is watching or listening. There is no need to perfect that song to be sung again. These would be love songs just and only for the Lord and just and only for that moment. Tell Him what you are thankful about and praise Him from your heart.

When you come together for times of worship with your church or other believers, never take God for granted. Church has no purpose unless God shows up or rather unless we show up to worship God in spirit and in truth. I don't want to go through the motions and mouth some words of a song or worship with my mind being elsewhere. Who would that bless? Consider stepping out or pausing in prayer to deal with distractions, then return to worship. I also don't want to be stuck in our modern inhibitions being concerned about what anyone else may think about the body language of my worship. I want to be there for the Lord. I want to stretch out my spirit to Him. I'll just move my hands and feet as He moves me. The point is to *bless His name.*

To a person who has not learned to worship, singing songs from a church hymnal or even with a rousing church band is uneventful, perhaps even a chore. This is mainly because there is no expectation of actually meeting with God.

For a person who has learned to worship, any form of God centered music will do or even no music at all. Good quality music and musicians can definitely add to the experience of worship. But when we are there to meet with God and *bless His name* these other things fade into their appropriate place in the background.

But I will sing of Your power; yes, I will sing aloud of Your mercy in the morning; for You have been my defense and refuge in the day of my trouble. To You, O my Strength, I will sing praises; for God is my defense, my God of mercy (Psalm 59:16-17).

The Practice of Fasting:

I have known brothers and sisters in the Lord who make fasting a weekly practice or even have a specific long term fast every year. By now you know what my counsel will be with regard to when you should fast: Seek the Lord, asking Him when and for what purpose or let it go and God will direct you to fast at appropriate times.

For the follower of Jesus, fasting is typically coupled with times of prayer. I can point out a few things which I have learned about fasting and I can share some related scriptures. But I cannot teach you about fasting because you will never learn anything about it until you practice fasting as part of seeking the Lord.

I'm no giant or great spiritual saint when it comes to fasting. Most of my days are filled with purpose and routine which includes eating. I tried to learn about fasting by just doing it. I would fast until late afternoon or evening and then have a time of prayer. The one thing that I discovered for myself from this was that coming to prayer just because I had fasted seemed to fall flat. It felt like I was bringing the horse but God was in effect saying 'where is the cart?' From this I understood that fasting was a tool to be used for bringing about a purpose and not an end goal in itself. Now, if I fast, it is because there is a reason; there is something that I need to know or deeply review with God or I need Him to take action.

The leadership group at my church will call us together from time to time to fast and gather for prayer. There is always a purpose for those times where, as a collective group, we are seeking God's direction for a certain part of the ministry. It is typical for this group to include times of personal examination during the prayer and I have gained both direction for and confirmation of my ministry efforts during those times.

Fasting is also an appropriate part of persistence. Remember our word for persistence; going on the offense (impudence) and placing an insistent or pressing demand (importunity). There will be times when we simply need God to take action. It would be very inappropriate for us to try to tell God what actions He should take or what His time-table should be. However, it is very appropriate for us to come asking, seeking, knocking on His door. Also, Jesus affirmed that there will be times when nothing is going to move without both fasting and prayer. Jesus arrived to find his disciples unsuccessful at casting a demon out of a child and so He did it Himself. *His disciples asked Him privately, "Why could we not cast it out?" So He said to them, "This kind can come out by nothing but prayer and fasting" (Mark 9:28-29).*

Somehow fasting helps us to get beyond our self. In denying ourselves food for the purpose of seeking the

Lord we are sharpened, perhaps more sensitive spiritually, and in a sense have laid aside our own interests. Perhaps this why some things can only happen when prayer is first backed by fasting? Learning a new spiritual practice with the Lord is like hunting for treasure, what will you find? Ask the Lord how you should engage in fasting and then go for it.

Through the prophet Isaiah, God made very clear to us the type of fast He is looking for. Take the time to read about this in *Isaiah Chapter 58*. Clearly God's idea of fasting far exceeds simply going without food and coming to prayer. He is looking for those who worship in spirit and in truth. Any passage of the Bible which ends with direct words from God like this should get our attention: *"Then you shall delight yourself in the LORD; and I will cause you to ride on the high hills of the earth, and feed you with the heritage of Jacob your father. The mouth of the LORD has spoken"* (Isaiah 58:14).

Humility, Meekness, and Waiting:

The concepts of 'humility' and 'meekness' certainly have their negative side. After all, who wants to be or feel weak? Doesn't the word of God tell us that: *those who wait on the LORD shall renew their strength (Isaiah 40:31)*? Indeed it does but why would I need my strength renewed unless I am weak?

The facts are upon us and we don't like them. The truth that is hard to face and even harder to let others see is that by ourselves we are indeed weak. If we are to come out from hiding then it is time for us to accept this about ourselves and learn to rejoice in the strength which only God gives.

Many a preacher has spent time trying to assure the congregation that meekness is not weakness. I believe that we are better served by understanding that at times

God will have us be weak and, in that weakness, we will experience His strength.

The Apostle Paul was definitely strong in the Lord and yet his life and missions for God often included times of weakness where he could not make it on his own. Three times he brought to the Lord what many think was a problem with his eyes. God neither healed Paul nor do we have an indication that God gave Paul any lengthy explanation of why not. But Paul understood and saw how it applied to the rest of his life, that in weakness he would know the strength and power of God. *And He said to me, "My grace is sufficient for you, for My strength is made perfect in weakness." Therefore most gladly I will rather boast in my infirmities, that the power of Christ may rest upon me. Therefore I take pleasure in infirmities, in reproaches, in needs, in persecutions, in distresses, for Christ's sake. For when I am weak, then I am strong (2 Corinthians 12:9-10).*

During feelings of weakness the first reaction from our fallen nature is almost always to move quickly and cover it up because we don't like how it makes us feel. This reaction of instant hiding is so strong that even relatively mature followers of Christ will fall into it as their first move given the right situation. Many times the best we can do is to recognize that this has occurred, return to an admission of weakness, and get with the Lord to find His direction of strength.

Moses exemplifies a man who matured into the position of living in his weakness and finding God's strength. *Now the man Moses was very humble, more than all men who were on the face of the earth (Numbers 12:3).* The Hebrew word translated humble also means lowly, meek, and even poor. Yet Moses' life is that of a history maker who, through the power of God, confronted the enemy, led a nation, established laws that are still in general practice, waged war, and secured a homeland. I would say that Moses knew his own limitations and instead of hiding them we see him repeatedly bringing those limitations before the Lord to discover strength.

Take some time with God to evaluate yourself with regard to meekness. Ask Him to train you in readily turning to Him as you encounter times when life is beyond your own strength: 'Lord continue to teach me who I am in you.' 'Lord let me always remember where I came from and where I am going.' 'Father, in those times when my soul would react in self-protection guide me back to your throne to find your strength.' 'Lord I want to experience the meaning of your word where it says: *Blessed are the meek, for they shall inherit the earth* (Matthew 5:5).'

Seeking God through Communion:

Jesus left His followers with two distinct ordinances: baptism and communion. I will avoid spending time on the theology of baptism but simply mention that it is typically a once in a lifetime event intended to proclaim our intention of following Jesus to others. On the other hand, Communion, or the Lord's Supper, is intended to be practiced repeatedly.

How often it is practiced is left up to our discretion. Some fellowships take communion every time they get together and some don't. The real questions are asked when we consider the intention and value of communion and how it relates to seeking God. *1 Corinthians 11:23-32* presents the Bible's clearest teaching on this subject so let's see what we can learn.

For I received from the Lord that which I also delivered to you: that the Lord Jesus on the same night in which He was betrayed took bread; and when He had given thanks, He broke it and said, "Take, eat; this is My body which is broken for you; do this in remembrance of Me." In the same manner He also took the cup after supper, saying, "This cup is the new covenant in My blood. This do, as often as you drink it, in remembrance of Me." For as often as you eat this bread and drink this cup, you proclaim the Lord's death till He comes (1 Corinthians 11:23-26). The words are clear: the intention of communion is that we might remember Jesus and in this manner proclaim His death until He comes. But why does Jesus want us to do this?

Do you remember my saying that in certain of our churches and circles of fellowship it is not OK to have questions and doubts? Well, in some of the same, it is also not OK to question anything either. I don't mean to pick on anyone but too often we do what we do because that is what is expected. However as a seeker of God it is high time to know 'why' we do what we do.

Asking 'why' is never an impertinent question before God. We learn and grow by asking, seeking, knocking. So why does Jesus want us to take a bit of bread and the fruit of the vine regularly remembering and proclaiming His death? A few things come to mind and I am sure you could find more if you were to take this passage before the Lord in meditation.

Remembering what Jesus did reminds me that He did it for me. Remembering His death reminds me that I stand on the firmest foundation; I have been accepted into the Kingdom by God Most High Himself. I remember that in God's sight the eternal punishment for my sins has been fully paid. I am reminded of the importance of being on mission with and for God to work with Jesus *'to seek and to save that which was lost' (Luke 19:10).* Proclaiming Jesus' death until He comes keeps me fixed on the end goal. No matter how hard life becomes down here there is a hope and a future which can never be taken away. This is at least part of 'why' Jesus wants me to remember and proclaim. It re-centers me and re-focuses me around the mission.

With that in mind, communion starts to become more than a dead ritual. Perhaps some of you have even rejected it as such or, like many, have just gone through the motions when it was time? I encourage you to revisit this experience in the new light of Jesus the very next time it comes up. Better yet, set aside a time with the Lord, get some bread, get some juice or wine or whatever you are comfortable with using and 'commune' with the Spirit of the Lord. Make it one of your special times of faith and you will be rewarded.

But let a man examine himself, and so let him eat of the bread and drink of the cup. For he who eats and drinks in an unworthy manner eats and drinks judgment to himself, not discerning the Lord's body. For this reason many are weak and sick among you, and many sleep. For if we would judge ourselves, we would not be judged. But when we are judged, we are chastened by the Lord, that we may not be condemned with the world (1 Corinthians 11:28-32). Communion comes with a warning. We are cautioned against taking it lightly.

The church in Corinth to whom Paul was writing had many problems with pride, division, error, and neglect of the poor and even drunkenness during times when they gathered to eat. It is important that we also examine ourselves when approaching Jesus' ordinance of communion. Is there a wrong we should make right first? Have we been saying 'no' to God with regard to something He has made clear to us? Have we been saying 'yes' but not following through? How are the relationships within the fellowship where I am taking communion? Am I *'discerning the Lord's body'*, His church and its needs or am I neglecting it? It is more than OK to let the bread and cup pass until I take care of any unsettled business that God reveals to me. It is more than OK; it is clearly what God expects of us as His followers. Perhaps a simple prayer before taking communion along with a bit of time to wait on the Lord for an answer is the best approach. *Search me, O God, and know my heart; try me, and know my anxieties; and see if there is any wicked way in me, and lead me in the way everlasting (Psalm 139:23-24).*

Putting It into Practice: (God's Promises for Those Who Wait)

By now I am sure you understand the two main facets of 'waiting on the Lord'. The first requires patience as I 'wait' for God to reveal something or to take an action. The second is that simple picture of the nicely dressed man at a high-end restaurant with the towel draped over his arm. He approaches your table and he asks, 'How may I serve you?' Of course that person is called 'a waiter' because he 'waits' on you.

Turn it around and it is you and I 'waiting' on the Lord, 'Lord, how may I serve you?' Better yet, instead of picturing the fancy waiter, picture Jesus who: *knowing that the Father had given all things into His hands, and that He had come from God and was going to God, rose from supper and laid aside His garments, took a towel and girded Himself. After that, He poured water into a basin and began to wash the disciples' feet, and to wipe them with the towel with which He was girded (John 13:3-5).*

Both types of 'waiting' are part of the seeker's connection with God. It is within this connection that Isaiah points out that: *those who wait on the LORD shall renew their strength (Isaiah 40:31).*

Many are the promises of God toward His children, servants, soldiers, and friends who 'wait' on Him. In closing this chapter, consider just one from Psalm 37 as strength for the faith which is growing within you:

For evildoers shall be cut off; But those who wait on the LORD, They shall inherit the earth. For yet a little while and the wicked shall be no more; Indeed, you will look carefully for his place, But it shall be no more. But the meek shall inherit the earth, and shall delight themselves in the abundance of peace (Psalm 37:9-11).

Chapter Nine

Waging War

For though we walk in the flesh, we do not war according to the flesh. For the weapons of our warfare are not carnal but mighty in God for pulling down strongholds, casting down arguments and every high thing that exalts itself against the knowledge of God, bringing every thought into captivity to the obedience of Christ (2 Corinthians 10:3-5).

The truths represented in these verses from Paul's letter to the Church at Corinth tell us directly that God has armed us for war. It is that great battle for the eternal souls of mankind and it rages in our day and age with or without our participation. The verses remind us that our weapons are not carnal, that is they do not issue from our old nature, the flesh. Instead they are mighty in God, issuing from His Spirit. When God shows up through us in word or deed, people become convicted of truth. Arguments are stopped and those things which would claim greatness over the knowledge of God are cast down. Within our own souls, every thought is challenged and brought into obedience.

What if God had an army that stood ready to do His will? He does. What if God had only a troop of soldiers whom He could use? In some situations that is all He has. What if He only had you through whom to make His-Story?

There are so many situations and encounters for which God specifically created you. In many of those, even when there are other soldiers for Christ, it will just be you and Jesus. At the very beginning of this chapter on waging war it is important for you and me to be able to make the commitment embodied in the old Christian hymn: 'Tho none go with me, still I will follow'.

God laid out His plans and Moses' mission as He spoke to Moses from the burning bush. He answered Moses' questions about the name of God and empowered Moses with a few miracles to prove that God had sent him. God tells him to go, but listen to Moses' next words. *Now therefore, go, and I will be with your mouth and teach you what you shall say." But he said, "O my Lord, please send by the hand of whomever else You may send" (Exodus 4:12-13).* Needless to say God was a bit angry and Moses went anyway, the rest is history.

Peter was up against this same dilemma in *John Chapter 21* when the risen Christ laid down Peter's mission. Peter feed my lambs, Peter tend my sheep. Peter understood that he was being directly called into responsibility for the first church to lead and to shepherd Jesus' other disciples both new and old. *Then Peter, turning around, saw the disciple whom Jesus loved following, who also had leaned on His breast at the supper, and said, "Lord, who is the one who betrays You?" Peter, seeing him, said to Jesus, "But Lord, what about this man?" Jesus said to him, "If I will that he remain till I come, what is that to you? You follow Me" (John 21:20-22).*

You follow me. God may have you work with or for other followers of His at times but we must never forget that the buck stops with us. We are called into this war in an individual, direct, and very personal manner. God did not create us so that He could look for *whomever else* to send when it came time to get the job done. God is looking to you and me through whom to enact His will and make His-Story in this current day and age.

"But what do you think? A man had two sons, and he came to the first and said, 'Son, go, work today in my vineyard.' He answered and said, 'I will not,' but afterward he regretted it and went. Then he came to the second and said likewise. And he answered and said, 'I go, sir,' but he did not go. Which of the two did the will of his father? (Jesus - Matthew 21:28-31).

Now in calling His soldiers into battle, would our Commander-in-Chief send out His troops unequipped? Certainly not and we are going to review the tactics of our enemy, the power to overcome, and our protective gear and weapons described in *Ephesians 6:10-20*. But first and of primary concern are our commission and general orders. Without clear direction from our Commander no amount of gear will matter in battle as we would not know how or where to carry the fight.

Here is your commission; it is the same as mine: *And Jesus came and spoke to them, saying, "All authority has been given to Me in heaven and on earth. Go therefore and make disciples of all the nations, baptizing them in the name of the Father and of the Son and of the Holy Spirit, teaching them to observe all things that I have commanded you; and lo, I am with you always, even to the end of the age." Amen (Matthew 28:18-20).* And here are your general orders; they are the same as mine: *But you shall receive power when the Holy Spirit has come upon you; and you shall be witnesses to Me in Jerusalem, and in all Judea and Samaria, and to the end of the earth" (Acts 1:8).*

The Enemy and his Tactics:

Finally, my brethren, be strong in the Lord and in the power of His might. Put on the whole armor of God, that you may be able to stand against the wiles of the devil. For we do not wrestle against flesh and blood, but against principalities, against powers, against the rulers of the darkness of this age, against spiritual hosts of wickedness in the heavenly places. Therefore take up the whole armor of God, that you may be able to withstand in the evil day, and having done all, to stand (Ephesians 6:10-13).

The first lesson we learn from this passage is that we are going to need all of the armor of God if we are to stand up to the enemy. The second is that this battle is not against flesh and blood, so we had better do a quick review of the tactics of our enemy.

Our enemy loves to use the truth to his advantage. The devil wages war by twisting truth. Remember Eve who gave in to temptation mixed with partial truth. Remember Jesus who endured the same but did not give in.

As much as he loves to use truth, the devil also strategically sows lies and is the author of much of the mistrust humans have toward one another. Jesus called Satan *'a liar and the father of it'* (see *John 8:44*).

Being excluded from the Spirit of God, the devil is a master at speaking into the spirit of self. His goals of planting temptations, lies, and mistrust are easily presented to humans since we ourselves are, or were, fallen in the same way. *For Satan himself transforms himself into an angel of light (2 Corinthians 11:14).*

Satan is the accuser of all those who follow Jesus. We are told that he works at this night and day (see *Revelation 12:10*). Remember how the devil accused Job before God? He has been doing the same against you and your fellow believers from the very start. His goal will always be to cause division among us and suspicion within us toward God and toward one another.

In *Isaiah 14:12* and *Revelation 20:3* we learn that the devil has weakened and deceived the nations of men. Do you ever wonder why peace escapes humanity? Who is behind the fact that our politicians just cannot seem to provide leadership?

Satan is the ultimate anti-Christ who counterfeits those things which are godly. In place of trust we have mistrust; in place of love we have lust.

The devil is known as the *'prince of the power of the air'* (see *Ephesians 2:1-3*). According to this passage we once followed him and all who are disobedient to Jesus are his followers. As such they can be expected to succumb to temptations and deceptions and live in opposition toward God and us. They give place to the devil and his schemes rather than to God because they are still lost. In my opinion, much Christian effort over the last 60 years was focused on insisting that non-Christians live morally. If that same effort had been focused on helping them know God and come to salvation we might be living in better times. Unbelievers cannot live morally because they are lost and under Satan's power, neither could we until we were saved.

The devil has legal authority over those things which have been surrendered to him. Remember Adam and Eve who surrendered their leadership of the world through abandonment of God's camp. The devil operates by permission. We clearly see that he could not touch Job without God's permission (see *Job 1:6-12*). If you are surrendered to God then the same protection belongs to you.

Finally, Jesus has overcome the devil, *that through death He might destroy him who had the power of death, that is, the devil, and release those who through fear of death were all their lifetime subject to bondage (Hebrews 2:14-15).*

Also, Satan knows that his time is short. *Woe to the inhabitants of the earth and the sea! For the devil has come down to you, having great wrath, because he knows that he has a short time (Revelation 12:12).*

The Power and the Price to Overcome:

Because of what Jesus has done we can successfully resist our enemy. *Therefore submit to God. Resist the devil and he will flee from you (James 4:7).* Through Jesus we can recognize and be victorious over the counterfeits of the devil: *that you put off, concerning your former conduct, the old man which grows corrupt according to the deceitful lusts, and be renewed in the spirit of your mind, and that you put on the new man which was created according to God, in true righteousness and holiness (Ephesians 4:22-24).* For more detailed instructions see *Ephesians 4:25-32* and *Colossians 3:8-10.*

The Apostle Paul had words of advice for us in regard to rescuing others who are still in Satan's trap: *And a servant of the Lord must not quarrel but be gentle to all, able to teach, patient, in humility correcting those who are in opposition, if God perhaps will grant them repentance, so that they may know the truth, and that they may come to their senses and escape the snare of the devil, having been taken captive by him to do his will (2 Timothy 2:24-26).*

God has provided for you and me to have the front line advantage in this war through preparation and readiness. *Be diligent to present yourself approved to God, a worker who does not need to be ashamed, rightly dividing the word of truth (2 Timothy 2:15).*

As unpleasant as it is, suffering will always be part of war and soldiers will always be called into personal sacrifice. *You therefore must endure hardship as a good soldier of Jesus Christ. No one engaged in warfare entangles himself with the affairs of this life, that he may please him who enlisted him as a soldier (2 Timothy 2:3-4).*

Paul is the best example we have of a warrior for Christ who suffered much for his involvement. *Remember that Jesus Christ, of the seed of David, was raised from the dead according to my gospel, for which I suffer trouble as an evildoer, even to the point of chains; but the word of God is not chained. Therefore I endure all things for the sake of the elect that they also may obtain the salvation which is in Christ Jesus with eternal glory (2 Timothy 2:8-10).*

The main passage we are studying clearly presents God's promise and intent when it tells us to: *take up the whole armor of God, that you may be able to withstand in the evil day.* It is God's intention that we be fully equipped and thereby able to stand. The power to overcome is from God, the price for us to overcome is that we must actively '*take*' His armor and put it to use.

God's Armament and Weapons:

Continuing to make our way through *Ephesians 6:10-20* we read: *Stand therefore, having girded your waist with truth, having put on the breastplate of righteousness, and having shod your feet with the preparation of the gospel of peace; above all, taking the shield of faith with which you will be able to quench all the fiery darts of the wicked one. And take the helmet of salvation, and the sword of the Spirit, which is the word of God; praying always with all prayer and supplication in the Spirit, being watchful to this end with all perseverance and supplication for all the saints (Ephesians 6:14-18).*

In my early days I can remember participating in prayer sessions where we: '*put on the whole armor of God*'. But at some point it struck me and I asked myself, when had I ever taken it off? Maybe I am simplistic but my solution to being ready is to leave the armor on rather than spending time in prayer to put it on yet once again.

After a time, any armor or armament becomes personal to the individual. We will find that it needs adjustment, cleaning, and care if it is to be kept in readiness. Would modern battlefield soldiers allow their rifles to remain clogged with mud after a march through wet terrain? They would be sorry during the next fire-fight if they did. Should we allow our skill with the sword of the Spirit to atrophy with disuse? It won't be much good in the battle if we do.

Stand therefore, having girded your waist with truth. At the trial, Pontius Pilate listened while Jesus spoke of His followers as those who are of the truth. Pilate responded with the question *'what is truth?'* (see *John 18:37-38*). This is a question to which the world does not have an answer but we who follow know that it is not a question of 'what' but of 'who' and the answer is Jesus who told us *"I am the way, the truth, and the life" (John 14:6).*

We are instructed to: *put on the Lord Jesus Christ, and make no provision for the flesh, to fulfill its lusts (Romans 13:14).* Put Jesus on, make yourself available, and get to know Him. Learn and practice His word, recognizing that here is the true King to whom we owe allegiance. Cling to, cleave to, and trust in Jesus Christ. Then in the power of that girding: *putting away lying, "Let each one of you speak truth with his neighbor" (Ephesians 4:25).* Also, *have no fellowship with the unfruitful works of darkness, but rather expose them (Ephesians 5:11).*

Put on the breastplate of righteousness. Though only God is truly righteous, having purity of all character quality and motive, this same Lord calls us to put on His provision of righteousness as our protective breastplate. The Apostle Paul wanted to: *be found in Him, not having my own righteousness, which is from the law, but that which is through faith in Christ, the righteousness which is from God by faith (Philippians 3:9).*

Don't run from righteousness just because you are not perfect or are afraid you might project a 'holier than thou' attitude. Remember that Jesus did not come to earth as God Most High whose example we can never live up to. Rather Jesus, Who is God the Son, came and lived as a true seeker and servant of God should and in so doing set us the example to follow.

There is no purpose in pursuing our own righteousness which we cannot obtain. However, God has called us to grow up and when we put on His righteousness we are affected by it, challenged by it, and encouraged by its daily presence to live righteously as Jesus did. This breastplate can stand up to the battles of life. This breastplate can absorb the blows that get past sword and shield. Our job is to make sure that this breastplate is protecting a heart that is loyal and true to the One Who provided the armor.

Shod your feet with the preparation of the gospel of peace. The Greek word for shod simply means to bind under one's feet, to put on shoes or sandals. The main focus in this portion of our scripture is being prepared by and with the *'gospel'* or good news, *'of peace'. Therefore, having been justified by faith, we have peace with God through our Lord Jesus Christ, through whom also we have access by faith into this grace in which we stand, and rejoice in hope of the glory of God (Romans 5:1-2).*

The Apostle Peter tells us that this preparation begins in our heart and conscience, which are the two pathways of communication for the Holy Spirit within our spirit, to speak into the emotions and mind of our soul. *But sanctify the Lord God in your hearts, and always be ready to give a defense to everyone who asks you a reason for the hope that is in you, with meekness and fear; having a good conscience, that when they defame you as evildoers, those who revile your good conduct in Christ may be ashamed (1 Peter 3:15-16).*

How will they know that we who come dressed for battle actually come in peace? How will they know that the battle for which we are prepared is not against our

224

lost fellow man but against the devil and his angels? They will know when you show up prepared with good news about peace from God, which is reflected in your good works done from the heart, and with a good conscience by the righteousness of Jesus Christ. Then the Gospel may receive a fair hearing among mankind. Get ready to walk in peace, which God has provided through Christ, and bring that peace into the history making of your daily life and God appointed destiny. For me, this requires daily choices and, in the past, has required greater efforts spent with God to root out of my life things that did not agree with His peace.

Take *the shield of faith with which you will be able to quench all the fiery darts of the wicked one*. Hailing all the way back into chapter four we learned that: faith is *the gift of God* (see *Ephesians 2:8*), *that faith comes by hearing, and hearing by the word of God* (see *Romans 10:17*). We know this gift of God exceeds the world's view of faith being blind or merely hopeful. We remember that the Greek word for faith in the New Testament is Pistis, pronounced pis'-tis, and meaning: persuasion, assurance, belief, faith, 'a belief based on knowing that I have heard' i.e. I am persuaded, I am assured and having the quality of knowing, not just hoping, that thus and such is indeed true. Through seeking we have also come to understand the meaning of these words from the New Testament: *But without faith it is impossible to please Him, for he who comes to God must believe that He is, and that He is a rewarder of those who diligently seek Him (Hebrews 11:6)*.

Now take the shield of faith as your main protective and defensive weapon in this war and make your stand. Many are the times in life when Satan will attempt to attack, harass, or toss some version or another of his fiery darts at the believer. From time to time, we may hear our fellow believers say that they are under attack when their circumstances or inner feelings get out of control. But consider this: our Lord and example Jesus Christ did not spend His time lamenting that He was under attack by the enemy. Jesus was always on the offensive.

Jesus was down here as the one from whom the wicked demons needed to cower in fear and not the other way around. Now, Jesus is here in you and in me and the deal is the same. We are that thing in the dark that the devil and his angels better be afraid of because here we come to wage this war, exposing them with the light of God. Listen to these words of our Master affirming that this is so: *But if I cast out demons with the finger of God, surely the kingdom of God has come upon you. When a strong man, fully armed, guards his own palace, his goods are in peace. But when a stronger than he comes upon him and overcomes him, he takes from him all his armor in which he trusted, and divides his spoils. He who is not with Me is against Me, and he who does not gather with Me scatters (Luke 11:20-23).*

Buck up soldier, it is high time to reject the religious and worldly ideas of our modern age which contain subtle fear of our enemy rather than the boldness to put him to flight.

I have noticed that the devil tosses most of his fiery darts at the weak. Satan likes to attack those at the edge of the pack who are wavering in their faith with regard to what God says about them. Spend the time with God to drill down into your soul and get rid of any remaining issues about who you are in the Lord. You can recognize these as the tape that from time to time tells you that you are no good and will never measure up or other discouragements. I would have to say that after these years of letting the Lord dig deep I really don't suffer many bold attacks from the enemy, or perhaps I just put them down about as quickly as they come up. If you lack courage, read the words of David in *Psalm 27* and notice how David's boldness relates to seeking the Lord.

Take the helmet of salvation. We covered salvation in Chapter Two, 'Taking the Biggest Step'. That free gift of God is the Lord's protective covering for your head. It is also a symbol of you and me living lives that are surrendered under His authority. We have been rescued from the raging ocean of sin and pulled into the safety of Jesus' mighty boat. There is work to do on this ship. There are activities that will assist Jesus in pulling many more to safety and a war against the forces which work to prevent Jesus' goal. But we must always remember that there is but one captain of this ship and it is not us.

The salvation we receive is the same helmet for every believer and should always remind us that we are on the same team. Perhaps the assignments of God will place me in a position of authority over some of my fellow believers and perhaps it will place me under some of them. I have certainly experienced both as part of what the Lord has wanted over the years.

To effectively wage war together, as the army of Jesus Christ, requires us to accept our assignments and acknowledge one another as fellow soldiers in the same cause. Throughout the scriptures we see that unity is foundational to power. Letting this helmet be our constant reminder of this is one of the precursors to victory. Forgetting our unity or letting the devil rob us of it is a sure precursor of defeat.

Take *the sword of the Spirit, which is the word of God.* Take notice the next time you see pictures or a movie where sword and shield fighting is involved. Sword and shield are used together by the skillful soldier to attack and defend. A fighter who loses shield or sword is at a great disadvantage to an opponent who has both.

How often do warriors draw their swords? For sure, they draw them when battle approaches but unless they have also drawn them many times in practice it may end up being a short fight.

Jesus used the written word of God: against the devil, as a means to teach truth, as a reminder of the path of God, and in His everyday situations. He was able to do this because He knew it intimately. By the way, what Bible did Jesus use and affirm as the word of God during His life and ministry? Oh, really? Well then perhaps we should make sure not to neglect that thing we call the Old Testament, as apparently Jesus assigned high value to it as the word of God (see *Matthew 5:17-19*).

Jesus also brought what He knew He had heard in prayer and in the moment from the Holy Spirit into play as His direction for how to face the challenges of ministry and daily living. *I can of Myself do nothing. As I hear, I judge; and My judgment is righteous, because I do not seek My own will but the will of the Father who sent Me (Jesus - John 5:30). Then Jesus said to them, "When you lift up the Son of Man, then you will know that I am He, and that I do nothing of Myself; but as My Father taught Me, I speak these things. And He who sent Me is with Me. The Father has not left Me alone, for I always do those things that please Him." As He spoke these words, many believed in Him (John 8:28-30).*

Would there really be benefit in writing further words to convince you of your need to get into and internalize the written word of God? Or is there value in attempting to further convince you of your need to listen to the Holy Spirit? Look around and you will see, our churches are filled with people whom we dearly love who seem to have never ending excuses for why they don't spend time in the Word or in seeking God. Don't be one of them, instead follow Jesus' example and maybe you will be used to wake up others. You will need *the sword of the Spirit* so don't let it rust in the scabbard.

Prayer, Watchfulness, Perseverance:
God's armored soldiers, now ready for battle, are to fight in full dependence on God. There will always be the small daily battles where we wrestle with our own self regarding choices in the Spirit which we know we should make. Not skipping time alone with God, following through on our commitments, following through on things God has shown us, and making good choices when it comes to relationships and care of our body which is His temple. There will also always be the need to reject the various temptations of the devil and at times put him in his place. At times the will of God will lead us in simple day-to-day living and at times God may require of us things that take us well out of our comfort zone. Such is the life of a soldier for Christ.

The one constant will be that we cannot do any of this independently. There will always be a need to depend on God in prayer and we may consider prayer to be the second offensive weapon of our armament after the *sword of the Spirit*. Jesus put it like this: *"I am the vine, you are the branches. He who abides in Me, and I in him, bears much fruit; for without Me you can do nothing"* (John 15:5).

Returning to the passage of our armament in *Ephesians 6*, it rolls right into this subject: *praying always with all prayer and supplication in the Spirit, being watchful to this end with all perseverance and supplication for all the saints — and for me, that utterance may be given to me, that I may open my mouth boldly to make known the mystery of the gospel, for which I am an ambassador in chains; that in it I may speak boldly, as I ought to speak (Ephesians 6:18-20).*

There are a number of things to notice about the prayer we are called to in this verse. It will definitely include supplication, which simply means to bring your requests to the Lord. We are also reminded to keep our focus on all the saints, our fellow believers, and not just on our own needs. This call to prayer is also fortified as a call to watchfulness and perseverance; we are to keep on asking, seeking, knocking, as we previously learned.

In these verses, the Apostle Paul also asks for prayer for himself that he may have what is needed to complete his work in the Lord. Taking a cue from this when we find that we have needs, we should also enlist other believers to pray for us. There is definitely power in practicing interdependence in prayer. *And shall God not avenge His own elect who cry out day and night to Him, though He bears long with them (Luke 18:7)?*

Have we messed up out there on the battlefield today? Then prayer should start with confession. *If we confess our sins, He is faithful and just to forgive us our sins and to cleanse us from all unrighteousness (1 John 1:9).*

We come to effective prayer with all respect toward the majesty of God. However, there are also many scriptures which indicate that God expects His people to make a bold approach to Him in the full knowledge of who we now are through Jesus Christ. The lowliest of us in the eyes of the world are the sons and daughters of God Most High. We are His servants, friends, priests, and even royalty. *But you are a chosen generation, a royal priesthood, a holy nation, His own special people, that you may proclaim the praises of Him who called you out of darkness into His marvelous light; who once were not a people but are now the people of God, who had not obtained mercy but now have obtained mercy (1 Peter 2:9-10).*

It is in the light of these truths about ourselves that we approach God confidently in prayer. We also know that there are conditions for answered prayer such that when we come before God as warriors of the Kingdom of Christ we will experience an effective prayer life. The Apostle John reminds us of the conditions and confidence involved in prayer. *And whatever we ask we receive from*

Him, because we keep His commandments and do those things that are pleasing in His sight (1 John 3:22). Now this is the confidence that we have in Him, that if we ask anything according to His will, He hears us. And if we know that He hears us, whatever we ask, we know that we have the petitions that we have asked of Him (1 John 5:14-15).

Ministering to Others through Prayer:
Nothing in the Bible says that it is more powerful to pray 'for' someone when they are not around than to pray 'with' someone regarding the issues of their life. However, there is a communication of loving and valuing which takes place when we pray 'with' a person regarding things near, dear, and important to them. This can be done on the spot, over the phone, or even typed back in response to an email or text message.

The Bible clearly assumes that we will minister to others through prayer. Prayer is universal for followers of Jesus and never referred to in scripture as a special gifting. In my opinion the truth is that many of us have just not walked through our fears about being open with prayer because it can take us beyond our comfort zone.

Part of our job in ministry is to recognize the culture into which we have been placed by God and use those cultural cues to further the work of the Gospel of Christ. In most of the western world, definitely in the United States, we have a culture which includes a sense of protection regarding individual privacy. It is often a false privacy but it must be respected because in praying 'with' another we are crossing over that person's boundaries and not just our own.

It is very important to get a sense of the felt need for privacy within the other person and perhaps suggest that we step into the next room to talk and pray rather than just laying on hands in public and blurting it out because I 'felt' led by the Spirit to pray for them.

What I am really saying here is that in ministering to others it is about them and not about you. The more you and I are able to grasp that and go against the flow of our own western cultural sense of 'individualism' the more fit and effective we will be in ministering to others.

In offering to pray for someone we should never assume that it is OK to just begin praying in their presence. Unless we already know that this is the case, we should always 'offer' to pray for someone. Once they say 'yes' then it is OK to surprise them by doing it right there on the spot. In my experience, people are often surprised when you start, but then they realize that they just said 'yes' and end up being blessed by it.

Suppose that a person you are talking to reveals something of their needs, hurts, or the issues of their life. Does the idea of offering to pray for them bring up hesitation for you? What do you think those hesitations are based upon? What would it take for you to work with the Lord and step out of your comfort zone in this area of ministry?

Dialog and spiritual discernment are indispensible when it comes to effectively praying with another person about their needs. As you read the New Testament gospels notice that Jesus often asked questions before ministering to people and we would do well to follow His example. A bit of dialog and discernment through a few gentle questions before prayer can help reveal what really needs to be prayed about. Often we will find that the issue they brought up is not what they need prayer for.

A person may bring up difficulties with financial issues but then, with a bit of dialog and discernment, we find that they are really angry because they feel their spouse is spending too freely and not respecting the family budget. Well, surely God can help them with the financial issue. But God is also way more interested in the two persons involved. We may end up praying for this person's ability to forgive, for their courage to peacefully approach their spouse about the issue, and for their ability to trust in and seek God for harmony and blessing in their home. Wow! Now we are quite a bit deeper than just mouthing some general prayer that God would somehow bless their finances. Don't forget to be a brother or sister to them in offering to follow up in a few days because that is how real ministry is effectively done.

How do we go about including dialog and discernment when it comes to working with others toward prayer? An old ditty goes something like this: 'I keep with me six serving men they taught me all I knew, their names are what and where and when and how and why and who'.

Ask them questions like: 'How does this issue make you feel?' 'Why do you think that you feel this way?' 'What do you think is really going on?' 'What do you believe is happening?' And then always spend the time to listen to their response.

Do you discern that their hearts and motives are in the right place? Is this the right timing for you to offer prayer? What is the Holy Spirit showing you in the moment? It is far more important to work with people than to rush to quick prayer. In doing so you are respecting their choice and their responsibility to open up to you or not. In the end, the person should know they were valued even if they choose to walk away. You will either get to minister to them in prayer today or likely they will return in the near future. Tomorrow is always another day so do not rush it, God is never in a panic. *Through the LORD's mercies we are not consumed, because His compassions fail not. They are new every morning; great is Your faithfulness (Lamentations 3:22-23).*

Overcoming Evil:

In calling the children of Israel to repentance and a return to godliness, God used a phrase which is important to understand. *Cease to do evil, learn to do good (Isaiah 1:16b-17a)*. Good is something all of us need to 'learn' how to do and develop in our lives so that we do it better. I devoted a chapter to this subject in my first book 'Breaking the Cycle of Slavery to Sin'. *But do not forget to do good and to share, for with such sacrifices God is well pleased (Hebrews 13:16)*.

Doing good is foundational to the furtherance of the Kingdom of God in this world. There is great power in doing good. When the people of God do tangible acts of good in the name of Jesus it can break down many of the misconceptions and lies which Satan has planted in our fellow man against the followers of Jesus. The scriptures directly tell us how evil is overcome. *Do not be overcome by evil, but overcome evil with good (Romans 12:21)*.

I know we would rather huddle in our churches and groups praying heartfelt prayers for our communities and nation, hoping that somehow God will take the upper hand and make changes. But as warriors for Christ we are that upper hand and the changes that overcome evil with good, if they are to happen in our day and age, will be done through us.

Seek the Lord on this with regard to what you and perhaps what your group should do. The power of God in this battle for souls is not always won by supernatural happenings. More often than not it is won by simple acts of goodness which is part of the 'fruit' of the Holy Spirit within us (see *Galatians 5:22-23*). *'Then the righteous will answer Him, saying, 'Lord, when did we see You hungry and feed You, or thirsty and give You drink? When did we see You a stranger and take You in, or naked and clothe You? Or when did we see You sick, or in prison, and come to You?' And the*

King will answer and say to them, 'Assuredly, I say to you, inasmuch as you did it to one of the least of these My brethren, you did it to Me' (Matthew 25:37-40).

Remember Those in Chains:

Remember the prisoners as if chained with them — those who are mistreated — since you yourselves are in the body also (Hebrews 13:3). At the end of the passage in Ephesians 6, which we have been studying in this chapter, the Apostle Paul asks the believers at Ephesus for prayer that: I may open my mouth boldly to make known the mystery of the gospel, for which I am an ambassador in chains.

Opening our daily newspaper, or perhaps our favorite news website, we are bombarded by the suffering and gruesome happenings all over our country and the world. One area we rarely receive any direct reporting on is the state and situation of our brothers and sisters in Christ who live in areas where they are minimized, bereft of opportunity, and often persecuted for the faith.

I can tell you from personal experience with believers in various parts of the developing world that they have not allowed their circumstances to stop them from serving Jesus Christ. Paul himself wrote much of the New Testament during his years of imprisonment for the Gospel. So we should support rather than feel sorry for our brothers and sisters whom God alone chose to place into those situations and history just as He has chosen what may be a different positioning and history for us. As a side note, to learn more directly about what is happening among your fellow believers around the world I recommend visiting www.persecution.com . There are other good web sources for this information but in my opinion Voice of the Martyrs has done an excellent job for many years and this is their website.

Now let's consider a few things as part of effectively waging war for Christ. A huge percentage of our world's population subsists on less than one or two dollars a day. Members of the body of Christ in those same areas are often minimized even further, being shut out from better opportunities by those of predominant religions. Yes, many are persecuted and even imprisoned as well, but this lack of economic opportunity is also another form of chains and so I submit that these are also worthy of our remembrance and prayers.

Followers of Christ are generally the ones in this world who have a purposeful care for the present well-being and eternal destiny of their fellow man. Because of this, when even the poorest of Jesus' followers is blessed or given opportunity, it ends up being shared with their neighbors.

Many of us who are holding this book live in circumstance where we have at least a few dollars to do with as we please, many of us have much more. If you have a warm place to sleep and little care about where your daily bread is coming from then be assured that you are one of the people at the party. You are indeed rich even if the culture within which you live does not recognize it as such.

All this suggests that those of us whom God has blessed and provided for should not neglect to ask Him what our role should be in regard to providing opportunity to our brothers and sisters around the world who suffer. Why else has God given us such access to know about events that affect them around the world? Part of waging war is for believers to seek God about their role in building up their less fortunate brothers and sisters in this day and age.

When a man or woman's family goes hungry day by day and shivers in the night, then that man or woman spends their self in attempts to provide. Things that we take for granted make a huge difference and, when they happen to families who also love Jesus, that difference overflows within communities.

A warm blanket can provide strength from the refreshment of a good night's sleep. Relatively inexpensive gifts of farm animals provide a source of food and income as well as a sense of stability within a home. Micro-loans, enabling farming or small businesses, restore a sense of purpose and capability to a man or woman in caring for their needs and the needs of their family. Water wells properly placed provide small country churches the opportunity for something life-giving to offer to their community and, in turn, often gain a hearing for the true words of life. Child sponsorship can fulfill the heartfelt hopes and dreams of poor but believing families for the future of their children as well as changing the entire course and future of that family's potential for prosperity. In so many simple ways we have the opportunity to impact the current and eternal destiny of God's Kingdom around the world. What would the Lord have you do?

There are many organizations which offer pathways into these types of involvement. It is fairly easy to ask any organization for their yearly audited statements, which should show the percentage of your money which actually makes it to those in need and outline the types of needs being addressed. Perhaps the Lord will give you a direct connection into a struggling inner-city or international church through someone you know and trust. As with all things it should be God's leadership we seek when making decisions about the extent of our involvement.

An Army's Morale and Sense of Community:

And let us consider one another in order to stir up love and good works, not forsaking the assembling of ourselves together, as is the manner of some, but exhorting one another, and so much the more as you see the Day approaching (Hebrews 10:24-25).

Life can be hard and all of us will go through hard times. Being a follower of Jesus will always have its challenges and even its measure of persecution. The Apostle Peter witnessed the discouragement of the rich man who went away because Jesus had called him to leave all and follow. Peter was clearly curious about where his own path was headed and what the reward might be. *Then Peter began to say to Him, "See, we have left all and followed You." So Jesus answered and said, "Assuredly, I say to you, there is no one who has left house or brothers or sisters or father or mother or wife or children or lands, for My sake and the gospel's, who shall not receive a hundredfold now in this time — houses and brothers and sisters and mothers and children and lands, with persecutions — and in the age to come, eternal life (Mark 10:28-30).*

God's promise to those who follow is that we will receive the fellowship of one another, where you become my brother, my sister, my mother and I become your brother, able to support and encourage one another through life. We are open to one another and able to share in one another's blessings of houses and lands and provision. It is also promised that this side of eternal life we will suffer persecutions which should serve to further bind believers together in community.

Praise and worship the Lord together. Express your thanksgiving both for one another and for God's providence to your group. Encourage one another daily in His word and Spirit as you see the day of Christ approaching. Can you see that God has specifically designed community this way so that each member of His army can prosper and live in high morale even in the darkest of times?

Learn together of His calling on your lives and become comfortable with how that may unfold over time. Feel your strength renewed as you seek the Lord with your fellow believers. Make a point of keeping your fellowships healthy, strong, and in good spirit.

In the glory of war we must consider the lot of the warrior throughout the centuries. Their lot is often one of privation, discomfort, and challenge. Warriors do not choose their battles but rather they obey. Warriors experience victory, defeat, gain, and loss. True warriors accept the battles which they are given and nothing should be beneath us when our Commander gives direction. What holds the individual warrior together is knowing that they can trust their commander implicitly and that they are part of a community of fellow warriors who rejoice together and often suffer together. Lastly, the warrior knows that their satisfaction in having fulfilled their purpose and destiny in this world and in their day and age comes from being faithful in the little things by which the Commander can then entrust them with greater (see *Luke 16:10-12*).

Spiritual Gifts, the Stealth Weapons of the Holy Spirit:
Spiritual gifts are the capacity of God's Holy Spirit to enable individuals in unique ways which are beyond mere learned talents and abilities. In many cases, it has become easier for modern western churches to ignore this subject or get stuck in controversies about the validity of 'lesser' gifts. However, battles are not won when we neglect or misuse our assets. Imagine a cavalry charge where each soldier leaves their sword behind. The main thing which God does not want us to do regarding spiritual gifts is spelled out for us by Paul: *Now concerning spiritual gifts, brethren, I do not want you to be ignorant (1 Corinthians 12:1).*
Throughout the New Testament we are encouraged to use both our spiritual gifting and our natural talents and abilities to serve God and one another. Oftentimes believers find it easier to express their faith through natural talents and abilities because they are natural to them, being present in us before and after salvation, and

because they are fully embraced and accepted by society as things common among mankind.

Spiritual gifts however are part of the new order for the saved person in Jesus Christ and therefore they come naturally to our born again spirits but not to our flesh. Nor are these 'gifts' embraced by society in general. My intention is to bring us to an understanding of God's purpose for the gifts and to whet your appetite to seek, appropriate, and walk in them. A general listing of those things which are referred to as spiritual gifts is drawn from a number of places in the New Testament as follows:

Manifestations of the Spirit from *1 Corinthians 12:4-11* include: Word of Wisdom, Word of Knowledge, Faith, Healing, Miracles, Prophecy, Discerning Spirits, Tongues and Interpretation of Tongues.

General Spiritual Gifts from *Romans 12:4-8* and *1 Corinthians 12: 28-31* include: Prophecy, Ministry, Teaching, Exhortation, Giving, Mercy, Apostle, Prophet, Teacher, Miracles, Gifts of Healing, Helps, Administration, Various Tongues.

Leadership Ministry Gifts from *Ephesians 4:11-12* include: Apostles, Prophets, Evangelists, Pastors and Teachers.

Celibacy (from *Matthew 19:10-12*).

Which of these gifts do you already recognize in yourself as being something which God has added to you by His Spirit? Perhaps you recognize some of the manifestations of the Spirit from *1 Corinthians 12* which seem to be ministrations which God brings through any believer whenever He wants to do so?

It is very important for us to avoid putting these things on a pedestal because they are intended to be part of the normal ebb and flow of the believer's daily life. In times of need a word of wisdom, a word of knowledge, or that deeper sense of discernment about a situation will roll into our minds. Some may call this inspiration or intuition, which are not uncommon among humans. As with everything else in creation which reveals the nature of the creator, inspiration and intuition in the lives of the lost are part of Jesus knocking on the door of their hearts to reveal Who He is. For the saved they become part of our daily expectation to walk with God and receive guidance from His Spirit.

Our second son came into this world with a number of complications. I remember the general panic with the doctor rushing the hospital staff into action and into the late night as the pediatrician tried to explain why bad things happen to good people. But from the very moment of his birth, God gave to me the gift of faith and I walked calm and beaming throughout because I knew that I knew that I knew that everything was fine. My friend simply said that these events were the opposition of the world to the advent of a new man of God. He was right and our son turned out perfectly healthy and is a solid God-fearing man today.

I have experienced, and also been used in, a number of healings and miracles which we will cover as a subject in our next chapter. I do not consider the use of unintelligible language in prayer and worship to be particularly wrong or out of place although in some churches it seems a bit overused. My experience with the gift of tongues has involved the ability to be clearer than normal in another language. One such day, my wife and I explained the Gospel to her brother, who spoke only German. I knew on the spot that my very limited command of that language was being supernaturally enhanced for the occasion and it was the day that he said 'yes' to Jesus setting his destiny forever.

Regarding gifts of ministry, the Lord has clearly led me in many of them from time to time but gifts of teaching, administration, and giving have greatly defined my roles within the body of Christ.

But earnestly desire the best gifts (1 Corinthians 12:31). Pursue love, and desire spiritual gifts (1 Corinthians 14:1). Have you begun to earnestly desire spiritual gifts? The Lord will reveal these to you as part of your unique identity within His Kingdom as you begin to seek Him about this. Like fingerprints, no one else will have your exact identity and no one else will be able to accomplish the roles for which God placed you alone into this stream of history.

Are you working with the Lord to actively exercise the spiritual gifting He has given to you? Many of the nuances of spiritual gifting are learned and grown into. Do not give up just because of a few failures; children don't give up on learning to walk just because they fall down at the beginning. *As each one has received a gift, minister it to one another, as good stewards of the manifold grace of God. If anyone speaks, let him speak as the oracles of God. If anyone ministers, let him do it as with the ability which God supplies, that in all things God may be glorified through Jesus Christ, to whom belong the glory and the dominion forever and ever. Amen (1 Peter 4:10-11).*

In truly seeking our spiritual gifting from God there are a few truths which need to be understood:

First of all, God's spiritual gifts come from God's grace and not by our merit. God is the One Who decides on and appoints the gifts among His followers as stated in *1 Corinthians 12:28.*

Next, the gifts are not actually given to an individual 'for' that individual but rather for the benefit of the body of Christ. (See 1 Corinthians 12:7). *Even so you, since you are zealous for spiritual gifts, let it be for the edification of the church that you seek to excel (1 Corinthians 14:12).*

Lastly, *1 Corinthians 12:31* tells us that we are to desire spiritual gifts and then makes sure we are pointed to *Chapter 13*, the chapter on love, as the better and higher way which must under-gird gifting and which gifting of itself cannot create. *But earnestly desire the best gifts. And yet I show you a more excellent way (1 Corinthians 12:31).*

Various tests and exams exist in order to aid believers in the discovery of their spiritual gifts. However, we can assume that the first believers and most of those who followed after did not rely much on paper examinations but rather on the Spirit of God and the discernment of fellow believers.

The Lord will always provide opportunity for you to exercise whatever spiritual gifts He is revealing to you. In my early days when the Lord was calling me into the gift of teaching I told my pastor that God had given me a clear call to preach His word. Pastor Harold simply said: there's my pulpit, be ready every Sunday for the next few months. That was challenging and Harold was faithful to follow up with me and discuss what I had preached each week. While that may be a bit unique, it should be understood that Harold was walking in his gifting as a pastor with the job of developing God's people. He knew me, discerned what God was doing in my life, understood that I was ready, and then gave me opportunity as the Lord led.

Understanding the Role and Importance of Prophecy:

Pursue love, and desire spiritual gifts, <u>but especially that you may prophesy</u>. For he who speaks in a tongue does not speak to men but to God, for no one understands him; however, in the spirit he speaks mysteries. But he who prophesies speaks *edification and exhortation and comfort to men (1 Corinthians 14:1-3).*

The Greek word translated as prophesy and prophesies in this passage is propheteuo, pronounced prof-ate-yoo'-o, meaning: to foretell events, divine, speak under inspiration, exercise the prophetic office.

Paul's dialog in *1 Corinthians 14* is clear regarding the everyday use of prophecy within the church as opposed to canonical prophecy which became Holy Scripture. Yet another example of the everyday use of prophecy is found in the Book of Acts which speaks of the Deacon Philip: *Now this man had four virgin daughters who prophesied (Acts 21:9).*

The normative flow of prophecy within God's Kingdom goes hand in hand with what we have studied about Jesus' stated purposes for sending the Holy Spirit:

However, when He, the Spirit of truth, has come, He will guide you into all truth; for He will not speak on His own authority, but whatever He hears He will speak; and He will tell you things to come. He will glorify Me, for He will take of what is Mine and declare it to you (John 16:13-14).

Most modern day western Christians have some apprehensions or even fears about the exercise of prophecy. In many cases it has become easier to focus on concerns about false prophecy than on the blessing and benefit from the normative flow of prophetic ministry within the church. Perhaps it's about our ability to trust one another? Perhaps it's about that feeling of being out of control? Perhaps we haven't done a good job of teaching and modeling the proper use of prophecy in our churches?

So how can we know if prophecy is from the Holy Spirit? God's word definitely gives us sufficient guidelines against which to judge words that are spoken along with the claim that the speaker heard them from the Lord. First of all, the scriptures are not talking about receiving wandering prophets who just happen to show up on your doorstep. God will take care of the level of conviction when a seaweed bedraggled guy who smells like he has been in the belly of a whale for three days shows up and calls a city to repent. In a normal flow of the gift of prophecy, God is sending word to His people typically through one of their own number whom they know and whose level of maturity is known among them. Why would God want to or need to send me word through someone else? I can think of a number of reasons which include: the limitations of each of us as individuals, God's desire that we work as a team and inter-depend on one another, and our tendency to get into situations where we are distracted by the world or are not listening to God.

For the gift of prophecy to be welcomed in a healthy way as a gift from God in our churches and fellowships the following guidelines from the scripture need to be respected:

There is no requirement that prophecy be wrapped in the words 'Thus saith the Lord!' More often than not a fellow believer may simply tell us what they believe the Lord is showing them. Prophecy will always line up with the written word of God, *for prophecy never came by the will of man, but holy men of God spoke as they were moved by the Holy Spirit (2 Peter 1:21).*

Is the prophecy from God? If there is any question about this then test it. *Do not quench the Spirit. Do not despise prophecies. Test all things; hold fast what is good (1 Thessalonians 5:19-21). Beloved, do not believe every spirit, but test the spirits, whether they are of God; because many false prophets have gone out into the world (1 John 4:1).* Is the one bringing the prophecy known to you as a mature and honest follower of Christ? Is the prophetic word in accord with the scriptures? If necessary take the prophecy back to the Lord in prayer and ask Him to confirm its meaning.

Is the one bringing the prophecy following the scriptural guidelines given in *1 Corinthians 14*?

But he who prophesies speaks edification and exhortation and comfort to men (1 Corinthians 14:3). He who prophesies edifies the church (1 Corinthians 14:3). Note that edification or 'to edify' is a seldom used English word which simply means to build up. In general, exhortation means to urge, advise, or caution. These guidelines tell us that the general purpose of this gift from God is to bring words which can: build up, encourage us to keep moving forward, or comfort us in hard times. This does not mean that God will never bring a word of warning or judgment but it certainly means that proclamations of warning and judgment are not the main function of the gift.

But if all prophesy, and an unbeliever or an uninformed person comes in, he is convinced by all, he is convicted by all. And thus the secrets of his heart are revealed; and so, falling down on his face, he will worship God and report that God is truly among you (1 Corinthians 14:24-25). In this guideline we learn that God intends for the gift of prophecy to be used to reveal secrets in a way that brings conviction leading to salvation. Our best example is Jesus, Who used the prophetic word properly to stir conviction in a group of men when He said: *"He who is without sin among you, let him throw a stone at her first." And again He stooped down and wrote on the ground. Then those who heard it, being convicted by their conscience, went out one by one, beginning with the oldest even to the last (John 8:7-9).*

A true prophet of God accepts their proper role within His church with submission to the words and guidance of others and without the need to dominate. *Let two or three prophets speak, and let the others judge. But if anything is revealed to another who sits by, let the first keep silent. For you can all prophesy one by one, that all may learn and all may be encouraged. And the spirits of the prophets are subject to the prophets. For God is not the author of confusion but of peace, as in all the churches of the saints (1 Corinthians 14:29-33).*

Ministers of God's New Testament:

And we have such trust through Christ toward God. Not that we are sufficient of ourselves to think of anything as being from ourselves, but our sufficiency is from God, who also made us sufficient as ministers of the new covenant, not of the letter but of the Spirit; for the letter kills, but the Spirit gives life (2 Corinthians 3:4-6).

In effectively waging war we must accept the mantle of responsibility which God has placed over us. We have been redeemed to serve His purposes and God alone is the one who enables us both to war and to win. Knowing that we have been made 'sufficient' as ministers by God Most High we clearly find our life through His Spirit as we seek God for daily living and destiny.

Putting It into Practice:

Because the weapons of our warfare are not carnal but mighty through God (see *2 Corinthians 10:3-5*) be serious about putting off the inclinations and deeds of your flesh. The battles of God are not won by using the tactics of this world.

Wait on the Lord daily seeking His direction for your life and renewing your strength (see *Isaiah 40:31*).

Invest yourself in time spent with the Lord to refine your faith. *Giving all diligence, add to your faith virtue, to virtue knowledge, to knowledge self-control, to self-control perseverance, to perseverance godliness, to godliness brotherly kindness, and to brotherly kindness love. For if these things are yours and abound, you will be neither barren nor unfruitful in the knowledge of our Lord Jesus Christ* (2 Peter 1:5-8).

Be sober and be vigilant, knowing the tactics of your enemy (see *1 Peter 5:8*). Be prepared and ready for Jesus, one of the servants of His house whom He can count on: *"Let your waist be girded and your lamps burning; and you yourselves be like men who wait for their master, when he will return from the wedding, that when he comes and knocks they may open to him immediately. Blessed are those servants whom the master, when he comes, will find watching"* (Luke 12:35-37).

Seek God for the specifics of a life that influences the world around you in His name. *Contend earnestly for the faith which was once for all delivered to the saints (Jude 3). Learn to do good; seek justice, rebuke the oppressor; defend the fatherless, plead for the widow (Isaiah 1:17).*

Endure hardships, keep and repeatedly bring yourself back on track as one enlisted by the Lord (see *2 Timothy 2:3-4*). Settle any issues you still have regarding worldly prosperity. God will take care of what you need as you follow Him and no one can serve two masters (see *Matthew 6:24* and *2 Corinthians 9:8*).

Put on the whole armor of God and don't take it back off.

The fate of this world in our day and age is in our hands: *if My people who are called by My name will humble themselves, and pray and seek My face, and turn from their wicked ways, then I will hear from heaven, and will forgive their sin and heal their land (2 Chronicles 7:14).*

And do this, knowing the time, that now it is high time to awake out of sleep; for now our salvation is nearer than when we first believed. The night is far spent, the day is at hand.

Therefore let us cast off the works of darkness, and let us put on the armor of light. Let us walk properly, as in the day, not in revelry and drunkenness, not in lewdness and lust, not in strife and envy. *But put on the Lord Jesus Christ,* and make no provision for the flesh, to fulfill its lusts (Romans 13:11-14).

Chapter Ten

Ministering Healing and Deliverance

Healing and Deliverance are two areas which were part of the regular and normal flow of Jesus' ministry. Jesus also declares His intention that His works are to continue through His people. *"Most assuredly, I say to you, he who believes in Me, the works that I do he will do also; and greater works than these he will do, because I go to My Father. And whatever you ask in My name, that I will do, that the Father may be glorified in the Son. If you ask anything in My name, I will do it"* (John 14:12-14).

Jesus certainly 'did' many different 'works' during His three year earthly ministry. He taught the truth of God, shared, gave, worshipped, prayed, had compassion on the multitudes, spread the Gospel, and laid down His life for all of us. In many ways these things have been the main focus and baseline of Christian life and ministry for over two thousand years.

In a sense, it has been easier for believers to involve themselves in these same activities and to mentally separate them from Jesus' other 'works', which are of a seemingly more supernatural nature, being: miracles, healings, and deliverance from demons. We have already discussed the two views which modern believers ascribe to Jesus. The first view focuses on Jesus having come to earth as God Almighty doing things which we could never and probably should never think of doing since we are not God. The second view focuses on Jesus, who is God Almighty, having lived an earthly life as our example of how a person who is properly connected to and seeking God should live. Which of these two views supports the words of Jesus, which we just read from *John 14*, where Jesus expects that His believers will do the works that He did?

Taking this one step further, we examine Jesus' motivations. All of the things which Jesus did and said, regardless of whether we would consider them natural or supernatural, were driven by His motivations. Jesus was clearly motivated by love and compassion; we see that theme again and again in the Gospels. However, His main motivation was obedience to the Father (see *Philippians 2:4-8*).

Jesus clearly let us know: *I can of Myself do nothing. As I hear, I judge; and My judgment is righteous, because I do not seek My own will but the will of the Father who sent Me (John 5:30)*. Quite a bit of the Gospel of John is devoted to teaching us about this connection between the 'works' of Jesus and Jesus being a 'Seeker' here to do the will of the Father. *For the Father loves the Son, and shows Him all things that He Himself does; and He will show Him greater works than these, that you may marvel (Jesus - John 5:20)*.

Now we come full circle. Historically, believers have found it easier to follow the 'works' of Jesus which are more natural, perhaps more privately done, and for which there may be no immediate expectation of results. Somehow it is easier to shy away from those 'works' of

Jesus which we seem to feel are more supernatural and where our own connection to Jesus might be questioned if our declarations of a miracle, healing, or deliverance produced no visible results. You see, for the most part we are often still scared; just find the right area of life and we can be found cowering and hiding with the rest. But it should not be so, was never intended by Jesus to be so.

God's way out of this dilemma is for us to recognize that all of Jesus' works, whether deemed natural or supernatural, were done in the context of seeking God to learn what should be done. When we finally come to this realization it will begin to dawn on us that we may have wasted quite a bit of our time on this earth in efforts to: teach, share, give, worship, pray, have compassion on the multitudes, spread the Gospel, and lay down our lives, for which we did not seek any direction from the Father.

In many cases, any fruit which resulted ended up being of God's mercy. However, a life lived upon assumptions of 'what would Jesus do?' is not the same as a life lived in the manner in which Jesus lived it, where He sought and listened to the Father in order to do the Father's will and finish His works. *Jesus said to them, "My food is to do the will of Him who sent Me, and to finish His work" (John 4:34).*

Imagine the immensity of healing and deliverance which would result from Jesus' worldwide church embracing life and ministry in this manner of Jesus, vs. living in assumptions about what Jesus would do. Can you and I get to that place where God is free to lead us in the 'works' of Jesus and even to where we do 'greater works' as Jesus said? Can we bring ourselves to see the miracle of God in simply sharing bread with the hungry as well as declaring to the lame *'arise and walk'*? Let's start by learning a few important things about two of those 'supernatural' areas of Jesus' works: healing and deliverance.

Note that as we continue through this chapter you will notice scripture references to 'signs and wonders' which surely include a greater scope than just healing and deliverance. Jesus stilled the storm on the Sea of Galilee, rescuing His shipmates from drowning. This was definitely a sign and a wonder to those who witnessed it. Perhaps the Lord has or will use you to manifest signs and wonders other than healing and deliverance? I don't doubt that He will as you stay open and ready for His use. However for purposes of this chapter, I will limit myself to a main focus on healing and deliverance which definitely constituted the main portion of the signs and wonders we read of in the Bible.

Healing and Being Healed:

My own experiences with healing have kept me in wonder with regard to how God operates. Over the course of my life in Christ I may have encountered more actual events of healing than I can count on my ten fingers but probably not more than I could count on both my fingers and my toes.

At times God has used me in healings. I don't sense that I have the spiritual gifts of healing or miracles in any constant sense, but I am open to being used in this manner. In my experience, which I believe to be supported by the scriptures, the body of Christ is intended to function as a whole. So long as we all remain willing and teachable the Lord will distribute among the members of His body the activities and gifting which will bring about the 'works' and 'greater works' which Jesus wants to accomplish (see 1 Corinthians 12:27-30).

Recounting some of my own experiences, there have been times when the Lord has used me to bring the compassion of healing to others. Fevers have departed and bones have knit as God moved me to pray for my own children at various times. My first pastor and I prayed over an elderly member of our church who was suffering at home from a broken rib. She leaped up declaring 'the pain is gone!' The next day she hiked up the double stairs into church. I have been a member of an elder's group through which God was pleased to heal a brother of cancer. The tumor remained and was surgically removed, however when diagnosed it was no longer the cancer which had been revealed by biopsy nor did the brother have cancer anymore.

There were other such events, some of which happened in the form of instant healings which I would call miracles. Others took time and responded to the Lord's grace as a course of events but in the end the people were healed just the same.

In my own body, two events stand out. My right knee had two surgeries over the years to repair a torn meniscus and around age 50 my left knee seemed to be headed toward surgery as well. I love the great outdoors and at this point I was wearing double knee braces to walk over hill and over dale. Neither of these prior surgeries was affected without seeking God in prayer and both times the results were positive but temporary. It was a guest speaker who stopped himself to say that God was showing him knees were to be healed. Everyone who has problems with their knees please stand up. Well, of course I stood up and he directed those near to us to lay on hands and pray. My knees were healed instantly. I have worn no braces these last few years and I can hike and exercise hard having what amounts to brand new knees, praise God!

My second event was considerably more drawn out but in the end it bore wonderful fruit. I had suffered for years with early enlargement of the prostate and had certainly sought the Lord for relief on a regular basis.

Working with a doctor, I had tried the available daily medications. Being an ex-addict, I absolutely hate being dependent upon a substance for my daily living. One drug was just too weak to get the job done. The other allowed me to relieve myself for the most part but I suffered every side effect until it was just killing me. By this time I had enlisted my church to pray weekly. I also asked our elders group for a session of prayer and they faithfully sought the Lord. Well, what happened? Because today I am fully healed and delivered from this condition.

I had come to the prayer room by myself one day just to wait on the Lord, and boom, He opened my mind and showed me that my lack of 'flow' was synonymous with a corresponding lack of flow from my soul and spirit toward my fellow man. It made perfect sense to me. It may not be obvious but I have always been a bit abnormally introverted where effort is required for me to engage with others. God was simply using the malady of my body to call me up another step in ministry. I had lapsed from my main gifting over the past few years into useful but not people-primary ministries and had also become absorbed by the demands of my day job. Having yielded this to the Lord, He now directed me to visit my doctor and ask for a permanent solution to my physical problem. The surgery I had was blessed from start to finish. I had an incredible day and night in the hospital surrounded by the best of people and have recovered to such an extent that I could make good money winning pissing contests against 20-year-olds. Praise God, the relief of being restored back to a function which I had taken for granted has restored my ability to sleep and my health. The direction God gave me for my spirit has also launched me back into the deep end of living out my gifting. In this, and in the restoration of my knees, I understand something of the heart of the sufferer and the gratitude of the healed.

I share these experiences here because there are at least a few things that should catch our attention. First of all, at times the Lord just simply heals in mercy, no strings attached. After all He loves us. At other times God is after something within the person and again, because of His love, He allows or uses circumstances of suffering to get at the core issue. Finally, medical knowledge and advancements have been a gift from God which many times He chooses to use. God is honored when He is our first stop and in being asked 'Lord what should I do?' We should neither despise nor make an idol of the gift of medicine and medical aide; not everyone on our planet has access to these blessings. I have been doubled over all night suffering from a kidney stone, which they say is the closest men get to experiencing childbirth. I sought the Lord and dragged myself into the ER where you can bet I valued both the skills of the people who know how to address a stone as well as the advanced painkillers that were available to me. Can you imagine me not praising God for having given such knowledge to men?

Where are the bulk of God's miracles taking place in our world today? Where are we seeing the most bona-fide cases of people being healed or delivered in Jesus name? We read about or see it first hand in the developing world where the poor, who are rich in faith, don't have much medical access.

Does that mean God will not work direct miracles or healings in western nations where medical access abounds? Not at all, but it might make us question how quick we are to run to the doctor before seeking the Lord. Also we should note that even the poor seek Him and are sometimes told 'no'. The Apostle Paul brought his own malady to the Lord three times and was told 'no' and given the reason for it (see *2 Corinthians 12:7-10*).

As in all areas of our lives, if we would follow Jesus, then the answer will be to ask God and do what He says.

In *2 Kings 20:1-10*, King Hezekiah was dying and the Prophet Isaiah had told him to put his house in order. Hezekiah had been a God fearing King his whole life and now he prayed to and wept before the Lord his God. The Lord sent Isaiah back to proclaim a healing which would add 15 more years to Hezekiah's life. It was not to be a miracle of instant healing but, as the Lord directed, the medicine of the day was applied and a sign was given to instill faith in recovery. What powerful things the gift of faith sent by God can bring.

The Nuts and Bolts of Ministering Healing:
If we are to work with God to minister healing, our first stop has to be a motivation check.

Is our focus on ourselves as a minister or appropriately on those in need of ministry? God is merciful and may use you in healing others even during times where you don't yet see a hidden pride. But be sure that He will also want to work such kinks out of you so that you can be a vessel cleansed and ready for His use.

What is it that you really want for the other person? To be sure, God is not likely to use us with much regularity in the lives of people we care nothing about.

Check your heart because it is natural to want to see others simply relieved of suffering which God has the power to do at any time. We can struggle internally in the face of suffering, especially when it involves the helpless. It can be very easy for us to fall into doubting and questioning God where our soul cries out the question: Why? While doubts and questions may be our natural reaction to a situation of crisis or suffering, they are not helpful or useful in resolving the matter at hand.

Consider this scene: you are involved in a traffic accident and you surely have a broken arm and a broken leg. Your abdomen hurts, so it is unclear whether there is any real internal damage or not. Your family and neighbors saw the whole thing and for the most part are rushing about in a panic. Your favorite cousin is sympathetically holding your hand but that's all they know how to do. What are you hoping for in this moment? You are hoping that someone, anyone, who is competent, level headed, knowledgeable, and not in a panic will show up and see what can be done for you.

It can be a struggle to be that competent, level headed, and knowledgeable person who is aligned in God's motivation for others and ready to be on the scene.

In searching the scriptures we observe two main avenues through which God has chosen to bring healing as well as other signs and wonders. The first is God's ability to simply heal or perform acts of power whenever He so chooses. The second focuses on dialog, discernment, and prayer. It is important for us to learn what to expect as normal within our role as ministers of God's Kingdom.

In reviewing God's choice to allow healing power to flow through or from individuals we learn from the experience of the multitudes in the ministry of our Lord Jesus Christ. *And the whole multitude sought to touch Him, for power went out from Him and healed them all (Luke 6:19*, also see *Matthew 12:15, Mark 3:10, Luke 5:17)*. In the same manner the testimony of Jesus continued after His resurrection. *Men of Israel, hear these words: Jesus of Nazareth, a Man attested by God to you by miracles, wonders, and signs which God did through Him in your midst, as you yourselves also know — (Acts 2:22)*.

This ministry of God's direct mercy continued through Jesus' Apostles: *so that they brought the sick out into the streets and laid them on beds and couches, that at least the shadow of Peter passing by might fall on some of them. Also a multitude gathered from the surrounding cities to Jerusalem, bringing sick people and those who were tormented by unclean spirits, and they were all healed (Acts 5:15-16). Then fear came upon every soul, and many wonders and signs were done through the apostles (Acts 2:43).*

When threatened with persecution if they continued these activities, the Apostles and believers prayed that God's mercy would continue. *"Now, Lord, look on their threats, and grant to Your servants that with all boldness they may speak Your word, by stretching out Your hand to heal, and that signs and wonders may be done through the name of Your holy Servant Jesus" (Acts 4:29-30).*

Healing and wonders were an active part of the ministry and missionary journeys we have on record for the early church. *Therefore they stayed there a long time, speaking boldly in the Lord, who was bearing witness to the word of His grace, granting signs and wonders to be done by their hands (Acts 14:3). Now God worked unusual miracles by the hands of Paul, so that even handkerchiefs or aprons were brought from his body to the sick, and the diseases left them and the evil spirits went out of them (Acts 19:11-12, also see Act 15:12).*

We are also given to understand by the scriptures that such ministry from God is to extend beyond Jesus and the original Apostles. *And Stephen, full of faith and power, did great wonders and signs among the people (Acts 6:8).* Mark records Jesus' words which once again affirm what we commonly call the Great Commission: *And He said to them, "Go into all the world and preach the gospel to every creature. He who believes and is baptized will be saved; but he who does not believe will be condemned. And these signs will follow those who believe: In My name they will cast out demons; they will speak with new tongues; they will take up serpents; and if they drink anything deadly, it will by no means hurt them; they will lay hands on the sick, and they will recover" (Mark 16:15-18).*

It is clear that at various times and through various people God has been pleased to simply let His merciful healing power and other miracles flow to touch and bear witness to individuals or multitudes. *Acts 14:3* tells us that God *'was bearing witness to the word of His grace.'*

In a deeper look into the scriptures, it becomes plain that those whom God used were walking in the same manner established by Jesus. They were here to do the will of God who sent them and to finish His work (see *John 4:34*). As Stewards of the grace of God, this manner should characterize everything we do. As we make the will of Him who sends us our primary focus, then God is free to use us in any manner He chooses. Do you sense that your own life is committed to God along these lines of being here in this world to do His will? Do you have any reservations regarding the extent to which He might use you in ministering healing?

Next let's examine God's choice to allow healing through dialog, discernment, and prayer.

In John Chapter 5 Jesus opens a dialog starting with the most important question of all. *Now a certain man was there who had an infirmity thirty-eight years. When Jesus saw him lying there, and knew that he already had been in that condition a long time, <u>He said to him, "Do you want to be made well?"</u> The sick man answered Him, "Sir, I have no man to put me into the pool when the water is stirred up; but while I am coming, another steps down before me." Jesus said to him, <u>"Rise, take up your bed and walk."</u> And immediately the man was made well, took up his bed, and walked. ... Afterward Jesus found him in the temple, and said to him, <u>"See, you have been made well. Sin no more, lest a worse thing come upon you"</u>* (John 5:5-9, 14).

In another example it seems that Jesus has to lead a blind man first into some hope before there was faith to be healed. *So He took the blind man by the hand and led him out of the town. <u>And when He had spit on his eyes and put His hands on him, He asked him if he saw anything.</u> And he looked* *up and said, "I see men like trees, walking." Then He put His hands on his eyes again and made him look up. And he was restored and saw everyone clearly (Mark 8:23-25).*

In one more example we see Jesus engaging what is likely the underlying issue of a family problem, the parent had issues with faith which were blocking a healing and deliverance for the child. *So He asked his father, "How long has this been happening to him?" And he said, "From childhood. And often he has thrown him both into the fire and into the water to destroy him. But if You can do anything, have compassion on us and help us." Jesus said to him, "If you can believe, all things are possible to him who believes." Immediately the father of the child cried out and said with tears, "Lord, I believe; help my unbelief!" (Mark 9:21-24).* Jesus then proceeded to cast the demon out of the child.

It is clear from these passages that Jesus used: dialog in asking questions, discernment regarding what the cause was and what to do next, and prayer sometimes verbally declared to seal the healing. From the example of the Apostles and other believers, as well as Jesus' own words, we are to go and do likewise.

Praying over Sickness: Physical, Spiritual, or of the Soul (mind/will/emotions):

Is anyone among you suffering? Let him pray. Is anyone cheerful? Let him sing psalms. Is anyone among you sick? Let him call for the elders of the church, and let them pray over him, anointing him with oil in the name of the Lord. And the prayer of faith will save the sick, and the Lord will raise him up. And if he has committed sins, he will be forgiven. Confess your trespasses to one another, and pray for one another, that you may be healed. The effective, fervent prayer of a righteous man avails much (James 5:13-16).

'*Is anyone among you sick?*' The Greek word translated here as 'sick' is Astheneo, pronounced as-then-eh'-o, meaning: to be feeble in any sense, diseased, impotent, weak, sick.

'And the prayer of faith will save the sick, and the Lord will raise him up.' The Greek word translated here as 'sick' is different, being Kamno, pronounced kam'-no, meaning: to work, to toil, to be weary, to tire.

From Vine's Expository Dictionary of New Testament Words we find: 'The choice of this verb instead of repetition of 'Astheneo' is suggestive of the common accompaniment of sickness, (being) weariness of mind (which is the meaning of the verb Kamno), which not infrequently hinders physical recovery'.

From the use of these two words it becomes clear that the focus of meeting with the sick person is first of all to assist them to come back to a basis of faith and rest in the Lord and what He will choose to do. It is the prayer of faith which saves the Kamno sick, person in weariness of mind, who has been: working, toiling, and is tired out over their 'Astheneo sick' infirmity. And then, it is the Lord who will raise him up; we cannot do that part.

When sickness or infirmity has taken over a life, the person is often in turmoil of mind. They have probably already been crying out to God but are still sick. There may be doubts. There are typically fears; just suggest the possibility of cancer and notice what effect that has on most humans.

In leading individuals into discovery of what God wants to reveal, and perhaps do, regarding their infirmity we return to dialog and discernment as the baseline for prayer. *'And if he has committed sins, he will be forgiven. Confess your trespasses to one another, and pray for one another, that you may be healed'* (James 5:15-16). It is very poor practice and often ineffective to merely pursue and pray for symptoms. There will be many times when a little child is sick with a fever and lacks the maturity to either cry out to God or review what might be going on. In these times we lay a simple hand on the child and wait a bit for God. Is there anything He wants us to know before we ask Him to heal the child? I have typically experienced success in praying for healing for children, they are not as 'gummed' up by fears and concerns as adults often are.

Notwithstanding, it is of the utmost importance to pursue root causes in order that the other person may truly be healed. First, seek the Lord together on the cause of the infirmity, then, take the time to work and dialog together. Maybe they did just fall down and break their arm? Don't presume that there is no more to it, rather ask the Lord if there is more to it or not.

I laid up in a gully with a dislocated shoulder crying out for God to just fix it. He did not just fix it and many hours later it was re-located in a hospital by competent staff. I asked the Lord later on what this could possibly have been about. After all, I was virtually alone out in the wild seeking the Lord all day and having the best day of my life when 'wham'!

God is good and He told me: 'you have to realize that this is the third time you have fallen down while out hunting'. In short, I was given to understand the need to govern my propensity to rush into things and to learn to be more cautious. God was definitely telling me that I had not been listening to His cues from the first two falls, where I did not get seriously hurt. Gordon, slow down before something really bad happens to you. I am listening now and have since learned better and more careful methods for traversing the wilds. We might question whether I was healed when my shoulder was put back in or whether I was healed once I understood and accepted God's message which led to straightening out my behavior.

Always lead the sick person regarding any necessary resolution. Is there a need to overcome doubts? Does their faith need to be re-strengthened? Are they in need of repentance, forgiveness, restitution, or perhaps setting their house in order? Fulfilling our part in the prayer of faith which saves the Kamno sick often involves helping a person to return to Jesus' path of faith and openness to God.

Reasons for Sickness:

Is the sickness or infirmity due to sin or iniquity in the person's life? Clearly the verses in James, *if he has committed sins,* as well as Jesus statement to the man at Bethesda (see *John 5:*14) and many other scriptures indicate that this is often the case. These matters may already be apparent to the person or will have to be discovered in seeking God. Confession and decision to follow through in dealing with the sin or iniquity is often required in order for healing to come. In many cases the sin will be of a manner which can be directly repented of and where there are steps of restoration which can be taken in seeking or offering forgiveness. In other cases iniquities can be very entrenched, entrapping people in cycles of repeating sin. As an example, the alcoholic is not likely to receive a renewed liver from the Lord without renouncing their abuse of alcohol. At the same time, regardless of modern scientific opinion, there is always a root cause for 'why' a person is drinking their self to death (or abusing drugs, or consumed by anger, or being sexually out of control, etc.). Without addressing such root causes in the case of iniquity, there is rarely success in offering simple prayers for healing of the bodily conditions which result from abuse. Don't get discouraged, there is always a way forward in Jesus. I offer my first book: 'Breaking the Cycle of Slavery to Sin' as a reference specifically addressing the deeper issues of freedom from entrenched sin and iniquity.

Is the sickness unto death? *In those days Hezekiah was sick and near death. And Isaiah the prophet, the son of Amoz, went to him and said to him, "Thus says the Lord: 'Set your house in order, for you shall die, and not live.'"* (2 Kings 20:1). In cases where the Lord reveals that the sickness or infirmity is unto death, we need to work with the person to heal the accompanying toil of their mind. There is no reason that the person cannot ask the Lord for life extension; Hezekiah did that and was rewarded. However, it is damaging and not helpful when we insist on praying for healing when the Lord has said that it is the end of the line. We must work to restore or bring the person into fully trusting the Lord with their life. Make sure they have help in getting their house in order and that they are not forsaken during the end of their time on this earth.

I recently attended a lunch with fellow employees from a previous job. We were there to say goodbye to one of our co-workers who was in the process of passing on from an aggressive cancer. Before the lunch I reviewed this in my mind and purposed to make sure and ask him some questions. How was he feeling about what was happening to him? What did he believe the Lord was saying? Did he have any fears about what was coming? I did ask and to my joy I discovered that this brother was deeper in the faith and more healthy in mind that most of us. He said he had bad days and good days. He was in hospice and had been told he only had a few weeks, but that was a year ago! He was seeking the Lord daily and living out whatever God was showing him. He also had a solid group of fellow believers in his church who were supporting him. What a breath of fresh air this brother was! These questions are valid and useful and more often than not we will discover fears, concerns, and a need for support when it comes to the business of dying.

Is the sickness for the glory of God? Perhaps there is a special way in which the healing will bring God glory? *Now as Jesus passed by, He saw a man who was blind from birth.*

And His disciples asked Him, saying, "Rabbi, who sinned, this man or his parents, that he was born blind?" <u>Jesus answered, "Neither this man nor his parents sinned, but that the works of God should be revealed in him"</u> (John 9:1-3). Reading in *John 9* we understand that this was a full grown man who had suffered this state of blindness his whole life. Jesus healed him and God was glorified: first in the neighbors who marveled at God's works hopefully awakening them, next in the Pharisees who despised God's works to their own destruction, and finally in the man who believed in Jesus receiving salvation for all eternity.

Is the sickness the result of the sin of others against this person or against humanity? Believers I have worked with in Nigeria have sent me photos of those maimed from acts of persecution. Our daily news is filled with the suffering of bystanders at the hands of the wicked. Unfortunately in our day and age, families often succumb to external pressures bringing hurt and damage to their own through words and actions. If sinful actions on the part of others are discerned to be the cause then we can simply pray for God's merciful healing. However, don't forget to assist the person to work through their troubled mind until they are at a place of peace and able to trust in and receive from the Lord.

'*Call for the elders of the church.*' Often in our day and age we don't always have elders in our churches that are versed in or willing to perform this function. I am blessed to be a member of a church where the elders are willing. In the worst case it may have to start with you both in taking your own infirmities to the Lord and in offering to follow through with others. Be willing to model this and be willing to call the elders of your church into this without condemnation. The worst that they can say is 'no' and then God is free through you to bring whatever example He wants to bring into your fellowship. It is fruitless to get mad at others who don't see something you think you see. Instead, seek the Lord to find out what you should do and then walk in obedience.

'The effective, fervent prayer of a righteous man avails much.' Without controversy, the scripture is telling us that healings, along with other signs and wonders, are blessed through those who are righteous. Without further review on that subject we know that this means a person who is redeemed through the salvation of Christ and also living in the honest flow of becoming a vessel cleansed and ready for the Master's use.

Not everyone gets well and the percentage is actually very low when we pray using the quick 'hope-so' kind of prayers that are typical among western believers in our day. As we have seen, there are often reasons for infirmity. It is not that God's arm is shortened. Rather, it is we who have not understood, employed, or at times been open to the effort which it often takes. In facing serious illness or injury we have often been a mixture of running to the doctor first and offering prayers of hope vs. prayers based on seeking and substance. In ministering healing, we have either had little to offer due to our lack of understanding or we have encouraged the same path of doctors and hope-so prayers.

How would the Biblical methods we have now reviewed change your approach in regard to seeking healing or ministering healing prayers for those in need? Can you see how all of these things hinge on your own connection with God and submission as His servant, ready to be directed and sent as Jesus was?

Ministering Deliverance:

Ministering deliverance involves exercising authority over demon spirits and leading individuals in recovering areas of life which they have surrendered to the evil one.

A Biblical understanding of the need for deliverance from evil spirits separates into two basic categories. First and most common is where the devil and demons exercise domination over one or more surrendered areas of a person's life. Secondarily a person could actually be possessed.

To begin with, it is important for us to know our enemy. The Apostle Paul indicates that Satan takes advantage through ignorance: *lest Satan should take advantage of us; for we are not ignorant of his devices (2 Corinthians 2:11).*

We have already covered this subject of knowing the enemy in chapters four, six, and nine. In short summary: we learned that Satan, and therefore every demon, is a sinfully self-focused creature the same as fallen man. Because of this he has no trouble at all planting directive decision urging thoughts, temptations, and suggestions into our minds. We also learned that God has already declared an end to the schemes of this madman (see *Isaiah 14:12-15*).

Next, as ministers of deliverance, as well as for any effective ministry, we must be spiritually prepared for battle. We have also covered this in chapter six Embracing Maturity and chapter nine Waging War. *Put on the whole armor of God, that you may be able to stand against the wiles of the devil (Ephesians 6:11).*

Ministering Recovery from Domination:

Demonic and even satanic domination of various areas of human life can be extreme to where we would say, 'That is a wicked person'. Jesus actually accused some of the Jews of this very directly. *You are of your father the devil, and the desires of your father you want to do. He was a murderer from the beginning, and does not stand in the truth, because there is no truth in him. When he speaks a lie, he speaks from his own resources, for he is a liar and the father of it (John 8:44).*

More commonly though is the level of domination found even in those we would not call wicked persons. A simplified example and anatomy of how domination enters from the father of lies and gets established in a person to the point where one or many areas of their life are in a frightful mess is as follows:

Father to Child: 'You will never amount to anything.'
Mother to Child: 'You are so stupid.'

There are two very common and natural responses, both being from our fallen nature, which result when a child is confronted by a parent like this. In either of these responses the lie which the parent spoke becomes internalized within the child.

The first response is: I guess I won't amount to anything, I guess I am so stupid. In this subdued response the child goes with the flow, accepting the lie as truth.

The second response is: Oh yes I will amount to something! No I am not stupid! In this rebellious response the child resists the flow, reacting to the lie to prove it wrong.

Both of these natural responses lead to bondage. Both are internalized by the child and become what the scriptures call iniquity or moral wickedness within our hearts which then drive us to actions or inactions. Both responses become the basis for behaviors that either go with the flow of the lie or specifically waste time resisting what is in actuality a lie to begin with. Rare is the child who will look up at their parent and say in healthy reply: 'that is not what Jesus says about me, that is not what God believes about me.'

Taking Adam and Eve as an example, in *Genesis Chapter 2* we see Eve, and then Adam, being told a lie by Satan. Their response was to go with the flow; they believed and internalized that lie initially resulting in the behavior of disobeying God. Now they, and all their offspring, are dominated by demonic moral wickedness which requires the deliverance of being born again through Jesus Christ to escape its foundational effect.

Considering the example of Saul of Tarsus who became the Apostle Paul we find that Saul had fully embraced the 'lie', actually many lies, of obtaining righteousness through legalistic religion, in his case Judaism. Embracing legalism as if it were truth resulted in behaviors that went as far as rounding up the followers of Jesus for execution. Saul was dominated, a tool of the devil, until Jesus delivered him by vision and then the ministry of prophetic prayer though Ananias (see *Acts Chapter 9*).

It may be apparent at this point that everyone not saved through Jesus is dominated by the devil. What may be less apparent is that even the saved can be holding onto areas in their lives where they have internalized lies and are producing bad fruit of bad behaviors because of this. In that sense they are also dominated in those areas of their lives. The good news is that Jesus came to set us free. *And you shall know the truth, and the truth shall make you free (John 8:32). Jesus said to him, "I am the way, the truth, and the life. No one comes to the Father except through Me"* (John 14:6).

As humans we are designed by God to yield ourselves and respond within a hierarchy of leadership and obedience. We are supposed to yield ourselves to God but often yield ourselves to lies instead. The scripture is clear that we are slaves to whom we yield ourselves, either to God or to un-godliness. *Do you not know that to whom you present yourselves slaves to obey, you are that one's slaves whom you obey, whether of sin leading to death, or of obedience leading to righteousness (Romans 6:16)?*

What godly decision could Eve and Adam have made that would have changed the course of human history?

Put yourself in the shoes of the child hearing from mom or dad that they are just no good. What godly decisions can be made by that child which would not lead into bondage? Are there decisions which you have made by which you are currently in bondage?

Recovery from domination is actually very basic; the lie believed or resisted must be exposed and then rejected as such. At the same time it needs to be replaced with a godly decision that does not lead to bondage.

Consider the following example: God involves you with a person who is always down on themselves, to the point where they cannot or will not involve themselves in service to the Lord even though they received Him and were baptized into the church. What might be the problem?

Let's assume that we are praying for them and God is working on them to the point where they see this and want to become free. By the way, it is impossible to help deliver a person who doesn't see the need. Remember Jesus question to the man by the pool of Bethesda in *John Chapter 5*: *"Do you want to be made well?"* At this point we can proceed in the same manner as with any infirmity; a bit of dialog and discernment coupled with prayer, perhaps over time, should reveal the lie upon which this area of their life is based. Ask sensitive but probing questions as the Spirit of God leads you. Why does this behavior exist in your life? What purpose is this behavior serving in your life? What happens inside of you when the need for this behavior arises? Challenge their belief system when it is out of true with the word of God. Why do you believe that? Get to the root issue which may include some time spent with them in quietly listening to the Spirit of God.

Let's assume the example where as a child they had accepted and internalized mom's words 'You are so stupid', and they now realize that this is the main root cause of their behaviors. Simple prayers can now follow where you lead this person in renouncing this as a lie of the devil and rejecting his control over their life. They also need to receive God's truth about themselves and to decide that His truth will be the new foundation for this area of their life from now on. The truth in this case may simply be revealed to them by the Spirit of God or may need some help from the scriptures, 'you are wonderfully made' (see *Psalm 139:14*), 'God is for me' (see *Romans 8:31-32*), 'the Father Himself loves me' (see *John 16:27*).

Do you see how domination has and does affect perhaps both yourself and the people you know? Satan incessantly works his schemes, enabled by our ignorance. Following Jesus is the path out of the dark woods of ignorance and deception.

Demonic Possession:

It is important to note that in all cases where we see Jesus dealing directly with delivering a person from demonic possession there is no real interaction with the possessed person until after they are delivered (for one example see *Luke 8:26-39*). At times Jesus seems to have needed to ask a few questions of the demon(s) or of others but He always dealt very directly with the demon itself.

What can we learn about ministering deliverance from demonic possession? This is an area of interest for me as well. My experiences in this area are few and in wanting to be a vessel cleansed and ready for my Master's use I would like to be armed with what understanding is available from the scriptures.

The scriptures indicate that we won't have to wonder, it will be very apparent that a demon is actually in control of and possessing a person. We don't see Jesus or the disciples in the scriptures having trouble identifying whether possession was involved. It may be constant control like the man possessed with a legion (see *Mark 5:6-10*). It may be during times of fits as seems to be the case in the boy whose father struggled with faith (see *Mark 9:14-29*).

Jesus and the Apostles did not see a demon behind every tree and certainly did not ascribe satanic influence to every wicked behavior they saw in man. It would seem that real instances of possession are most common in areas of the world where idolatry abounds. Whereas we understand that a physical idol is nothing, yet the Apostle Paul has given us to understand that these are deceptive demons which are worshipped by those who believe in them (see *1 Corinthians 10:18-22*). We can rejoice if the Lord has us living in an area where such is not common. On the other hand may we always be ready to assist in rescuing the possessed as the Lord leads.

Ministering in a migrant camp, there was a young girl whose behavior was evidently not her own. God only knows what must have happened to her. In the end she would not allow me to pray for her and in such a case there would have had to be some willing adult authority who could insist that she receive ministry. I have known one other man who shifted between four very distinct personalities at every attempt to expose what was really going on in his life. Both of these were very apparently matters of possession and I sensed that the Holy Spirit affirmed this.

In all cases Jesus is recorded as having directly commanded demons rather than talking to the possessed person about their possession. Demons were also subject to Jesus' followers in His name. Jesus sent out the 12 Apostles and again the 70 disciples with power and they returned saying that even the evil spirits are subject to us in your name (see *Mark 6:13* and *Luke 10:17-20*).

From this we understand that demons do not get a choice regarding whether or not they will obey the follower of Christ and we should never give them one as this is a strict matter of authority. In one case Jesus allowed them to enter pigs but there was never a bargain about whether they could continue to possess the person. As mentioned in our section on healing, we do see Jesus dialoging with the father who was in unbelief and needing to believe before his child could be delivered. Unbelief within the child's family may have been the root cause for this possession; Jesus insisted on addressing it before commanding the demon to depart.

At times Jesus seemed to need to identify the demons by name before having full command over them. The reason for this is not fully apparent although in the case of *Luke 8:30* it did clarify that there were many to be cast out and not one. The demons definitely knew who Jesus was (see *Mark 1:34*). They also know whether or not you are a follower of Jesus. The sons of Sceva got a beating from a possessed man because although they were not followers of Jesus they thought they would give deliverance a try (see *Acts 19:13-17*).

Jesus has directly commissioned His followers to have power over the enemy. *"Behold, I give you the authority to trample on serpents and scorpions, and over all the power of the enemy, and nothing shall by any means hurt you. Nevertheless do not rejoice in this, that the spirits are subject to you, but rather rejoice because your names are written in heaven"* *(Luke 10:19-20)*. In explaining how He cast out demons Jesus said, *if I cast out demons with the finger of God, surely the kingdom of God has come upon you. When a strong man, fully armed, guards his own palace, his goods are in peace. But when a stronger than he comes upon him and overcomes him, he takes from him all his armor in which he trusted, and divides his spoils (Luke 11:20-22)*. Along with this example of being the stronger who overcomes we are also told that the gates of Hades will not prevail over Jesus' church and: *"I will give you the keys of the kingdom of heaven, and whatever* you bind on earth will be bound in heaven, and whatever you loose on earth will be loosed in heaven" (see Matthew 16:18-19). These scriptures are yet another example of Jesus' intention that His followers would do His *'works'* and *'greater works'*.

We can rest assured that it is God's will to deliver those who are tormented by possession and to bring healing into this world. Jesus was here to fulfill the will of the Father and we have been placed into history and redeemed in order to carry on that same purpose.

The word which God sent to the children of Israel, preaching peace through Jesus Christ — He is Lord of all — that word you know, which was proclaimed throughout all Judea, and began from Galilee after the baptism which John preached: how God anointed Jesus of Nazareth with the Holy Spirit and with power, who went about doing good and healing all who were oppressed by the devil, for God was with Him (Acts 10:36-38).

Inasmuch then as the children have partaken of flesh and blood, He Himself likewise shared in the same, that through death He might destroy him who had the power of death, that is, the devil, and release those who through fear of death were all their lifetime subject to bondage (Hebrews 2:14-15).

Putting It into Practice:

Ministering Healing and Deliverance are two of the many facets of ministry into which the Lord may choose to lead you. At the same time they are definitely part of the greater whole of life and ministry under Jesus' leadership. Having a clear grasp of scriptural truth in these areas will keep us from error. However knowledge can only take us so far and, as with any other area of seeking the Lord for daily living and destiny, ministering healing and deliverance can only be learned through an openness to engage in and experience them with the Lord. Step out as the Lord leads you, rely on His promises in which we do taste and find that the Lord is good.

Chapter Eleven

Conclusion
(Where we have been and where we are going.)

We have covered a considerable array of concepts and scriptures over the last ten chapters. All focused on a baseline and foundational theme which God has woven carefully throughout His word the Bible.

My grandchildren love to play treasure hunt. I write clues on small slips of paper, each leading to the next clue and the last one leading to some small 'treasure'. I'm careful to distribute these in such a manner as: 'next to the toaster', 'on the backyard swing', 'under Grandma's pillow', and so forth such that the little nippers are rushing from one end of the house to the other and back again following the one or two who can read. And the Lord God said: *And you will seek Me and find Me, when you search for Me with all your heart. I will be found by you, says the LORD (Jeremiah 29:13-14).*

We have been on a bit of a treasure hunt together through the pages of this book and I hope that at every turn you have found Him, Who is and always will be our treasure, the Lord Jesus Christ Himself. We have understood that we were: 'Created on Purpose'. We have engaged with the salvation of God in: 'Taking the Biggest Step'. We understand what it takes to be a person who is: 'Seeking God for Who He is'. We know the implications of being created: 'In the Image of God'. We are coming into our own in: 'Interacting with His In-dwelling Spirit'. We are being cleansed and readied for the Master's use as we face the necessity of: 'Embracing Maturity'. Our feet are solidly on the path of: 'Becoming a Friend of God'. We are living in His presence daily: 'Waiting on the Lord'. We have joined God's army willing and ready for: 'Waging War'. We understand the fundamentals and are available to God for: 'Ministering Healing and Deliverance'.

From here the path leads only forward as you and I follow Jesus each day and remain open and sensitive to the leadings of His word and Spirit. As it is written: *for in Him we live and move and have our being (Acts 17:28).*

We remember Peter's question, *"But Lord, what about this man?"* And we also remember Jesus response, *"what is that to you? You follow Me"* (See John 21:21-22). In remembering, we understand that the call of God is an individual contract between each of us and our Lord. We are not here to learn new things just to teach them by word of mouth to others. We are also not tasked with insuring that everyone else follows. We are here to take up our own responsibility and follow Jesus.

In doing so we become that fruitful branch connected to the vine of Christ. *"I am the vine, you are the branches. He who abides in Me, and I in him, bears much fruit; for without Me you can do nothing"* (John 15:5). We become an example which will affect and whet the appetite for God of those whose lives He enables us to touch. They are drawn by His love, repulsed by their fears. In our hopes they are drawn in again to receive their own contract of salvation through Christ and begin to follow. This is the great commission where you and I fulfill the call of Jesus to: "*Go therefore and make disciples of all the nations, baptizing them in the name of the Father and of the Son and of the Holy Spirit, teaching them to observe all things that I have commanded you; and lo, I am with you always, even to the end of the age.*" Amen (*Matthew 28:19-20*).

In comparison to many of the largest civilizations of past history, our current North American societies seem to be reaching their peak. Having married a European, spent quite a bit of time there, and studied some of their current affairs, I would say that the other half of the western world is a bit farther along the downhill slide than we are in North America.

What do I mean by that? Perhaps you have heard the common axiom that history repeats itself? Perhaps you have heard it in a bit stronger form: that those who ignore their history are doomed to repeat it.

History fascinates me almost as much as human behavior. I have worked at self-education with regard to history and in particular have sought those books specifically written by those who were there. Pretty much any review of history will show that human civilizations go through very predictable cycles.

In a quick sketch, some of the top shelf cycles are: rebellion and revolutions, civil wars, wars with their neighbors, followed by: potential greatness if the upper hand is won, periods of innovation, periods of strength, potential prosperity. When peace and prosperity last, the populace goes soft and becomes selfish. Their politicians in-fight and squabble for power, abandoning the interests of the people. The military is diminished by politicians who fear that they won't get away with their schemes in the presence of a strong military. These lost human reactions in the face of prolonged periods of peace and prosperity have historically always brought about the end of such societies.

Where is David's and Solomon's Jewish Kingdom? Where are the Greeks? Where are the Romans? Where are Byzantines? These latter two were even 'Christian' Empires. There are other examples but let us ask: where are the Europeans and Canadians going and what of America? We enjoy such blessing from God but, without controversy, our self-centered societies have increasingly tossed God and His ways behind our backs. God's pattern for the removal of societies was expressly outlined to the Hebrews (see *Leviticus 18:24-29* and *20:22-23*). We do find many history changing reformers during their time, who turned the people back to righteousness. But in the end Israel rejected their God and was rejected as a nation. In short God has not allowed selfish societies to continue forever. He either gives them over to their enemies or over to a people more deserving. Sometimes that happens from within.

Dear reader, it will never be society that acts to fulfill the will of God or allows God to use them as a His-Story making vessel to bring forth His Kingdom and salvation to mankind in our day and age. On the contrary it will be you and me who, as seekers of God for daily living and destiny, will be used of God to do His will. Jesus clearly told us: *"Not everyone who says to Me, 'Lord, Lord,' shall enter the kingdom of heaven, but he who does the will of My Father in heaven. Many will say to Me in that day, 'Lord, Lord, have we not prophesied in Your name, cast out demons in Your name, and done many wonders in Your name?' And then I will declare to them, 'I never knew you; depart from Me, you who practice lawlessness!'"* (Matthew 7:21-23).

Into what adventures will God call you as you seek Him during your moment under the sun? Take up the mantel which God has bestowed upon you. *Seek the LORD while He may be found, call upon Him while He is near (Isaiah 55:6).* The alternative is to remain marginal and miss your destiny.

Appendix A

The Importance of God's Word

As newborn babes, desire the pure milk of the word, that you may grow thereby, if indeed you have tasted that the Lord is gracious (1 Peter 2:2-3).

Your word is a lamp to my feet and a light for my path (Psalm 119:105).

How can a young man cleanse his way? By taking heed according to Your word. With my whole heart I have sought You; oh, let me not wander from Your commandments! Your word I have hidden in my heart, that I might not sin against You (Psalm 119:9-11).

All Scripture is given by inspiration of God, and is profitable for doctrine, for reproof, for correction, for instruction in righteousness, that the man of God may be complete, thoroughly equipped for every good work (2 Timothy 3:16-17).

Be diligent to present yourself approved to God, a worker who does not need to be ashamed, rightly dividing the word of truth (2 Timothy 2:15).

So then faith comes by hearing, and hearing by the word of God (Romans 10:17).

The grass withers, the flower fades, but the word of our God stands forever (Isaiah 40:8).

Heaven and earth will pass away, but My words will by no means pass away (Jesus - Matthew 24:35).

O earth, earth, earth, hear the word of the LORD! (Jeremiah 22:29).

He who has My commandments and keeps them, it is he who loves Me. And he who loves Me will be loved by My Father, and I will love him and manifest Myself to him (Jesus - John 14:21).

Oh, that they had such a heart in them that they would fear Me and always keep all My commandments, that it might be well with them and with their children forever! (Deuteronomy 5:29).

But grow in the grace and knowledge of our Lord and Savior Jesus Christ. To Him be the glory both now and forever. Amen (2 Peter 3:18).

Appendix B

Biblical Interpretation

The Bible has something to say about every aspect of our lives. To gain clarity from the Bible it is important that we understand what is being taught regardless of whether we initially believe it or have yet incorporated that teaching into our lives. If otherwise, then we end up with a collection of opinions or even misinformation rather than a true understanding of what is being communicated, (See *Psalm 119:105*).

Most likely we will always have a few questions that can only be truly satisfied in eternity. This is simply because few things can be fully understood without experiencing them and we are not there yet. For the most part the words and message of the Bible are plainly spoken, needing no interpretation at all. They simply mean what they say and no amount of 'interpretation' will change that.

The word 'interpretation' may make it sound complicated. However let me assure you that God has gone to great lengths to make sure that His word is fairly straightforward and not really that hard to understand. Here are the basic things which you should know:

1. In many places the Bible claims to be the Word of God.

What the Bible teaches can only be truly understood in the light of understanding this claim (or at least understanding that this claim is being made). *2 Timothy 3:16*, reveals much of the purpose of God's Word, it is: *for doctrine, for reproof, for correction, for instruction in righteousness, that the man of God may be complete, thoroughly equipped for every good work.*

2. The Bible is not of any private interpretation; rather it is inspired by God through men.

Knowing this first, that no prophecy of Scripture is of any private interpretation, for prophecy never came by the will of man, but holy men of God spoke as they were moved by the Holy Spirit (2 Peter 1:20-21).

Because of this truth we should not accept any person's private version of what the scriptures mean for today especially when such teaching is in opposition to the obvious message of the Bible.

Jesus and the writers of the New Testament warned us that many false teachers would come. Jesus said we would know them by the fruit of their lives (see *Matthew 7:16-20*). In general these are people with their own agenda, often greedy for gain, and interested in having others follow them. In many cases they are not aware of their own deception. This is yet another reason why we need to know the word of God for ourselves rather than blindly following anyone else.

3. Scripture should be used to interpret scripture. (The use of religious traditions to interpret scripture often leads to division rather than truth.)

If you have a question about what a passage means, try finding other passages in the Bible which will shed light on the same subject. Typically you will find quite a few. Like the Bereans of old, if you will apply yourself in study, then you will find that God has designed the Bible in a manner that will satisfy much of your curiosity.

Then the brethren immediately sent Paul and Silas away by night to Berea. When they arrived, they went into the synagogue of the Jews. These were more fair-minded than those in Thessalonica, in that they received the word with all readiness, and searched the Scriptures daily to find out whether these things were so. Therefore many of them believed, and also not a few of the Greeks, prominent women as well as men (Acts 17:10-12).

Division among Christians from different groups regarding various interpretations of the Bible has been going on through the centuries. In many cases it is shameful and does not serve the cause of Jesus Christ. We should remember that if another person claims to believe the basic Gospel of Jesus Christ (found in: *1 Corinthians 15:3-4*) then we have every reason to treat them as a brother or sister in the Lord even if they don't worship and serve exactly as we do.

Separation because of differences should be limited to the short list given in scripture (see *1 Corinthians 5:*11). This list tells us that we should not fellowship with someone who claims to be a Christian but is living immorally.

Other than these, disagreements about scripture should not be turned into a basis for whether or not we can fellowship together as believers.

4. Context is King! The message of any Bible passage is to be understood within the context that it was given.

Simply put: any scripture taken out of the context within which it was give can be easily misunderstood or misused. Many un-biblical teachings are founded upon scriptures taken out of their context. True context should always include understanding the purpose, setting, and situation in which the scripture is given.

It never hurts to spend some time learning about the historical settings and periods of time in which the Bible was written. What was it like to be a shepherd or to live under the dominance of Rome? Were people actually different or did they just have different pressures of necessity and circumstance? What if there were no hospitals or doctors to go to when you were ill or injured? Many around the globe in our 'modern' world still live today almost as the people of the Bible did.

Sadly, the most common example of scripture used out of context in our day and time is found when greed becomes the focus of the faith. In such settings the scriptures about giving are twisted to suggest that God wants the believer to be rich and prosperous with worldly wealth if they will only give to support certain organizations. Such 'prosperity doctrines' provide TV preachers with fancy suits but in the end followers are either disappointed or idolatrous toward money. The watching world is turned off by the greed of what they believe to be the church and the legitimate need of local congregations for monetary support is negatively impacted.

5. Biblical Symbolism. Was that meant to be taken literally?

A passage or statement from the Bible can be considered symbolic if the scripture says it is symbolic. Otherwise consideration should be given to whether or not that scripture should be taken literally.

For example a vision given to John in *Revelation Chapter 17* is of a harlot sitting on a beast. Many things are said within the chapter but at the end the angel clearly tells John that the vision is symbolic. There may be a number of things we could learn and spiritually discern from this chapter. However we are to understand that what John saw represents a city and not an actual woman on a beast. *And the woman whom you saw is that great city which reigns over the kings of the earth (Revelation 17:18)*. On the other hand this same chapter includes an angel speaking to John. There is no hint given of any symbolism and we are to understand that an actual angel from God spoke to John.

6. English Bible Translations: Three types and the general reasoning and purpose of each.

Biblical interpretation begins with the translation which you chose for yourself. The translator or translation teams who worked to create each version used specific rules and methods of approach. Because of this it is valid and important to learn something about who the translators were, what they might have believed, and what rules and methods they used when working on the English version of the Bible you may plan to use for reading and study. If there is a foreword or introduction to the translation in the front of your Bible then it would be a good idea to read it.

The first type of Bible translation can be considered 'Word for Word'. This includes translations that strive to give a corresponding English word for each Hebrew or Greek or Aramaic word from the original texts of the Bible. The goal of the translators was to strive for accuracy and typically the body of known manuscripts, fragments, and references which existed at the time were used. These are very useful in general reading, word studies, and in determining life impacting decisions based on Bible doctrine. Prominent versions: King James (KJV), New King James (NKJV), American Standard (AS), New American Standard (NAS).

The Revised Standard Version (RSV), New Revised Standard Version (NRSV), and Amplified Bible (AMP) are also considered 'Word for Word', however my understanding is that they lean very heavily on what the translators considered the two oldest large Bible Manuscripts while discounting many manuscript excerpts which are even earlier or from the same time. Their footnotes call into question a few parts of the Bible based on that premise, most notably the story of the woman caught in adultery in *John Chapter 8* and the last verses of *Mark Chapter 16*.

The second type of Bible translation can be considered 'Same Sense'. This includes translations that strive to give the reader a more accurate sense in English of what the Bible is saying in its original languages. These can be very useful for making the Bible understandable to today's Bible student. However they are not the best source for word studies and may not always be the best source when making life impacting decisions based on

Bible doctrine. Prominent versions: New International Version (NIV), New Living Translation (NLT). It is my understanding that the NIV also followed the same methods as the RSV/NRSV.

Lastly a Paraphrase is a translation, or modification of a translation, that has been put into the author's or authoring group's own words. These are usually created for a purpose, such as making the Bible very understandable for first time readers or making the Bible understandable to children or those of a lower educational level.

Be aware that some paraphrases lean toward traditional or denominational teachings. Paraphrases can be very useful for a first Bible or as a Bible choice, depending on the paraphrase and the target group of readers. Not having read all of them the only one I can recommend is the New International Reader's Version (NIRV). Many others exist including: The Way, Today's English Version (TEV), Good News Bible (GNB), and The Message (MSG).

Note that the New World Translation was created by the Jehovah's Witness group specifically to support their teachings. These include teaching that the Father and Jesus are separate gods and rejection of the born again experience where one receives the Holy Spirit. Because of this most followers of Jesus consider them to be a pseudo-Christian cult. This author does not recommend use of that book for serious reading or study of the Bible.

Above All: Seek the Lord and ask Him to show you the context and meaning of Bible passages and how they may apply to your life today.

Appendix C

Disciple me Lord! Bible Study

The study of God's Word, the Bible, has a central role in developing people as followers of Jesus Christ. In living out the gift of teaching, my goal is two-fold. First, that I may be used to teach the Word of God after the manner of Jesus and the Apostles. Next, that I may be used to train others in methods sufficient for each person to connect with the Lord and allow Him to develop them as His followers.

Study the Bible with Dependence upon God:

From *John 14:25-27* we read these words of Jesus: *"These things I have spoken to you while being present with you. But the Helper, the Holy Spirit, whom the Father will send in My name, He will teach you all things, and bring to your remembrance all things that I said to you."*

The work of God's Holy Spirit as well as God's intention to teach, train, and bring up the willing soul in His truth and lifestyle is apparent though-out scripture.

The Bible is studied best when we approach our Lord in dependence upon Him as our ultimate teacher and the revealer of truth. Open your Bible to *John Chapter 14* and this time read *verse 23* to get a more complete sense of just how close and intimate God wants to become with you.

Pray:
Before you start your reading and studies take a few moments to come to quiet prayer. Just quiet yourself before the Lord not asking anything, not wanting anything, not saying anything. Wait on Him for just a bit in full dependence. He knows what you need. He knows you are coming to read and study His Word. See *Isaiah 40:30-31*, come and renew your strength.

After some quiet waiting now ask the Holy Spirit to guide you as you study, to teach you all things, to bring to your mind what you have already learned and to show you how it all connects.

A THREE FOLD APPROACH

1) Inductive Bible Study:
Induction is a transfer of flow that happens when we get close to a source.

Inductive Bible Study focuses on getting close to the source by asking basic questions of the passage under study: *who, when, where, what, how, and why*. In addition, it is important to look at the context or setting in which the teaching is occurring so that we gain a proper framework for understanding what is being done and said.

It is often very helpful to start by simply reading through all of the passage being studied before going back to ask inductive questions.

Grab something to write with and re-read each scripture portion one section at a time. Make notes by using the following questions as applicable:

o Who are the main persons involved?
o Is there an importance to When and Where this is taking place?
o What action is happening and How is it being accomplished?
o What is being taught by these passages?
o Why is this happening or why is this being taught?

2) Capture and process any insights you have gained and any questions which the scriptures have brought up for you.

As you study the Word of God under the guidance of the Holy Spirit, you will gain insights. Take some time to record and process those insights. Do those insights ring true when compared to what you know about the rest of the counsel of the Bible? Do other scripture verses or passages come to mind which support those insights?

What questions do you have about what is being said, done, or taught in these passages of scripture? Do you know other scripture passages which give an answer to those questions? What do you think the answer(s) might be?

Spend some time with God asking Him to give you greater depth of understanding especially concerning any questions you have. It is the hungry soul which gets fed (see *Luke 1:53*). Bring your insights and any remaining questions to your Bible study group or believing friends for discussion.

3) Discern and put into practice the Life Applications which the Lord is showing to you.

As you know by now, God's Word, the Bible is filled with challenging and life changing applications which reveal the will of God to the willing. We should always expect to come away changed from our encounters with our Lord.

Look for and record life applications from your studies of the Bible. These may be commandments of God, direction on how to live, or perhaps from personal insights the Lord has given you during study. A life application, against which we choose to alter some aspect of how we have been living, should be solid and apparent rather than speculative or unsure. If there is no conviction that it is God's will for your life then move on to something else.

Spend some time with the Lord in reflection to discern how a particular application can be put into practice in your life. Life change involved in becoming a solid disciple of Jesus Christ, takes time and effort. Often details are gained and insights expanded only when we put God's word into practice with Jesus. Better to make solid application of one thing that we are certain is the will of God for us, than to make half starts on many things. Have patience, we are God's work in progress and He will use us to fulfill His purposes.

Be diligent to present yourself approved to God, a worker who does not need to be ashamed, rightly dividing the word of truth (2 Timothy 2:15).

Appendix D

Overcoming our Sinful Nature

True definitions of right and wrong are rightfully established by God. He is the ultimate authority by Whom and from Whom and for Whom are all things. Therefore, God is the only fully legitimate source of truth. Two things accompany the existence of right and wrong and these are: moral choice and consequences.

As we have seen in our studies, God presented moral choice and consequences to the very first humans in a simplistic form. It was right for them to partake of everything which God had given freely to them. However, regardless of beauty or desirability, it was wrong to partake of those things which had not been given to them.

Far beyond crossing over any particular forbidden line, man has always had the choice of whether or not we will remain in God's camp under God's authority or whether we will join the camp of those who disobey God and reject His will. Historically, the latter has most often won out even in the face of experienced consequences.

Humans, both as a race and as individuals, have consistently chosen to join the camp of those who disobey

God. Those of us born into this race are driven both by heritage and by decision. The scriptures clearly teach us that we are born with sinful natures disconnected from God (see *Romans 3:23*). Before that moment of time when we may choose to receive God's free gift of salvation, we are only able to make our choices based on our sinful nature.

We are also given to understand by the scriptures that God accepts our repentance and reception of Jesus Christ and then assists us over a lifetime to both overcome our sinful nature and to flourish in the new life which Jesus brings (see *Ephesians 1:3-6*). This is contrary to the religions of man which attempt to deal with sin where one must first do enough good to be accepted. Because of this love and patience on God's part the redeemed people of God should have a new desire to fully suppress and emerge from the bondage of our sinful nature.

One of the best proofs we have of the existence of our sinful nature is our sense of potential consequences should we sin. Because of this, most morally wrong choices are made when humans believe that no one is looking. God has given us a sense of personal privacy in that others cannot read our minds nor see through walls. However this sense of privacy was never intended to exclude God and His ever present Spirit. *And there is no creature hidden from His sight, but all things are naked and open to the eyes of Him to whom we must give account (Hebrews 4:13).*

Furthermore there are clearly times when we choose to drop our morality and blatantly shake our fist of rebellion at God. We want what we want when we want it. Times of weakness and great failure are often accompanied by inner feelings which we have not resolved such as loneliness, anger, or hurt. Drugs and alcohol also act to bring down our God given moral defenses. Often in these feelings or states we feel justified in the moment to do things we later regret.

The Apostle Paul asked the appropriate question and from his experience provided the only true answer. *O wretched man that I am! Who will deliver me from this body of death? I thank God – through Jesus Christ our Lord! (Romans 7:24-25)*. Paul recognized that if he willfully continued in sin after having been so powerfully saved through Jesus Christ that his life on earth would be wasted amounting to death and spreading death among others (see *Hebrews 10:26-31*). Paul also recognized his own powerlessness over sin and that only through making choices in the Spirit of God would he receive victory and glorify God with his life. *And if Christ is in you, the body is dead because of sin, but the Spirit is life because of righteousness. But if the Spirit of Him who raised Jesus from the dead dwells in you, He who raised Christ from the dead will also give life to your mortal bodies through His Spirit who dwells in you (Romans 8:10-11). For if you live according to the flesh you will die; but if by the Spirit you put to death the deeds of the body, you will live. For as many as are led by the Spirit of God, these are sons of God (Romans 8:13-14)*.

Tackling the practical side of overcoming our sinful nature by putting to death the deeds of the body through the Spirit of God includes coming to grips with the mechanics of fear. Put us in the right situation and fear arises automatically even within the soul of those who are saved.

Fear has a proper purpose, God's intention is for fear to arise as a warning that we are headed for danger or that we are approaching a moral cross-roads which includes consequences. When fear arises in the form of warning, we must ask God what path to take or take the obvious path that God has shown. Even in times of temptation we know that God always provides a path that leads toward righteousness (see *1 Corinthians 10:13*).

Secondarily, fear arises when we know that we have sinned and that there will be consequences. Those consequences may include punishment for crime, broken relationships, or a measure of sickness or poverty. Perhaps they will include a halt in our walk with God until we deal with the sin. Either way in the midst of this sort of fear we are faced with choices.

The best choice we can make in fear of consequences is of course to come clean with God and with our fellow man. Approach God with what we know we have done and seek His forgiveness and reconciliation through Jesus Christ. True godly sorrow, which seeks restoration, is then ready to do whatever God reveals as necessary to restore life. The sorrow of the world, in effect being sorry I was caught, brings no release and perpetuates death. (See 2 *Corinthians 7:10*).

It has been my experience that we rarely run immediately to God to pursue reconciliation. Although immediate repentance would serve us best, it seems that our fallen nature typically struggles a bit before we come clean. Gaining a better understanding of that struggle can actually help us make our decision all the sooner. I can remember my earlier days in Christ when I would sin or stumble crossing some line of temptation which I knew I should not have crossed. The pattern that would follow is common to man being similar to the initial reaction we have seen in Adam and Eve. Our first response is to hide. Disregarding for a moment the impossibility of actually being able to hide from God, we must recognize what this pattern looks like if we are to short circuit it.

We have sinned and we know it. This is almost immediately followed by attempting to hide from God, from others, and from our self. The feelings of fear are those of exposure and nakedness. Our first reactions usually include a measure of working to convince our self that we have not actually sinned, were justified in what we did, or that someone else is at fault. We tell ourselves that we are not afraid, after all who knows about it and what will really happen anyway. We struggle with trying to feel not exposed and not naked.

Our immediate mode toward others who may be involved is one of self-protection. We deflect the truth of the situation from ourselves and blame it on others. (See the reaction of Adam and Eve in *Genesis 3:6-13*). All of this is then followed by guilt which, however we may choose to bury it or justify ourselves, remains with us until such time as we come clean with God.

It used to take me about three days to run this cycle of self-justification while under the constant light of truth from the Spirit of God. After my initial self-preserving actions I would wallow in guilt and self-condemnation and then inevitably succumb to the pressure of His love calling me back to Himself.

One day a fresh thought struck me. I hated wallowing in guilt and self-condemnation and I loved walking with God. I had been through this cycle many times which had always resulted in being down and defeated for about three days and then returning to God to get back up and going once again. What if I short circuited the three days of self-inflicted punishment and chose instead to return to the Lord as immediately as possible after having stumbled? After all it was not God who was keeping me bound in guilt and condemnation but myself.

Try this the next time you are confronted with a wrong that you have done. Take notice that there is an almost automatic cycle of hiding, self-protection, and guilt. What is preventing you from simply coming clean with God? Is it because you know that He will require you to apologize or make restitution to those you have wronged? My big mouth often got me into trouble which led to these same struggles. My answer to this dilemma was to choose the step of immediate apology any time I had clearly offended someone with my words. In choosing this acceptance of consequences, I actually found it became much more natural for me to hold my tongue than to wag it, a very freeing experience.

Fear also results and arises within us when we are confronted with almost any situation where we may be implicated in wrong doing. Regardless of whether such implication involves real fault, assumed fault, or just the displeasure of another, there is usually an immediate rising within our soul.

As mentioned, this automatic reaction is from our sinful nature which moves to protect self. There can be an almost instant hiding, blaming, and deflection of attention through self-justification.

What should reaction to implication be from a person with a renewed and Spirit controlled heart and conscience? Surely those of us who follow Jesus should be able to mature to a point where we seldom react in self-protection. Two incidents happened to me in the same week which caused me to pull myself up short and spend a bit of time with the Lord to question the operation of my soul and how I could function within these situations as He has intended. The following are learned functions which are contrary to our sinful nature but which, over time, the Spirit of God can help us to develop into as we: *by the Spirit ... put to death the deeds of the body:*

First, instead of reacting, empathize with your accuser who is the offended party. Let them know that you understand the concern or feelings they are presenting. If they are truly an enemy, then your good response will heap hot coals on their head revealing whether or not there is a path upon which to proceed further or not (See *Romans 12: 17-21*).

Next, if possible learn the facts about the accusation. In the case of my first incident I went ballistic over a large bill I had received but then when I called to discuss it politely I found it to have been sent in error. I had frustrated myself for no reason whatever. In my second incident strong feelings began to arise and I began to move toward self-protection. This is when I stopped myself and spent the time with God to take a deeper look at what was really going on. That accusation also ended up being based on a presumption on the part of another and was resolved when the facts were laid upon the table.

In taking the time to learn the facts we gain two opportunities. First we can bring clarifications which may resolve the issue fully or partially by removing assumptions. Second it is important that we take responsibility and ownership of our actions and choices when they are indeed ours, no hiding.

Offer to discuss the matter. If the other party is willing, we should offer to listen to their perspective. In turn perhaps they will listen to our perspective. If we discover that our actions or choices have wronged the other, then here is the perfect opportunity to apologize and see if we can agree on what will make it right. In overcoming our own sinful nature it is important for us to take ownership of our part and leave others free to choose to own their part or not. We may or may not be able to come to an agreement if the matter is complicated by their actions. God requires repentance from sin on my part but does not require me to make concessions based on the sinful choices of others.

Lastly in overcoming our sinful nature during conflicts, we must forgo blame and counter blame, as well as reciprocity where we 'get the other person back'. All of our decisions should be made in the Lord and we should never make decisions or second guess godly actions just to appease the angry or in reaction to a threat.

Treading on Serpents and Scorpions
Poems for the Path

"Behold, I give unto you power to tread on serpents and scorpions, and over all the power of the enemy: and nothing shall by any means hurt you." (Luke 10:19 KJV)

The following collection of my poems is offered for use during times of meditation, reflection, and prayer before the Lord. Over the course of about a year I felt inspired to write each one. I had never really written any poetry before and have certainly never studied poetry as a subject or read many of the poems of others. However it was a joy to just sit with the Lord and let them flow.

In some manner or another each of these helped me to express myself toward God and take His life and truths deeper within. Without doubt, as you continue upon the path of seeking the Lord, He will lead you in various acts of worship which will build up both yourself and others. Some of those will be new for you as writing a bit of poetry was new for me.

Each poem is accompanied by a passage of scripture which is followed by simple definitions and clarifications of a key word or two. I hope you will find these of use and blessing.

There is Nothing Deeper

There is nothing deeper than the love of God for me,
Forgiving my transgressions, Setting my soul free.
Though often times I have despised
that inner still small voice,
And fallen victim to temptation
strengthened by poor choice,
The Love of God is deeper and He lifts me back on high,
Repentance and godly sorrow restores a sinner such as I.

Through the years that I had wandered
and the years that I was led,
I've experienced nothing deeper than
His great and mighty love.
Jesus comforts us in sorrow and He calls us to His cross,
The Lord guides us when we are perplexed
and leads us when we're lost.
He supplies us mighty power from
the Holy Spirit within,
That we might spread His Gospel truth
and fully live for Him.

There is nothing deeper than the love of God for us,
Redeemed, Restored, Rejoicing, in Jesus Christ we trust.

Ephesians 3:14-19
For this reason I bow my knees to the Father of our Lord Jesus Christ, from whom the whole family in heaven and earth is named, that He would grant you, according to the riches of His glory, to be strengthened with might through His Spirit in the inner man, that Christ may dwell in your hearts through faith; that you, being rooted and grounded in love, may be able

to comprehend with all the saints what is the width and length and depth and height-- to know the love of Christ which passes knowledge; that you may be filled with all the fullness of God.

"depth": profundity, i.e. extent; mystery, deep-ness, deep things, depth

Be Still

Be still my soul within me,
Prayer just can't be rushed.
God will answer every question,
Your job is to hush!
So often times I bring my pain and woes before His feet,
God often waits until I'm done before He lets us meet.

Exodus 14:13-15
And Moses said to the people, "Do not be afraid. Stand still, and see the salvation of the LORD, which He will accomplish for you today. For the Egyptians whom you see today, you shall see again no more forever. "The LORD will fight for you, and you shall hold your peace."
And the LORD said to Moses, "Why do you cry to Me? Tell the children of Israel to go forward."

"Stand Still": to place, to station, offer, continue: present selves, stand fast, stand forth

Holding Myself Open

I choose life this day Lord Jesus,
In my powerlessness I choose Your power,
I wait on Your Spirit and beautiful grace in the quiet hour.
The under-girding goal of this day is to remain and
abide in You,

Staying connected through each activity,
to Your words remaining true.
Holding myself open and ready for use
that You may have your way,
Abiding, remaining, bearing Your fruit,
in Your presence I choose to stay.
Seeking Your face,
Accepting Your gracious voice in faith.
My amen pleads: 'let it be so',
Your Amen states: 'so it shall be'.
Come Lord Jesus that so it shall be,
My daily hopes rest in Thee.

John 15:1-8
"I am the true vine, and My Father is the vinedresser. Every branch in Me that does not bear fruit He takes away; and every branch that bears fruit He prunes, that it may bear more fruit. You are already clean because of the word which I have spoken to you. Abide in Me, and I in you. As the branch cannot bear fruit of itself, unless it abides in the vine, neither can you, unless you abide in Me. I am the vine, you are the branches. He who abides in Me, and I in him, bears much fruit; for without Me you can do nothing. If anyone does not abide in Me, he is cast out as a branch and is withered; and they gather them and throw them into the fire, and they are burned. If you abide in Me, and My words abide in you, you will ask what you desire, and it shall be done for you. By this My Father is glorified, that you bear much fruit; so you will be My disciples.

"Abide": to stay (in a given place, state, relation or expectancy), abide, continue, dwell, endure, be present, remain, stand, tarry for

Designed to Go Forward

Now and then we may need to retreat,
Yet to get where we're going we walk forward on our feet.
The Living Lord has purposed it that way,
Eyes in front to guide us through the day.
This physical creation holds lessons for our soul,
To grow in Jesus it's forward we must go.
Toward forgiveness, love, and truth,
Away from bitterness, hate, and lies.
The Master's path it lies ahead,
The devil's lies behind,
Let's follow His Spirit's eyes and feet,
Surrender to Jesus instead of retreat.

Hebrews 10:36-39
For you have need of endurance, so that after you have done the
will of God, you may receive the promise:
"For yet a little while, And He who is coming will come and
will not tarry.
Now the just shall live by faith; But if anyone draws back, My
soul has no pleasure in him."
But we are not of those who draw back to perdition, but of those
who believe to the saving of the soul.

"draws back": to withhold under, to withhold out of
sight, to cower or shrink, to conceal, to reserve, draw or
keep back, shun, withdraw

"of those who draw back": shrinkage, timidity, apostasy,
draw back

I Did Not Wait

Stayed up late and Rose up late,
No excuse I did not wait.
Now the house is abuzz there's no private place,
Had to hurry to get ready,
I did not wait.

Early morning stressed and sickly,
After work worn and tired.
All day long under my own power,
A pretty average day.

I did not rise and did not soar,
My strength was un-renewed,
I did not pray or seek today,
I did not wait on You.

Isaiah 40:28-41:1
Have you not known? Have you not heard? The everlasting God, the LORD,
The Creator of the ends of the earth, Neither faints nor is weary.
His understanding is unsearchable. He gives power to the weak,
And to those who have no might He increases strength.
Even the youths shall faint and be weary, And the young men shall utterly fall,
But those who wait on the LORD Shall renew their strength;
They shall mount up with wings like eagles, They shall run and not be weary,
They shall walk and not faint.
"Keep silence before Me, O coastlands, And let the people renew their strength!
Let them come near, then let them speak; Let us come near together for judgment."

"But those who wait on": to bind together (perhaps by twisting), collect, to expect, gather together, look, patiently, tarry, wait for or on or upon

The Treasure of God's Word

Gold and Silver are rarely neglected lest hidden
by some evil plan,
Lest lost at sea or lost through fire something
the owners did not intend.
Yet great treasure lies hidden in God's Holy Word
awaiting for all to find,
A treasure of Love and a treasure of light which God
forged for all mankind.
Why is that treasure so often neglected,
hidden, rejected, abused?
Sometimes it's ignorance or hardness of heart,
Sometimes because it's misused.
The Sword of the Spirit that great spiritual steel,
It drives off the lies of our foe.
It's a lamp to our feet and a light to our path to protect
us from failure and woe.
Jesus knew what was in the heart of all man,
The selfishness, fears, and the greed.
It is these things that keep us away from His Word from
the light of that treasure indeed.
His Word demands change if we will have light,
Repentance brings forgiveness from above.
If we would be the sons and the daughters of the King,
We must practice His untainted love.
Step out from your fears and open the Word,
With a prayer for God's Spirit to renew.
And through all your life Jesus will heal all your strife,
As His lamp lights the way for you.

John 5:24 "Most assuredly, I say to you, he who hears My word and believes in Him who sent Me has everlasting life, and shall not come into judgment, but has passed from death into life."

"has passed", to change place, depart, go, pass, remove

Submission to the Mission

Submission, Submission,
Come under God's mission,
To seek and to save,
Requires all His brave,
To submit.

In morning or evening on your knees,
Seeking not ourselves to please,
Walking where the Lord's light shines,
Yielding to His Spirit's times,
In unity with Jesus so divine,
Now we are under His mission.

Through each day with one another,
Submission places faith in God.
Peace or battle, Joy or sorrow, all points in between,
We find our life, He brings forth goodness,
on His mount it shall be seen.
For the people under God's mission.

James 4:6-7
But He gives more grace. Therefore He says: "God resists the proud, but gives grace to the humble."
Therefore submit to God. Resist the devil and he will flee from you.

"Submit": to subordinate, to obey

<u>Let God Choose</u>

Through the strength of Jesus surely I can do all things,
Though not all things are profitable only what He brings.
God reveals which works through seeking,
In faith I say 'I'll try',
But what the Kingdom of God is needing,
Are servants who will choose to die.
Our heart and flesh are deceiving and
will readily limit the Lord,
In dying with Christ we're enabled,
To trust and obey His Word.
Will God ask to much of us? Will He go to far?
We can never make any progress
when it's us who set the bar.*
Our loving Father will not demand above what we can do,
But expect him to stretch and bring us beyond the level
of what we knew.

Ephesians 2:10
*For we are His workmanship, created in Christ Jesus for good
works, which God prepared beforehand that we should walk in
them.*

"Workmanship": a product, fabric, thing that is made,
workmanship

"Prepared beforehand": to fit up in advance, ordain
before, prepare afore

*Setting the bar, as in high jump or pole vaulting.

The Lord Has Seen It

The unseen witness of everything,
Knows the sad heart, sees the merry who sing.
He beholds all the evil,
And beholds all the good,
From each lie of the devil,
To peace-loving brotherhood.
The Lord has seen it.

Daily prayers to Him are sent,
The prayer of the needy who can't pay the rent,
The prayer of the selfish who want their own way,
The prayer of repentance from hearts gone astray.
The Lord has seen it.

What does the Lord do with all that He sees?
With that which He hears and then how He feels?
He does what He does and He'll do what He'll do,
His choices aren't guided by counsel from you.
God considers the evil, considers the good,
Heard the poor ones cry and for them He stood.
We know that He looks and we know that He sees,
Because just to save us He died on a tree.
The Lord has seen it.

So in Him we'll trust when we don't know the way,
Hold fast to our faith, trust God and pray,
And know in our hearts that surely it's true,
The Lord does see me and He also sees you.
The Lord has seen it.

Hebrews 4:13
And there is no creature hidden from His sight, but all things are naked and open to the eyes of Him to whom we must give account.

"All things": all, any, every, the whole, (including all the forms of: falling off or away, decline, deterioration, deviation as from faith or from a standard)

Two Sides of Solitude

Isolate:
Won't see nobody,
Don't know their names,
Don't worship God,
Life's all the same.
Depressed, alone, I suffer through,
Day to day with no help from you.
I'm safer in this Island home,
The down side is I'm all alone.
My fears are not good company,
But mostly I'm afraid of what it means to live free.

Openness:
I've made my choice I'll come about,
Gonna embrace my God with a quiet shout.
I'll spend my quiet times with Him,
Finding strength to live and reject my sin.
Strike down those fears,
Send them away,
Back to the devil,
I refuse to play.
Solitude now means more to me,
It's a happy place to where I flee.
There I meet Jesus in His Word and prayer,
To listen to His Spirit and give Him my care.
Together in solitude's secret we give,
We fast, we pray, that others may live.
We find the directions so vital for living assured,
A life that's more open, abundant, secured.

Psalms 91:1-2 (see verses 3-16 as well)
He who dwells in the secret place of the Most High shall abide under the shadow of the Almighty. I will say of the LORD, "He is my refuge and my fortress; My God, in Him I will trust."

"in the secret place of": a cover
"my refuge": a shelter

Why?

Such a tiny question filled with mighty power,
Ask it in humble seeking prayer in your brightest
or darkest hour.
Who and What and When and Where and
How reveal the facts,
But Why is the question that seeks the motive
of where the heart is at.
And in the heart are found the roots both evil and sincere,
The evil roots cause bad fruit (sin),
Sincere roots bring forth good.
If I pull off a bad fruit and throw it away surely it will
grow again,
Unless through the seeking question Why ? God reveals
the root of my sin.

Psalm 27:7-14
Hear, O LORD, when I cry with my voice! Have mercy also upon me, and answer me.
When You said, "Seek My face," My heart said to You, "Your face, LORD, I will seek."

"Seek", "I will seek": to search out (by any method, specifically in worship or prayer), to strive after, ask, beg, beseech, desire, enquire, get, make inquisition, procure, make request, require, seek for

Extending Christmas

Presents and packages, do we need more?
Preparing the meals, trips to the store.
The world has made Christmas become many things,
A bike or a pony, maybe a ring.
Surely giving reflects God's own desire,
We'll read about Jesus as we sit by our fire.
Jesus is God's gift to us and all man,
To deliver us from Satan, that is the plan.
How perfect is God's gift that does not depend,
On position or wealth or on status of men.

His gift is for all of us, the captive the free,
Those rich and poor, and those in between.
So bless one another on this and all days,
Give from the heart but do not let it stay,
Only between those whose equals you are,
To share Christ your gifts will need to reach far.

Prayer is a gift that the poorest can give,
Make a friend of the lonely helping them live,
Warm clothes or a blanket to fend off the cold,
Share your food with the hungry,
preach the Gospel, be bold.

How perfect the gift that does not depend,
On position or wealth or on status of men.
Such gifts are for all, the captive the free,
Those rich and those poor, and those in between.
Merry Christmas Lord Jesus!

Matthew 25:34-36
Then the King will say to those on His right hand, 'Come, you
blessed of My Father, inherit the kingdom prepared for you from

the foundation of the world: for I was hungry and you gave Me
food; I was thirsty and you gave Me drink; I was a stranger and
you took Me in; I was naked and you clothed Me; I was sick and
you visited Me; I was in prison and you came to Me.'

"you blessed": to speak well of, to bless (thank or invoke
a benediction upon, prosper), bless, praise

My Meditation

Eyes to see and ears to hear,
You're my meditation.
I've a heart to understand 'cause,
You're my meditation.
Thoughts revolve around Your Word,
And how You'd have me live and serve,
Now I hold back no reserve for,
You're my meditation.
Father, Jesus, Spirit of Light,
Reveal to me the path of Life,
As I wait here 'neath Your sight,
Lord You're my meditation.

Psalms 119:97-99 Oh, how I love Your law! It is my meditation
all the day. You, through Your commandments, make me
wiser than my enemies; for they are ever with me. I have more
understanding than all my teachers, for Your testimonies are
my meditation.

"Meditation": reflection, devotion, meditation, prayer

The Spirit of Fasting

Fast to seek God,
Fast to know Him,
Fast to understand.
Cover the mouth,
Abstain from food,
Seek mercy for our land.
When perplexity, confusion,
or darkness are striving to prevail,
Find the answers as are needed,
draw near through Christ's torn veil.
Set your life to serve God daily and
you'll be welcome there,
It's His intent to provide His servants
with answers to their prayer.

Isaiah 58:4b, 6-9 (Chapter 58:1-14 are all about Fasting)
You will not fast as you do this day, to make your voice heard on high.
Is this not the fast that I have chosen: to loose the bonds of wickedness,
to undo the heavy burdens, to let the oppressed go free, and that you break every yoke?
Is it not to share your bread with the hungry, and that you bring to your house the poor who are cast out; when you see the naked, that you cover him, and not hide yourself from your own flesh? Then your light shall break forth like the morning, your healing shall spring forth speedily, and your righteousness shall go before you; the glory of the LORD shall be your rear guard. Then you shall call, and the LORD will answer; you shall cry, and He will say, 'Here I am.'

"Fast": to fast, cover over the mouth

<u>Simplicity is...</u>

We worry, we're anxious, we fret and moan,
This exalts the devil to the throne.
Nag and argue, claim our rights,
Is this really the Holy fight?

To cease from strife and over-think,
Accept God's rest and from Him drink,
This would be simplicity.

To listen to other's becoming aware,
Then taking them to the Lord in prayer,
Assuring them that Jesus cares,
This would be simplicity.

Accepting the gifts that we've been given,
Thanking and Praising our Lord in Heaven,
This would be simplicity.

Simplicity puts a foot on the neck
of our enemy Satan's head,
His sneaking ambitions to control are
discovered and shed.
He'll not be exalted where Jesus is feared,
The devil to the dungeon, Our Lord be revered.
Let us walk with our God in Simplicity.

2 Corinthians 1:12 For our boasting is this: the testimony of our conscience that we conducted ourselves in the world in simplicity and godly sincerity, not with fleshly wisdom but by the grace of God, and more abundantly toward you.

"Simplicity": singleness, i.e. sincerity (without dissimulation or self-seeking), or generosity (copious bestowal)

The Perfect Church

In looking for the perfect church
one thing we must understand,
There has not been a perfect church and
that's because of man.
The Lord knows what He's doing and
what He has called into being,
It's all us believers: hearts, minds, and wills,
which have some trouble seeing.
And that's because when born again
we start as babes afresh,
We don't begin in Christ anew
full-formed in righteousness.
Our sinful natures need conquering
if we are to live for Him,
To remove the walls between us all
we have to get rid of sin.
Not just putting off the bad we must put on the new,
Created for good works in Christ: beautiful, bold, and true.
Over the years as we focus on Him
we grow in the nature of Christ,
We learn to trust, to love and obey,
warming our hearts of ice.
In a church where we share this journey,
With the struggles that growing brings,
We can minister one to another,
Overcoming in all of these things.
To such a church the Lord will draw:
men, women, and children too,
Bringing them into Jesus so that they will be renewed.
And maybe that is what it is to be the perfect church,
Formed by the Lord, blessed with His Love,
a jewel of great worth.

Hebrews 10:23-25
Let us hold fast the confession of our hope without wavering, for He who promised is faithful. And let us consider one another in order to stir up love and good works, not forsaking the assembling of ourselves together, as is the manner of some, but exhorting one another, and so much the more as you see the Day approaching.

"Assembling": a complete collection; especially a Christian meeting, assembling, gathering together

END

Printed in the USA
CPSIA information can be obtained
at www.ICGtesting.com
JSHW080832170923
48379JS00001B/15

9 781593 308148